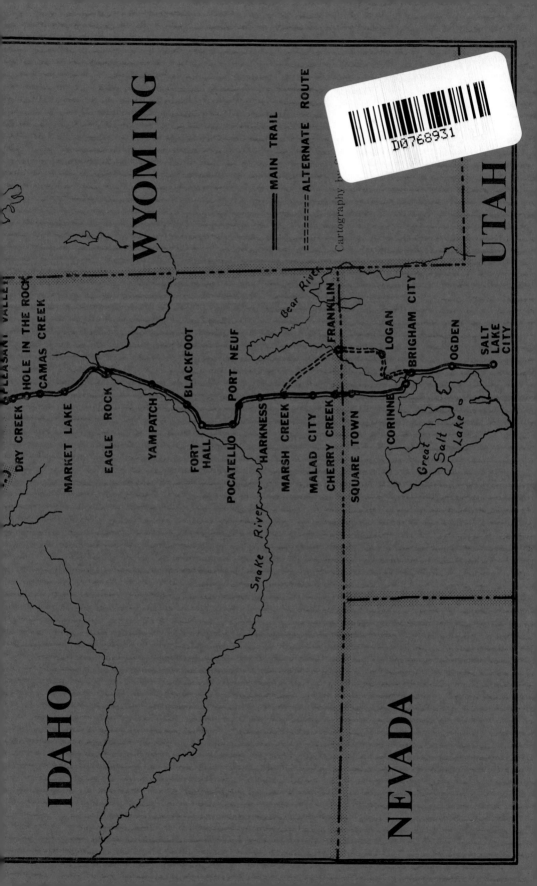

NORTH TO MONTANA!

Betty M. Madsen received her Master's Degree in Linguistics from the University of Utah. She has co-authored several articles with her husband, Brigham D. Madsen, and was formerly assistant editor of *Language in American Indian Education*. She is currently Thesis and Dissertation Editor for the Graduate School of the University of Utah.

Brigham D. Madsen received his Ph.D. in History from the University of California, Berkeley, and is presently Professor of History at the University of Utah. He has written *The Bannock of Idaho*; *Corinne: The Gentile Capital of Utah*; *The Lemhi: Sacajawea's People*; *The Northern Shoshoni*; and edited *Letters of Long Ago*. In 1977 he received a Distinguished Teaching Award from the University of Utah.

Main Street, Helena, Montana Territory, 1874. *Montana Historical Society, Helena.*

NORTH TO MONTANA!

Jehus, Bullwhackers, and Mule Skinners on the Montana Trail

by
Betty M. Madsen
and Brigham D. Madsen

University of Utah Press
Salt Lake City

Volume thirteen of the University of Utah Publications
in the American West, under the editorial direction of
the American West Center.
S. Lyman Tyler, Director

Library of Congress Cataloging in Publication Data

Madsen, Betty M   1917–
    North to Montana.

    (University of Utah publications in the American
West ; v. 13)
    Bibliography: p.
    Includes index.
    1. Montana Trail--History. 2. Transportation--The
West--History. I. Madsen, Brigham D., joint author.
II. Title. III. Series: Utah. University. Publica-
tions in the American West ; v. 13.
HE356.A17M3   388.1'0978   78-60240
ISBN 0-87480-130-3

For Karen, David, Linda, and Steven

Contents

Illustrations

Preface

The story of the trail from the Great Salt Lake to Helena and Fort Benton never has been told adequately, an omission we hope this book will remedy. Our objective has been to compose a narrative as accurate and complete as possible that will be of interest to general readers as well as to scholars. The focus of the book is the Montana Trail, and we have not attempted to integrate our research with more general spheres of study such as the national transportation industry, land settlement patterns, business development, or influence on Indian policy. We had hoped to furnish a statistical analysis of the amounts of goods shipped along the Montana Trail during the 1860's and 1870's, but we have been unable to locate records supplying adequate information. Appendix E summarizes our best estimates.

We believe that only history in detail gives a true picture of what actually occurred; therefore, we have liberally illustrated the narrative with anecdotal material. The experiences of the people who traveled the road to Montana—by foot, by horseback, by freight wagon; and by stagecoach—are the details of history that make events live again.

For anyone undertaking a history of travel, it soon becomes apparent that there are no solid blocks of archival material awaiting the investigator. The research consists of a long search for bits and pieces of information fragmented among diaries, government reports, and frontier newspapers. News stories sometimes may be vague or puffed up by prideful local editors, but they are still a most rewarding source.

Because of the scattered nature of the available information, we have followed a chronological format with a few exceptions where it has seemed necessary to pause and examine specific topics in depth, such as the development of toll roads, rival steamboat freighting on the Missouri River, or the construction of the Utah Northern Railroad.

Our journey along the Montana Trail has led us to search in many places, and we are grateful to the scholars who have helped us. We would especially like to express our appreciation to the staffs of the Library of Congress, the National Archives, the Utah State Historical Society, the Montana State Historical Society, the Idaho State Historical Society, the University of Montana Library, the Montana State University Library, the University of Utah Library, the Utah State University Library, the Brigham Young University Library, the Church of Jesus Christ of Latter-day Saints Historical Department, the Bancroft Library, the Huntington Library, the William Andrews Clark Memorial Library at Los Angeles, and the Idaho Falls, Pocatello, Blackfoot, and Deer Lodge public libraries.

In addition, we owe a special debt of gratitude to Colin Sweeten, County Clerk, Oneida County, Malad, Idaho; the late Charles Bovey of Virginia City, Montana; Lewis O. Brackman of Helena, Montana; and Dr. Merrill D. Beal of Pocatello, Idaho.

We should like especially to express our appreciation to Dr. Stanley R. Davison of Western Montana College and to Dr. Everett L. Cooley and the late Thomas M. Schmid of the University of Utah who carefully read the original manuscript and made valuable suggestions for its improvement. We appreciate, too, the expertise of Peggy Lee of the University of Utah Press, whose editorial skills and perceptive judgment have contributed significantly to this volume.

Introduction

The Montana Trail was a shorter version of the well-known Oregon-California Trail, but differed significantly in that it was a north-south, rather than east-west, route. Freighters, stagers, and emigrants outfitted at the settlements in northern Utah for a dash across the barren plains of eastern Idaho to the verdant valleys of Montana some 400 to 500 miles away. To these travelers, the Continental Divide at Monida Pass, gateway to Montana, seemed almost as formidable a barrier as the Sierra Nevada was to east-west travelers. Unlike the more fortunate early Californians who could be amply supplied by sea with necessities and even luxuries the year round, delivery of goods for isolated Montana settlers was subject to many uncertainties. The only water access to the Montana settlements was the unreliable Missouri River route—usable for only a few months during high water on the river. And in winter, on the only passable road into the territory, blizzard conditions and freezing weather had to be battled again and again by freighters and stage drivers moving supplies and emigrants across the Continental Divide at Monida Pass.

Because the Northern Shoshoni and their neighbors had known and used this "natural" route for generations, in the early years of the nineteenth century trappers for the British fur companies easily marked for themselves the road from the Great Salt Lake to the Beaverhead country.

With the building of Fort Hall at the junction of the Oregon-California trails and the increase in transcontinental travel, the federal government became interested in acquiring Oregon territory and dispatched several expeditions to explore roads into the northern Rockies. Captains Hood, Frémont, Stansbury, and Mullan described in turn the wilderness connections between the Great Salt Lake and the mountain heights of Idaho and Montana.

A Mormon settlement at Fort Lemhi, Idaho, and a trading post established by John Owen in the Bitterroot Valley reflected the increasing interest in wagon travel to the north. The discovery of gold transformed the first modest trickles of wheeled vehicles into a deluge moving toward the mineral-rich areas of Grasshopper Creek, Alder Gulch, and Last Chance Gulch in Montana. Using every means of transportation, from "shanks' mare" to stagecoach, the impatient miners soon marked out a dusty thoroughfare across the sage plains of the Snake River Valley and the backbone of the continent. Poorly organized and haphazard freighting outfits followed. Trade was slowed briefly in late 1862 by troubles with the Shoshoni until General Patrick E. Connor effectively halted Indian depredations by his massacre of several hundred Shoshoni at the Battle of Bear River.

Soon settlers, attracted by tales of sheltered valleys and fertile meadows, began trekking to Montana—usually by covered wagon and oxteam, but occasionally by horse and buggy. This migration quickened during the 1860's—particularly after completion of the transcontinental railroad. The iron horse eliminated the long wagon journey from Omaha to Salt Lake City and deposited settlers at Corinne, Utah, where outfits could be purchased for the trip to Montana.

The first seven years of freighting along the Montana Trail, from 1862 until the arrival of the Central and Union Pacific railroads, saw the introduction and adaptation of different transportation methods to frontier travel. Pack trains were used in the first year or two to move supplies from Washington Territory via the Mullan Road, and occasionally mule trains could be seen traveling north from the Great Salt Lake. But mostly a traveler would encounter slow, plodding oxen or mule team outfits pulling wagons along the road to Montana. The types of wagons used, the methods employed in training animals, the comparative merits of oxteams and mule or horse outfits, or the responsibilities of wagon bosses were just a few concerns of freighting in the 1860's along the Montana Road.

Many of the first eager freighters were outfitted with war-surplus teams and wagons left over from the Utah War and auctioned off at Camp Floyd, Utah. A number of Mormon farmers-turned-freighters acquired equipment in this manner and joined the more **permanent** freighting companies in taking goods to Montana. Bandits, bad weather, and accidents along the way failed to impede the flow of goods, and an established pattern of about eight months' freighting each year developed, interrupted only by the winter blizzards that closed Monida Pass.

Of all the supplies transported to the northern mines in the early years, nothing approached the importance of flour. Scarcity of this precious commodity led to riots in the camps one year and encouraged freighters to deliver immense stocks through 1869 in an effort to corner profits in the fluctuating Montana markets—though many frequently lost as well as gained from rapidly changing prices.

Other companies mined profits on the trail by transporting passengers to the new towns of western Montana. Jack Oliver's Bannack City Express provided a primitive means of travel for the first two years of settlement until Ben Holladay drove him out of business in 1864. Two years later this "Stagecoach King" decided to avoid competition from the coming railroad and sold out to Wells, Fargo & Co., which continued service until arrival of the Union and Central Pacific lines. Wells Fargo was to establish a fairly stable route, with fixed home and swing stations. All three of these first stage companies also carried the mail, the fastest means of communication until a telegraph line connected Salt Lake City and Helena in 1866.

The more human side of staging had to do with the kinds of coaches, jerkies, or mud wagons used to bounce passengers back and forth to and from Montana. The drivers, or jehus, as they were known, were the leading players in the drama of the long, rough trip. The hazards of coach travel were many—the weather, the danger of accidents, or the soul-chilling cry of "Hands Up!" from the highwaymen who infested the road. The most famous holdup was probably the Great Portneuf Stage Robbery of July 13, 1865, an event that received widespread newspaper coverage and demands for an end to the lawlessness on the Montana Trail.

Another serious consideration for freighters and stagers was the continuing exorbitant expense of tolls at ferries, bridges, and on many roads, none of which received more than minimal upkeep from their grasping owners. In Utah tolls were charged on the road north from Salt Lake and at the Bear and Malad river crossings. The Idaho segment of the route north became the possession of the contentious William Murphy, who operated the

Oneida Wagon Road Company from Malad to the Montana line until his death opened the way for H. O. Harkness to take control by marrying Murphy's widow. The chief travel obstacle in Idaho was the Snake River, which was finally bridged at Eagle Rock, to the relief of many frightened emigrants and anxious freighters. After crossing Monida Pass, travelers encountered toll roads, bridges, and ferries in the mountainous areas of Montana. The chief link in the north-south route was the Beaverhead Wagon Road, although so many charters were quickly granted then disapproved that it was difficult even for regular customers to keep track of who was taking tolls on any particular road, bridge, or ferry. In all three territories, citizens were delighted when legislatures took control away from the private chartered companies and eliminated the costly tolls which had increased the prices of goods shipped to Montana.

From time to time other routes into the isolated region were tried, but none was kept open for more than a brief period. The one persistent rival of the road from Salt Lake City was the Missouri River. Except during low-water years, shipping by steamboat was more convenient and cheaper and, for passengers, easier, though more time-consuming. Many believed completion of the transcontinental railroad heralded the end of river transport; to their surprise, shipment of bulk goods by steamboat not only continued, but grew in volume during the 1870's. Only with the entry of the Northern Pacific Railroad into Montana did the river lose its place as the favorite for transportation of heavy goods such as mining machinery.

The driving of the Golden Spike on May 10, 1869, immediately changed the transportation pattern for Montana and eastern Idaho; the new town of Corinne, Utah, became the main freight transfer point north. Establishment of this Gentile settlement in Mormon Utah led to a political and economic rivalry that did not end until the narrow-gauge railroad bypassed the wagon road from Corinne, settling the question. From 1869 to 1879, Corinne was the end of the trail for weary travelers to and from Montana and the great freight terminal for goods going north. Corinne was Montana-minded in its heyday and was more an appendage of that territory than a part of Utah.

The much greater surge of travel north was perhaps the

most significant transportation aspect after 1869. Stagecoach travel became more regular in the 1870's and grew in volume as emigrants and settlers were attracted to the northern valleys. The firm of Gilmer & Salisbury took over the stage lines from Wells Fargo in 1869 and continued to operate the route until completion of the Utah Northern Railroad ended through business. The stations along the route changed little during this period, and the usual discomforts of travel—accidents, holdups, and bad weather—permeated travelers' accounts. In 1874, extension of the Utah Northern Railroad to Franklin, Idaho, changed the southern terminus of the railroad to that town.

Freighting in the 1870's revolved around a few large, well-organized, and efficient companies, with the Diamond R firm the most important. Four trips a year were usually planned by the wagon masters of the various trains. More and more, return cargoes of rich ores from the silver mines of Montana filled freighters' wagons. Fast-freight and express lines were established at higher rates for speedier service, and the volume of business grew tremendously. Mormon farmers and occasionally Mormon outfits continued to freight, but made up a much smaller percentage of the business than in earlier years.

The Utah Northern Railroad was initially a Mormon project designed to link the northern Utah settlements with Salt Lake City. Later promoters tried to extend the line northward to tap the rich markets of Montana, but the Panic of 1873 halted these attempts. Only when Jay Gould of the Union Pacific stepped in and negotiated control of the line did the narrow-gauge finally push through Idaho and into Montana. Prior to this, Corinne and Franklin engaged in competition for the Montana trade, with Corinne coming out the unexpected victor until 1878, when the railroad pushed past Franklin and Corinne expired as a freight transfer point and a Gentile town.

The advance of the Utah Northern Railroad across Idaho created difficulties in providing passenger and freight transportation from the changing railheads. The pattern was usually one of insufficient wagons to haul goods in the spring until higher rates enticed freighters to come to the railhead in the summer and fall. As more and more pilgrims began to depart for Montana from the railroad, they faced a shorter and less fearsome coach ride than in the early days. By March 1880, the tracks were at Monida Pass, and everyone rejoiced at the end of the divide as a major obstacle.

As the railroad penetrated Montana, the Gilmer & Salisbury line began to do enormous business. Competition with other lines and the difficulties of providing passenger service were just a few of the problems of managing a stage line. The joining of the Utah Northern Railroad and the Northern Pacific at Garrison, Montana, in 1884 finally ended the story of the Montana Trail.

The importance of the Montana Trail as a prerailroad overland arterial highway has been neglected. The newspapers of many Montana and Utah towns were filled with the comings and goings of freight outfits and stagecoaches, and to the citizens of the time, such an oversight would have seemed incredible. For a vital twenty years the road was crowded with travelers and wagons. The many memoirs left by those who traversed the road contribute to the richness of Western Americana and tell a story of true hardship with rare humor. The Montana Trail was the lifeline tying Montana to "civilization" as the jehus, bullwhackers, and mule skinners of the day drove their animals and wagons north with the supplies necessary for life in the faraway Territory of Montana.

NORTH TO MONTANA!

Abbreviations for Primary Source Collections

BL	Bancroft Library, University of California, Berkeley
BYUL	Brigham Young University Library, Provo, Ut.
DUP	Daughters of the Utah Pioneers, Salt Lake City, Ut.
HL	Huntington Library, Pasadena, Ca.
ISUA	Idaho State University Archives, Pocatello, Idaho
LDSHD	Church of Jesus Christ of Latter-day Saints Historical Department, Salt Lake City, Ut.
MLUU	Marriott Library, University of Utah, Salt Lake City, Ut.
MSHS	Montana State Historical Society, Helena, Mont.
MSUL	Montana State University Library, Bozeman, Mont.
NA	National Archives, Washington, D.C.
USHS	Utah State Historical Society, Salt Lake City, Ut.
USLC	U.S. Library of Congress, Washington, D.C.
WCML	William Andrews Clark Memorial Library, Los Angeles, Ca.

1

The Trail to Beaverhead

The first miners to pan gold on Grasshopper Creek in the mountains of western Montana in 1862 soon realized how far their new home was removed from any base of supply. A mountain mass in central and northern Idaho effectively stopped any transportation except packtrains from the Pacific Coast of Oregon and Washington; hostile Indians soon blocked the Bozeman Trail through Wyoming; Fort Benton on the upper Missouri River was 150 miles away, with a long water route down to St. Louis; and Salt Lake City was more than 350 miles to the south. Of the four possible routes, the one by boat between Fort Benton and St. Louis appeared to be the most promising, but because the water level varied from year to year and delivering supplies by river craft proved to be erratic, the people of Montana looked to Salt Lake City as a more reliable source. The Montana Trail was to acquire prime importance in the delivery of goods to western Montana and add a new north-to-south dimension to the usual east-to-west pattern of travel common in the trans-Mississippi West.

Present-day Highway 91 very closely follows the Montana Trail as it runs through gently sloping and open valleys with the rather low Monida Pass (6,823 feet) through the Continental Divide its only serious obstacle. When Captain J. Howard Stansbury returned from a military reconnaissance of the route between Salt Lake City and Fort Hall in 1849, he pronounced it "the best natural road I ever saw." [1] But Stansbury was a latecomer who traveled only the segment of this north-south trail that ran from the Great Salt Lake to the Beaverhead country in

---

[1] Captain J. Howard Stansbury, *An Expedition to the Valley of the Great Salt Lake*, p. 93.

western Montana. Centuries of animal migrations, chiefly buffalo, had marked out trails later followed so regularly by nomadic Indians that well-defined roads came to be superimposed upon the old game paths.

Early Visitors

Early visitors to the region, mostly trappers of fur-bearing animals, had not thought of the road as a possible thoroughfare for wagons. Indeed, the typical Mountain Man simply followed whatever course led from one beaver pond to the next, being concerned with direct routes to the nearest point of civilization only when his packhorses were laden with beaver pelts. From the accounts of trappers and other early travelers in the region, however, one may trace without too much difficulty the growth of the trail as it developed into an occasionally used wagon road.

The few written records left by fur hunters offer only sketchy accounts of landmarks noted and routes taken between the Great Salt Lake and the Great Falls of the Missouri River. The Lewis and Clark journals are significant exceptions, and the detailed description of their journey from the Great Falls of the Missouri to Three Forks, up the Jefferson and Beaverhead rivers, then across to Lemhi Pass and the Salmon River country is the first written record of what came to be a section of the main north-south route through western Montana. Between Twin Bridges and the confluence of Red Rock and Black Tail Deer creeks, Lewis constantly refers to the "Indian road" his party was following. The expedition leaders decided to take the westerly course up Red Rock Creek as it appeared to be more traveled and to lead in the right direction to a crossing of the Continental Divide. A rocky promontory in the valley south of present-day Dillon was known to the Indians as "Beaverhead." Lewis used this name to identify the entire valley and the river flowing through it.[2]

Other early explorers and traders failed to record any Indian roads they may have followed farther to the south. For example, members of the Astoria expedition of Wilson Price

---

[2] Bernard De Voto, ed., *The Journals of Lewis and Clark*, p. 183.

Beaverhead Rock in 1868 from Alfred E. Mathews' *Pencil Sketches of Montana* (New York: Alfred E. Mathews, 1886). *Montana Historical Society, Helena.*

Hunt in 1811 recounted the hazards of canoeing down the Snake River past Eagle Rock (present Idaho Falls) and the Fort Hall bottomlands, but made no mention of any well-worn trails following the banks of the river through the Shoshoni–Bannock homeland. It seems likely that some of the Hunt group may have worked north across the Rocky Mountain chain and down into Beaverhead country during 1812.[3]

The first recorded fur-hunting junket to this remote country was led by Donald McKenzie in 1818. In the three years following, he discovered and named Black Bears Lake and made known to British authorities a broad region from the Utah–Idaho border well up into western Montana. This marked the beginning of the well-known Snake Expeditions of the British-owned Northwest Company and Hudson's Bay Company from Fort Walla Walla to the Beaverhead, upper Snake River Valley, and Bear River regions. After Finan McDonald had directed a relatively little-known fourth Snake Expedition in the area, Alexander Ross established Flathead Post in western Montana in late 1823 and led trappers on a fifth trip across the backbone of the Rocky Mountains south into the upper Snake River Valley.

The following winter, 1824–25, the British fur traders encountered the first organized group of American trappers to challenge the British command of the Snake country. Parties from the Rocky Mountain Fur Company, organized in 1822 by Americans William Henry Ashley and Andrew Henry, wintered in Cache Valley in northern Utah and at the mouth of the Weber River. With their leader, Jedediah Smith, some of the Americans came upon a party of destitute Iroquois trappers from the Ross expedition who asked for aid in finding their way back to the Ross camp. Seizing the opportunity to see new country and examine the British base of supply, Smith found Ross and traveled with him over the Continental Divide north to Flathead Post.[4]

The man who was perhaps most accurate in describing the area, and certainly the most verbose of these early trapper leaders, was at Flathead Post ready to launch a sixth Snake

---

[3] Washington Irving, *Astoria*, pp. 254-62.
[4] Harrison Clifford Dale, ed., *The Ashley–Smith Explorations*, pp. 55-98.

Expedition when Ross and his unwelcome American companions arrived in 1825. Peter Skene Ogden was to lead his motley crew of British, French-Canadian, and Indian trappers back and forth across Monida and Lemhi passes to the Snake River and Portneuf River country for the next five years. Ogden was probably first to record the feelings later experienced by numerous freighters and travelers as they learned to cope with the dryness of the summers and the severity of the winters on the road to Montana. While crossing the plains of Idaho in the spring of 1825, for instance, Ogden found grass for his horses near Three Buttes but no water; later, he found water at a river but no grass. His frustration prompted him to write, "what cursed Country it is." In 1827-28, at a camp on the Portneuf, he experienced perhaps the worst winter of the fur trapping era. Horses, buffalo, and antelope starved and froze to death by the hundreds. On December 13, while a huge storm raged, Ogden wrote: "The Snake [Shoshoni] Chief this day informed me that they had already lost 10 Horses from the Severity of the weather, and requested me to cause a change, *poor creature* little is he aware of my influence of conducting the business *above*, had I any, long since for my own comfort and interest I should have made use of it, but alas, I have none." [5]

From 1825 to the coming of overland travelers along the Oregon Trail in 1840, British and American fur companies carried on a ruthless competition during their indiscriminate wanderings in search of beaver. The British, being better organized and having a more consistent objective of denuding the Idaho-Montana country of furs, tended to dominate and eventually almost eliminate the independent American fur hunters. Although there was no wagon traffic during this period and packhorses were the sole means of transport through the wilderness, the constant search for furs began to mark out the main arteries of travel, particularly the one from the Great Salt Lake to the Beaverhead and Bitterroot regions via the Portneuf-Snake River complex and Monida Pass. The first sign of permanent human habitation in the area came when Nathaniel J. Wyeth

---

[5] Glyndwr Williams, ed., *Peter Skene Ogden's Snake Country Journals*, p. 35; E. E. Rich, *The History of the Hudson's Bay Company*, vol. 2, pp. 588-89; Merrill D. Beal and Merle W. Wells, *History of Idaho*, vol. 1, pp. 137-63.

established Fort Hall in 1834.

Wyeth, with one transcontinental trip already to his credit, had contracted to supply the Rocky Mountain Fur Company with trading goods for 1834. When the Rocky Mountain parties repudiated their contract with him, he built a fort near the confluence of the Portneuf and Snake rivers and attempted to sell his $3,000 worth of goods to sovereign Mountain Men. The Hudson's Bay Company then built Fort Boise to draw the trade away from Wyeth. The uneven contest resulted in Wyeth's selling Fort Hall to the British, who were in control of both Idaho forts by 1838. But there were now places to attract travelers, and a wagon-wheel maze of trails began to converge on the post at Fort Hall.[6]

Even though the Rocky Mountain trappers could rather easily find their way along the various routes, their knowledge of the terrain was not shared by government officials in Washington, D.C. When the Honorable Caleb Cushing of the House of Representatives demanded to know what was going on at the headwaters of the Missouri and Snake rivers, his request was passed from hand to hand in the War Department until it fell to the lot of Captain Washington Hood in the Bureau of Topographical Engineers to come up with an answer. The resulting report was not derived from actual surveys but from information supplied by two trappers who had been in Captain Benjamin L. E. Bonneville's party—a fact acknowledged in the letter of transmittal written by Captain Hood's superior.[7]

In this 1839 report, Captain Hood and his trapper informants provide a very early official description of the headwaters of the Missouri and the "Big Snake or Lewis" rivers. In one detail he told how the name of the "Malade, or Sickly river of the Big Snake" had originated when trappers were made ill by eating the flesh of beaver that had fed on a species of poisonous parsnip growing along the banks of the stream. The captain also described an "easy passage through the mountain-height [Bannock Moun-

---

[6] Beal and Wells, *History of Idaho*, vol. 1, pp. 164-98.

[7] Captain Benjamin L. E. de Bonneville obtained a leave of absence from the U. S. Army (1832-34) to lead a "scientific" expedition to engage in the fur trade in the northern Rocky Mountain area. As a commercial venture his project was a failure, but he became well known as a result of turning his journals over to Washington Irving, who described Bonneville's explorations in *The Adventures of Captain Bonneville*.

tains], . . . to be found from the valley of Bear River to the great Shoshone valley through the ravines of either the Pents-Neuf or Blackfoot river." After explaining that the " 'burnt-up' piece of land" comprising the Snake River Valley was worthless as farm-land, he qualified his statement by saying that there were two exceptions: one at Fort Hall and the other at "Jervey's Market," today's Market Lake (a marshy area that became an important "market" for replenishing supplies, "being a choice resort of Buf-falo, from which the party daily obtained the amount of provision required for its sustenance"). Captain Hood concluded his report with the statement that there was no map of any accuracy in existence "which will tend in any degree to enlighten travelers in their journeyings towards the mouth of the Columbia River." [8]

Explorers and Pioneers

Undaunted by the national government's lack of knowledge of the Rocky Mountain areas, pioneers were already gathering in the Midwest to begin a trek across the new Oregon Trail to the Pacific Coast. The Bidwell party left eastern Kansas in May 1841 and was fortunate to have Father Pierre Jean De Smet as one of the group, since the preceding year the Jesuit priest had jour-neyed to a meeting with the Flathead Indians at the Three Forks of the Missouri and was acquainted with the route. De Smet and his party were headed back to the Flathead country, where they would build St. Mary's Mission on the right bank of the Bitterroot River about twenty-eight miles above the mouth. At Fort Hall the missionary group left the California-bound pioneers and headed up the Snake River with one wagon and three carts they had created from their covered wagons. With these wheeled vehicles they crossed the main Snake River below Henry's Fork, losing three mules and some baggage in the process. They passed Market Lake and started north across the Snake River Plain, the "most barren of all the mountain deserts." Complaining about the "sandy plain," Father De Smet recorded that during the eight days it took to cross, the travelers supported life by fishing,

---

[8] NA, Abert to Poinsett, Mar. 18, 1840, "Letters Received by the Topo-graphical Bureau."

while their animals had to "fast and pine" because of the scarcity of grass. At the end of this "fatiguing journey" of over a week, they "entered into a beautiful defile . . . [later known as Pleasant Valley], pleasing and abundant, . . . watered by a copious rivulet." De Smet named this passage the Father's Defile and thus became the first to take wagons across Monida Pass on the Continental Divide into the country of the Beaverhead.[9]

In 1843, four years after Captain Hood's report and two years after the Bidwell Party had broken the trail, a negligent Congress was prodded by Senator Thomas Hart Benton to dispatch his son-in-law, Lieutenant John C. Frémont of the United States Army, to survey the Oregon road as far as South Pass. Frémont further elected to reconnoiter the country around the Great Salt Lake. Entering Malad Valley from Cache Valley by way of Weston Creek, the expedition moved south to Bear River and crossed it about five miles above its delta. They found a "broad plainly beaten trail" along the front of the Wasatch Mountains leading to the Weber River. After a boating trip on the Salt Lake, Frémont and his detachment of troops returned north by recrossing the Bear River and following the Malad River up to the Great Basin Divide and over to the headwaters of Bannock Creek. A journey of seven or eight miles down this small stream brought them to the "plains of the Columbia," where the Snake River "Sage Desert" spread across many miles to the Three Buttes. After easily fording the lower Portneuf River and traversing a nine-mile stretch of road, they arrived at Fort Hall. Frémont's decision to go by way of Bannock Creek, instead of crossing the Malad Divide to Marsh Creek and the upper Portneuf, established a pattern for later travelers who chose to follow the example of the "Great Pathfinder." But it was not until the gold rush that freighters began to follow the Portneuf Canyon route to Fort Hall. Lieutenant Frémont's survey of the southern half of the Montana Trail could now be linked with De Smet's description of the northern half.[10]

In the mid-nineteenth century, several major factors developed emphasizing the pivotal position of Fort Hall and the

---

[9] Hiram Martin Chittenden and A. T. Richardson, eds., *Life, Letters, and Travels of Father Pierre-Jean de Smet, S.J.*, vol. 1, pp. 231–316.

[10] Allan Nevins, ed., *John Charles Frémont*, pp. 232–58.

Inside view of Fort Hall in 1849. *U.S. Signal Corps, National Archives.*

growing importance of the road from the Great Salt Lake north to the Bitterroot Valley. First was the increasing flood of emigrants along the Oregon Trail. By the time these pioneers reached Fort Hall, many were desperately in need of supplies and were deciding to abandon all nonessential items to prepare for the last dash across the deserts of southern Idaho or northern Nevada. The bargain-basement atmosphere prevailing at Fort Hall, where a sharp trader could make comfortable profits, attracted many former Mountain Men. Trappers from western Montana joined road merchants and established an informal trade in horses and other goods between Fort Hall and the northern areas.

The key figure at Fort Hall was the chief agent, Richard Grant. The Mormon High Council at Salt Lake City met with Captain Grant on December 7, 1847, "on the subject of opening a trade with the Hudson Bay Company." Grant suggested the High Council send a letter to the Hudson's Bay board of management explaining that there were presently 3,000 settlers in the Salt Lake Valley, that 10,000 were expected within a year, that 2,000 acres of winter wheat had been planted, and that another 3,000 acres of spring crops would be sowed. The Mormon leaders indicated they would have some money and peltries to exchange for "sugar, coffee, tea, bleached and unbleached domestic or cotton cloth, cotton drillings, . . . blankets, iron, steel, powder, hollowware . . . and such other articles as may occur to you of use and that will warrant so lengthy a land carriage." The High Council also promised to "influence . . . the channel of trade in your favor" if the Hudson's Bay Company would send trade goods directly to Salt Lake City. A year later, on November 19, 1848, Captain Grant arrived in Salt Lake from Fort Hall with a pack train laden with "skins, groceries and other goods, and opened a store in the morning on the south side of the Old Fort." But by April of 1851, the "History of Brigham Young" recorded a reversal in this trade pattern, noting that a "small party arrived from Fort Hall in search of provisions and Indian trading goods." The balance had shifted. From this time on, Salt Lake City became the supply base for the northern areas. With a settlement at Fort Hall and a much larger one at Salt Lake, the incentive for trade between the two isolated spots of civilization inaugurated wagon traffic along the road laid out by Frémont.[11]

The last factor was the discovery of gold in California, which added thousands of impatient and improvident would-be miners to the homeseekers thronging the transcontinental wagon roads. The United States government now recognized the importance of the Fort Hall crossroads by sending Colonel William M. Loring in August of 1849 to settle his mounted riflemen at a cantonment near the fort.[12]

The fact that the army command at Fort Hall was relying heavily on Utah and the Mormons was reported by the quartermaster, Lieutenant S. K. Russell, as early as October 1849 in a letter to his superiors. In August Lieutenant Russell was ordered to send to Salt Lake City for a supply of potatoes to prevent scurvy among the troops. The price demanded by Mormon farmers was $8 per bushel, an amount Russell refused to pay because he considered it exorbitant; however, he was ordered to purchase the potatoes anyway "for let the price be what it may it is absolutely necessary that the Troops should have them." [13]

But the Fort Hall Mounted Riflemen were not the only ones in distress. In October 1849, Mormon Apostle Wilford Woodruff wrote that 500 wagons between South Pass and Fort Hall were "helpless; teams drowned in crossing streams, died from want of grass, road blocked at passes by broken-down wagons." The government officials at Fort Hall dispatched an express to gather these destitute pioneers into Salt Lake Valley, for they "must die if they had not help." Of the 35,000 travelers with 60,000 animals who passed over the Oregon Trail in 1849, Woodruff estimated that approximately 3,000 "gold emigrants" intended to winter in the valley.[14] The road to Fort Hall was fast becoming an authentic thoroughfare.

[11] LDSHD, Brigham Young, "Journal History," Dec. 7, 1847, pp. 1-2; BL, "History of Brigham Young," Nov. 1848, p. 26, and Apr. 1851.

[12] NA, "Office of the Quartermaster General, Consolidated Correspondence File, 1794-1915," box 363.

[13] NA, Russell to Gibson, Oct. 10, 1849, "Office of the Quartermaster General, Consolidated Correspondence File, 1794-1895," box 363.

[14] LDSHD, Brigham Young, "Journal History," Wilford Woodruff to Pratt, Cambridgeport, Mass., Oct. 13, 1849.

Roads North

The press of travel that year in the Fort Hall–Salt Lake region prompted the War Department to dispatch Captain Howard Stansbury with a survey party to explore the Great Salt Lake and adjacent valleys in order to lay out roads. The captain had intended to accompany Colonel Loring's Mounted Riflemen, but arrived late at Fort Leavenworth and journeyed directly to Salt Lake City instead. He left his main party at work on surveys while he took a small group to Fort Hall to pick up supplies, crossing the Bear River at present Collinston, Utah. This was to become the main fording point on the Bear River. Later he referred to the relatively low Malad Pass as "one of the handsomest passes" he had seen, marking it out as an easy route for use by future travelers.

In his published report of the reconnaissance, Captain Stansbury italicized his statement that the survey had demonstrated "the entire practicability of obtaining an excellent wagon-road from Fort Hall to the Mormon settlement upon the Great Salt Lake." He emphasized also that "Although when we passed there had not been even a track broken, so favourable is the surface of the country that I transported my provisions over it without the slightest difficulty, loading my wagons with not less than thirty-five hundred pounds each." [15] But even the enthusiastic captain had to recognize the problems of seasonal weather along his road when the following January an express he dispatched to Fort Hall "failed, owing to the deep snow." [16] From Hudspeth's Cutoff at Malad Springs, hundreds of emigrants had already followed the well-defined road to Salt Lake City, but Stansbury marked out a new wagon road north across the divide to Bannock Creek following the earlier line-of-march of his fellow officer, John Charles Frémont.

Four years after Stansbury's explorations, another army officer demonstrated that a serviceable wagon road lay northward from Fort Hall along the route traveled by Father De Smet. In 1853 Lieutenant John Mullan, as part of the Isaac I.

---

[15] Captain J. Howard Stansbury, *Exploration and Survey of the Valley of the Great Salt Lake*, p. 93.

[16] BL, "History of Brigham Young," p. 71.

Cantonment Stevens twenty-five miles south of Missoula. Lieutenant John Mullan's camp in 1825. *U.S. Signal Corps, National Archives.*

Stevens exploration for a northern railroad, was dispatched from Fort Owen to survey the area from the "Bitter Root ranges of mountains" to Fort Hall "to connect with the survey of Frémont." [17] His expedition left the Bitterroot Valley on November 28, a time of year sure to prove or disprove the possibility of wagon traffic to and from Fort Hall. At the head of the valley he reported that wagons coming from Fort Hall crossed the Continental Divide at this point, but he advised that loaded wagons traveling south would find the going difficult because of the steep grades. Continuing through Red Butte Valley, he crossed the Rocky Mountain chain a second time at Medicine Lodge Pass, followed Medicine Lodge Creek to the Snake River Plain, and reached Market Lake over "a very rocky sage-covered road, where no trace of a trail had ever been made." Mullan's party then forded the Snake River and reached Cantonment Loring, five miles above Fort Hall, by way of an "excellent road."

After a five-day rest Mullan turned back across the Snake River, over the Camas Creek desert to "high Bank Creek Canon" (today's Beaver Creek Canyon), and reached the divide at Monida Pass by another "very excellent road." An eight-inch fall of snow there was no surprise to the lieutenant, who knew that "this range is reported . . . as being a range where snow falls early, and at times exceedingly deep." The expedition then followed Red Rock Creek and the Beaverhead River to the Jefferson Fork and came by way of the Big Hole River to "Big Hole Mountain," crossing it to Deer Lodge Valley. They arrived back at Fort Owen on January 10, 1854.[18]

In his final message to his superiors, Mullan said the route back was "a much better though longer" road and "is by far the better wagon road: in a word, there is no difficulty whatever in the passage of wagon trains by this route." [19] While a few wagoneers had already used this natural road, the publication of the military reports of Frémont, Stansbury, and Mullan officially

---

[17] "Northern Pacific Railroad Exploration Survey, Letter from Isaac I. Stevens to Lieutenant Mullan, Fort Owen, St. Mary's Valley, October 8, 1853," U.S. Congress, *Senate Exec. Doc. 78*, p. 61.

[18] "Report of Exploration of a Route for the Pacific Railroad from St. Paul to Puget Sound," by Isaac I. Stevens, U.S. Congress, *House Exec. Doc. 129*, pp. 315–48.

[19] Ibid., p. 535.

affirmed the possibility of much more extensive wagon transport from Salt Lake to the Beaverhead and undoubtedly influenced the decision of later emigrants to head for Montana.

The Beginning of Wagon Travel

John Owen, an early Montana resident, inaugurated the first somewhat regular trade between the Bitterroot Valley and Forts Hall, Benton, and The Dalles, but, of greater importance to later chroniclers, he kept a daily journal recording the beginnings of organized freighting from Salt Lake City to western Montana. Owen probably came into the Oregon country in 1849 with the troops commanded by Colonel Loring. By the following year he had left the army and appeared at St. Mary's Mission on the Bitterroot. The Jesuit fathers, discouraged by the indifference and estrangement of the Flathead Indians, decided to lease the mission to Owen with the understanding that it would revert to the fathers within a stated time. Here the ex-sutler built Fort Owen, which soon came to be a base for trading in the Bitterroot area as Fort Hall was in the Snake River region. When the post was completed in 1851, Major Owen made an extensive trip to Fort Walla Walla by way of Fort Hall.[20]

The first extensive wagon traffic along the southern section of the newly surveyed road was stimulated by the establishment of a Mormon colony on a branch of the Salmon River. With eleven wagons, forty-six head of oxen, twenty-one cows, three calves, seven horses, three dogs, and sundry provisions and seed grain, twenty-seven men left Ogden on May 17, 1855, to follow the Frémont–Stansbury route across the divide from the Malad River and down Bannock Creek to Fort Hall. Then, following the route laid out by De Smet and Mullan over a "barren and thirsty country," the missionary party branched off near Mud Lake to ascend Spring Creek (now Birch Creek) to the divide separating that stream from the Salmon River drainage. Traveling along the "east branch of the Salmon river," the group chose a site for Fort Lemhi for their mission among the Shoshoni and Bannock

---

[20] *The Journals and Letters of Major John Owen,* ed. Seymour Dunbar and Paul C. Phillips, vol. 1, pp. 31–37.

Fort Owen, Montana, date unknown. *U.S. Signal Corps, National Archives.*

Indians of the area.[21]

The Mormon officials kept in constant touch with Lemhi, their most northerly branch, by wagon, packtrain, and mail packets on saddle horses. As soon as a fort and homes could be built, other Mormon emigrants arrived, including wives and children. Winter slowed but did not stop the wagon trains. In the middle of December of the first year, nine of the Fort Lemhi missionaries appeared at Fort Hall after having traveled through snow about fifteen inches deep. When the Mormon teamsters stepped into chief agent Captain Richard Grant's cabin, he was sitting up in bed, and in great astonishment at the arrival of visitors in the dead of winter, "threw up his hands exclaiming: 'My God, and where do you come from?' " Continuing to Salt Lake City across the Bannock Range, the missionaries found the snow so deep that one day they made only three miles, "the snow having to be tramped down by the brethren in front of the cattle before they could pass." [22]

Mormon Traffic North

By 1857 the settlement at Fort Lemhi was so successful that Brigham Young decided to visit the far-off colony. On April 24, a party of 115 men, 22 women, 5 boys, 168 horses and mules, 54 wagons and carriages, and 2 light ferry boats left Salt Lake on the "grand excursion," proceeding without incident via the Bannock Mountain road to the "great Shanghi Plain" of the Snake River. The visit of Brigham Young and his entourage marked the high point of the Mormon settlement on the Lemhi River. The following winter, emboldened by the presence of General Albert Sidney Johnston's Army of Utah at Camp Scott in Wyoming, about 200 Indians attacked Fort Lemhi on February 25, 1858, and in late March the missionaries abandoned the post and returned to Utah, leaving behind a forlorn ghost town and a well-marked road to the Salmon River area. Brigham City in northern

---

[21] HL, B. F. Cummings, "Journal—Salmon River Mission," pp. 1–73; USLC, Gilbert Belnap, "Autobiography," pp. 47–50; Beal and Wells, *History of Idaho*, vol. 1, pp. 249–52.

[22] John V. Bluth, "The Salmon River Mission," *Improvement Era*, vol. 3 (Sept. 1900), p. 810.

Utah again became the most northerly settlement of importance on the road to Montana.[23]

Several attempts were made to provide a primitive passenger and mail service to points north of Salt Lake City. In November of 1851, Phineas H. Young and Son announced a two-horse "Stage Carriage" to Brownsville, Utah, leaving Salt Lake City on Mondays and Thursdays at 7:00 AM and arriving in the northern Utah village at 6:00 PM. One-way fare was $2.00 per passenger.[24] A further service was provided by Mormon teamsters who were sent out from the General Tithing Office in Salt Lake City to collect butter, eggs, and other goods as tithes, and who were "at liberty at their discretion... to carry passengers and freight." Rates were to be $.04 a mile for passengers without baggage and freight $3.00 per hundred pounds "to be paid in advance or upon delivery." The order was signed "Brigham Young, Trustee in Trust." [25]

Mail service to Box Elder (Willard), Utah, was started in 1853, and shortly afterward Brigham City was receiving semi-weekly postal delivery based on a schedule of a day and a half from Salt Lake City. The postal department had already taken a giant step by announcing a mail route 800 miles long from Salt Lake City by way of Forts Hall and Boise to The Dalles in Oregon. The schedule called for departure from Salt Lake City on the first of the month and arrival at The Dalles by the end of the month, with another month for the return trip.[26] These early routes were not for faint-hearted pilgrims. A *Deseret News* report for Christmas 1852 stated that the carrier bringing the

---

[23] Brigham D. Madsen, *The Bannock of Idaho*, pp. 92–110; *Deseret News*, June 10, 1857. When David H. Burr, surveyor general of Utah Territory, issued his annual report in September of 1856, he listed Mound Fort and Bingham Fort ("two small settlements surrounded by mud walls" just north of Ogden) then a twelve-mile stretch of sage plain, "an indifferent settlement, called Willow Creek," and a final village called Box Elder. North of this, except for a few isolated dwellings and a way station in Malad Valley, there was no human habitation. "Annual Report of Surveyor General of Utah," U.S. Congress, *House Exec. Doc. 1*, p. 545.

[24] *Deseret News*, Nov. 29, 1851.

[25] Kate B. Carter, comp., *Our Pioneer Heritage*, vol. 5, p. 20.

[26] Ralph L. McBride, "Utah Mail Service Before the Coming of the Railroad, 1869," M.S. thesis, Brigham Young University, 1957, pp. 31–34; *Deseret News*, Dec. 25, 1852.

Oregon mail into Salt Lake City had lost six mules and horses on one trip.[27]

Traders to Montana

Since the early 1840's, Mountain Men, Mormon settlers, and other Rocky Mountain inhabitants had engaged in a disorganized but constant trade with Oregon Trail emigrants. Bargains in cattle, horses, and wagons, as well as in miscellaneous equipment, could be purchased at very low prices along the trail. The livestock was driven to the valleys of western Montana for a period of "rehabilitation" and then returned to Fort Hall to be sold for a good profit. John Owen took part in this commerce, as did Captain Richard Grant and other businessmen. At Fort Hall the fattened cattle and horses were traded to discouraged pioneers—one good animal for two jaded ones.[28] Mormon farmers also dealt in flour and other farm commodities along the Oregon road. One of them recorded rather pessimistically that in 1854 he had made one trip up the road with a cargo of flour. Not only had he received little profit, but "the profanity I heard and the drunkenness I saw served to completely cure me from going on all other trips of the kind in the future."[29] Nonetheless, Owen, Grant, and many others who were unperturbed by such considerations were back on the road every summer offering their wares to the weary travelers.

Most of the trade with Montana had been carried on by means of packtrains, but in 1852 an old Mexican trapper, Emanual Martin, drove an oxteam into the Beaverhead Valley, and soon other enterprising traders were using wagons to expand their merchandising operations.[30] Owen noted with surprise on November 1, 1854: "I discovered fresh Waggon tracks & was at a loss to Know whose teams they were So I concluded it best to return When on reaching the fort I found it to be Mr. Van Et Ans with two Waggons from Salt Lake down for the purpose of

---

[27] *Deseret News*, Dec. 25, 1852.

[28] Owen, *Journals and Letters*, vol. 1, p. 46; James M. Hamilton, *From Wilderness to Statehood*, p. 385.

[29] USLC, Belnap, "Autobiography," p. 46.

[30] Hamilton, *From Wilderness to Statehood*, p. 131; George F. Weisel, ed., *Men and Trade on the Northwest Frontier*, p. 38.

buying horses." [31] Van Etten was a Mormon freighter from Salt
Lake City who had decided to haul goods into the Bitterroot
Valley to trade for Flathead Indian horses. From 1854 to 1861 he
made regular yearly trips, spending the winters along the Bitterroot.[32] From the time he noted Van Etten's arrival in 1854, John
Owen matter-of-factly recorded in his journal the comings and
goings of other wagon freighters from Salt Lake City, indicating
the increasing traffic along the road via Fort Hall and Medicine
Lodge Pass.[33]

Freight wagons continued to make the arduous trip from
Utah to the Bitterroot in the final years of the 1850's. At the same
time, wagon traffic within the valleys of western Montana began
to take on more importance, though the relatively trackless
wilderness afforded no easy trip for the traveler.

James and Granville Stuart

However, the long, lonely haul by wagon connecting Salt
Lake City with points north was soon to change. Near Malad
City, the last isolated outpost on the way to Fort Hall, an unexpected illness and change of plans in the summer of 1857 were to
have a profound effect on the lives of two brothers and on the
future of Montana. James and Granville Stuart left California in
June to visit the States. At the head of Malad River on the Hudspeth's Cutoff, Granville became ill. While he recovered at the

---

[31] Owen, *Journals and Letters*, vol. 1, p. 88.

[32] Weisel, ed., *Men and Trade*, pp. 97-98.

[33] During the summer of 1856, Owen noted that Van Etten brought two
wagons, each drawn by four yoke of oxen, and a number of men into the
Bitterroot country, including George Goodwin, James Brown, Bill Madison,
and Frank H. Woody. The firm of Hooper and Williams of Salt Lake City sent
three wagons with this party, driven by George and Frank Knowlton, Arch and
Alma Williams, Merrill, Portugee Louis, and Robert Heyeford. Other traders
listed by Owen as stopping by his fort in 1856 are "Harris and Barr [Burr] to
Salt Lake City ... a Mr. Ogden to Fort Hall and return ... a Mr. Adams from
Salt Lake City ... and Neil McArthur to Salt Lake City and return." Later in
the season, Neil McArthur entered the valley with three oxteams; with him
were Louis R. Maillet, James Holt, Jackson, and Bill West. Frank H. Woody
also reported that John Owen and P. M. LaFontaine returned from Fort Benton
that season bringing the first goods over that road by oxteam. Weisel, ed., *Men
and Trade*, pp. 97-98; Owen, *Journals and Letters*, p. 88; Frank H. Woody, "A
Sketch of the Early History of Western Montana," in *Contributions to the
Historical Society of Montana*, vol. 2, pp. 93-97.

camp of Jacob Meek, Meek convinced the Stuarts that the Mormons would not allow anyone to travel east because of the Mormon War. The Stuarts decided to join some passing Mountain Men planning to winter in Montana. Needing supplies for the trip, James Stuart and Meek went to Malad City to buy staples from Bishop Ezra Barnard, "who ruled the settlement, as was always the case among the Mormons." They hoped Barnard could be persuaded to part with some of his goods at a profit despite Brigham Young's warning not to trade with Gentiles (non-Mormons). The bishop agreed to sell them a quantity of flour, bacon, coffee, and sugar, provided Meek would bring his wagon to the settlement at midnight, get his supplies, and then drive the rest of the night so as to be far away by daybreak.[34]

Thus provisioned, the Stuarts joined the Mountain Men. Crossing Monida Pass in October, Granville was awed by the "wonderful change [that] appeared in the country. Instead of the gray sagebrush covered plains of the Snake River, we saw smooth rounded hills and sloping bench land covered with yellow bunch grass that waved in the wind like a field of grain." [35]

After a winter spent living in elk-skin lodges at the mouth of Blacktail Deer Creek, the Stuarts left for Fort Bridger in March of 1858, but encountered six feet of snow at Pleasant Valley near Monida Pass and were forced by a driving snowstorm to return to their camp on Red Rock Creek. The party finally crossed the pass in June to find Camas Creek, which the summer before had been a "beautiful little clear stream flowing through the sagebrush," now out of its banks and forty yards wide. They had to swim their horses across. At Eagle Rock on the Snake River, which later became the major crossing point since it was the only spot narrow enough for a bridge, the Stuarts were awestruck by the river flowing through two gaps in the lava. They estimated the Snake to be 100 feet deep, and Granville recorded that the water flowed with such velocity "as to make us poor devils giddy to look at it." Continuing their difficult journey, they reached Fort Bridger, traded some of their horses, and headed for Camp

---

[34] Granville Stuart, *Forty Years on the Frontier*, ed. Paul C. Phillips, vol. 1, pp. 118-23; Granville Stuart, "A Memoir of the Life of James Stuart," in *Contributions to the Historical Society of Montana*, vol. 1, pp. 37-39.

[35] Stuart, *Forty Years on the Frontier*, vol. 1, p. 124.

Floyd south of Salt Lake City to buy surplus army equipment and supplies. It was two years before they returned to Montana, but something they had found during their travels was certain to bring them back.[36]

---

[36] Ibid., pp. 130–44; Stuart, "A Memoir of the Life of James Stuart," in *Contributions*, pp. 43–45.

2

Gold Seekers Throng the Road

The stormy weather that delayed James and Granville Stuart's journey to Fort Bridger in 1858 gave them an opportunity to visit Gold Creek, where a French halfbreed named Benetsee had discovered gold in 1852. The Stuarts, too, discovered gold in the vicinity. After spending two years accumulating the stock, tools, and supplies necessary for mining, they managed to return to western Montana in the fall of 1860 without bringing a horde of fortune seekers with them. Initially, relatively few people showed any interest in working the low-paying deposits, but when John White discovered gold in paying amounts on Grasshopper Creek on July 28, 1862, his find confirmed the rumors growing since February 1852, when John Owen had first reported finds on the Bitterroot, and the rush was on.[1]

At the time of the strike on Grasshopper Creek, men were swarming to the Clearwater River mines in Idaho, where gold had been discovered in 1860. In fact, so many were pouring into Salt Lake City from Pikes Peak, from the East, and from California en route to the new mines that the editor of the *Deseret News* was moved to "speak out against the allurements of reported mountains of gold" and warned the "young and inexperienced . . . [that] there are greater riches than the possession of 'filthy lucre.' " [2] Many of those already in Idaho were eager to move to greener pastures, and many en route to Idaho changed their minds and headed for the new gold fields on the upper Missouri.

An unidentified New Mexico freighter heading for the Salmon

---

[1] Merrill D. Beal and Merle W. Wells, *History of Idaho*, vol. 1, p. 283; Granville Stuart, "A Memoir of the Life of James Stuart," in *Contributions to the Historical Society of Montana*, vol. 1, pp. 40–46; Granville Stuart, *Forty Years on the Frontier*, vol. 1, pp. 133–56.

[2] *Deseret News*, May 28, 1862.

River mines from Denver in the fall of 1862 may have accelerated the rush to Beaverhead. He had reached Sublette's Cutoff before hearing news of the "Grasshopper diggings," and his employees threatened to abandon their wagons if he did not change his course. He compromised by delaying the train while he rode to Salt Lake City to verify the rumors. He promised to give a truthful report and go to Grasshopper Creek if there were reason to believe gold in paying amounts actually had been discovered. His greeting on returning from Salt Lake City, was, "Yoke up, boys—I guess we'll go to Gras." At the new gold camp he sold his fifty loads of merchandise at startlingly high prices and immediately returned to Denver. Cautious and indefinite reports were still being received there, but he dispelled all doubts by exhibiting his treasure in a bank window—a milk-pan brimful of shining gold dust, and plainly labeled, "from the 'Gras. diggings.' " [3]

Hungry Miners

Supplies for established mines in Idaho were being packed in from Salt Lake City and Walla Walla. The rugged terrain and the weather frequently delayed freighters, often reducing the miners to destitute circumstances, especially if they were very far from new towns. With most of the freight still being directed to the Salmon River mines, the men at Grasshopper diggings found themselves in an increasingly precarious situation. "They were in that chronic state of miners, out of provisions, and knowing they could not live on gold." There were 75 men at Grasshopper when C. H. Howard arrived from Wisconsin on August 30, 1862, and 200 or 300 more soon joined them. Despite the lack of supplies, many wanted to remain for the winter and work their claims as long as possible, so a few men offered to make a trip to Salt Lake City and bring back provisions. Although it was 430 miles away, the Mormon capital was the nearest place where clothing, food, and mining tools could be obtained. Before the volunteers were ready to depart, however, a freight train pulled into the valley on September 8 loaded with provisions, including a full supply of the alcoholic refreshment known as "Valley Tan." [4]

---

[3] *Historical Sketch and Essay on the Resources of Montana*, pp. 49–50.

[4] Francis M. Thompson, "Reminiscences of Four Score Years," *The Massachusetts Magazine*, vol. 6 (1913), p. 66; *Deseret News*, Nov. 19, 1862.

This train belonged to Joseph and Charles Woodmansee, brothers who were veteran merchants and freighters from Salt Lake City and Ogden.[5] Accompanying them were many more miners, among whom, no doubt, were some emigrants who had banded together to journey from the East to the Salmon River mines and who were described by Emily Meredith in a letter to her father. Apparently this group's plan was to go by way of Deer Lodge to the Mullan Road and over the mountains to the Idaho mines, a route frequently taken by miners. Shortly after crossing the Snake River, they "fell in with a train of forty Murphy wagons loaded with flour and beans... from Utah... on their way to dispose of their lading at Deer Lodge." [6] The committee directing the emigrant train decided to follow these freighters. However, at the junction of Rattlesnake Creek and the Beaverhead River, the travelers came upon the now famous sign painted in tar on pieces of packing box:

> Tu grass Hop Per digins
> 30 myle
> Kepe the trale nex the bluffe

The committee held another conference and decided to divert the train to the new diggings. The next morning they took the "trale nex the bluffe," followed by the Mormon freighters, who were always alert for prospects of a better market for their goods.[7] The Woodmansees sold their merchandise easily at $25 per hundred pounds and even asked $30 for some of it. When they returned to Salt Lake City in November, the *Deseret News* reported that they had "made a snug little fortune, and ... brought back ... not a little of the 'dust.' " [8]

The trainload of freight provided only temporary relief. With the influx of several hundred new emigrants, the scarcity of goods became so acute that many of the worried miners returned with the Woodmansee train to winter in Salt Lake City. On October 15,

---

[5] Edward L. Sloan, comp., *Gazeteer of Utah, and Salt Lake City Directory*, pp. 150, 179.

[6] Emily R. Meredith, *Bannack and Gallatin City in 1862-63*, ed. Clyde McLemore, Bannack City, Idaho, Apr. 30, 1863, p. 4.

[7] Ibid.

[8] *Deseret News*, Oct. 15, Nov. 12, 1862.

1862, a company of twenty-five men from Grasshopper arrived in
Salt Lake with nine ox teams and six mule teams, planning to return to Montana with supplies of 2,500 to 3,000 pounds per team
before winter set in. J. Gammill set out with his two wagons loaded
with 7,000 pounds of flour, and as late as November, a Mr. Menden-
hall started for Grasshopper diggings with a six-wagon train.[9]
Some of the Montana men remained in Utah to be among the first
to take spring supplies into the camp. Fortunately for those who
stayed in Montana, the weather was unusually mild, so supplies
could be hauled from Salt Lake all winter. Many felt that if the
snows had been as severe as they were in other years, "the whole
population might have perished from starvation." [10]

Making Do

Provisions were spare even so, and the shortages often served
to sharpen the creative and inventive imaginations of those having
gold or funds they had brought with them, as well as those who had
run out of money long before arriving at the gold fields. Tales of
the initiative displayed by several of the early residents provide an
interesting insight into the emigrants' way of life that first winter
in Montana. The Merediths, for example, had arrived "with but
little provision and no money," but Mr. Meredith "went to making
hay," probably from the wild grasses in the area. Although he felt
sure that he would be able to sell it in the wintertime for $100 a ton,
he needed the money immediately and sold the hay for $12 to $20 a
ton. As soon as he had accumulated $100 and "enough ahead to send
two yoke of oxen and a wagon," he succumbed to the lure of speculative freighting.[11]

Schoolmates William B. Carter and B. C. Bennett had been
bound for California through Salt Lake City when they heard of
the strike in Montana, but they heeded an older brother's admoni-
tion to always go to the newest camps, and headed north. To finance
the change of plans, they sold Bennett's pistol and arrived in Ban-

---

[9] Ibid., Oct. 15, Nov. 12, Dec. 10, 1862.
[10] BL, "Bancroft Scraps, Utah Miscellany," vol. 109, pp. 2, 13, 44, 109, 705;
BL, "Bancroft Scraps, Montana Miscellany," vol. 90, p. 12.
[11] MSHS, Mrs. Emily R. Meredith, "Experiences and Impressions of a
Woman in Montana, 1862–1863," p. 6.

nack with six pennies between them. They were soon back in business, though, having sold the pennies to a jeweler for $.75 each because he needed them to make alloy. By trading in this manner for a few months, Carter was soon able to join others speculating in freight.[12]

Resourceful miners created what they needed from the materials at hand. George Bruffey and a blacksmith friend made a pick from old metal, but they could not afford $2.50 for a new handle, so they broke up a discarded wagon and made handles out of the tongue and axletrees.[13] Another man, Joseph T. Walker, melted empty cans to make a part for a sawmill, then lubricated his machinery with castor oil—at $40 a gallon. Not even the packing crates were wasted, but were used to cover the dirt floors of many tents.[14]

Perhaps the most resourceful man of all that winter was Sam Hauser, who handled one shortage with great finesse. The men of his mess, by great fortune, had acquired a single gallon of molasses to last the entire winter. One night they returned home to find Sam inspecting a mouse that had apparently drowned in the molasses. The other men lost their taste for molasses immediately, but it didn't seem to bother Sam. He continued to enjoy the delicacy all winter until he had consumed it all. Then he casually asked the men why they had "quit on molasses." James Stuart replied that he "liked molasses but not well enough to eat it after a mouse had drowned in it." Only then did Sam confess that he had killed the mouse first and smeared it with molasses afterward.[15]

No doubt previous experience provided several people with the know-how and inventiveness for "stretching" a barrel of whiskey. Regular whiskey sold for $.25 a glass, but Red-eye could be made for much less: to two barrels of water, one added a few plugs of tobacco, some camphor, and a "little stricknine to give it tang." This, mixed with one barrel of whiskey, would produce three barrels of Red-eye, Valley Tan, Mountain Dew, Bug Juice, Tanglefoot, Jersey Lightning, or whatever name seemed suitable. The only

[12] M. A. Leeson, ed., *History of Montana*, p. 984.
[13] George A. Bruffey, *Eighty-One Years in the West*, p. 41.
[14] MSHS, Joseph T. Walker, "A Trip Across the Plains, 1863, 1865," p. 13; Lulu Ferebauer, "The Critical Years," in *The Idaho Story*, vol. 1, p. 89.
[15] Stuart, *Forty Years on the Frontier*, vol. 1, p. 238.

Contemporary view of hotel and Skinner's Saloon in Bannack. The sign on the saloon reads, "Bannack 'Grasshopper Diggings' 1862. First Important Gold Camp In Mont. First Capital Mont. T. 1864–1865. Headquarters Vigilantes and Road Agents." *Photograph by Betty Madsen.*

The Bannack jail, built in 1862 by Sheriff Henry Plummer. *Photograph by Betty Madsen.*

trouble was that there was often too much "tang" at the bottom of the barrel, and it was so dangerous when the level got low that a man could drop dead from the effects of too many glasses. "A man went to the happy hunting grounds cross lots when he got to drinking in the mines." [16]

At times, though, it was cash that was in short supply, and many relied on the good will of merchants and shopkeepers in extending credit. James and Granville Stuart gave up mining and opened a store in Bannack in the winter of 1862-63 when they discovered there was more money in merchandising than in searching for gold. They closed the Bannack store in April and reopened it in Virginia City in November 1863.[17] Meanwhile, they kept a record not only of accounts owed to them, but also of the manner in which the accounts were "squared." Of the sixty-two accounts listed on thirty-seven pages, twenty were squared by death or violence. Some of these entries were:

House Brothers, July 21, 1863 — "This acct was squared by Ed House dying of small pox at Walla Walla, and his brother Freeman leaving the country."

Henry Brooks, July 8, 1863 — $139.91 — "This acct was Squared by his getting accidentally Shot & Killed at Uncle Ben's Gulch.... Some drunken fellows began shooting in a saloon & poor Brooks who was outside went to a window & peeked in just in time to meet a bullet coming out & was mortally wounded."

Old Phil (The Mountaineer) The Man Eater. Philip Gardner — $28.75 — "This acct was squared by the roof of the Cal Exchange falling on & killing him on the 24th of April 1864 at Virginia City, M.T."

George Carhart, July 8, 1863 — $106.43 — "This acct was Squared by his getting accidentally killed by a pistol shot fired in a drunken row in Skinner's Saloon at Bannack City in July 1863 & in which another man was mortally wounded - After George's death his estate amounting to 5 or $6000[00] passed through hands of 3 or 4 administrators who absorbed all the money & his debts have never been paid—"

---

[16] Michael Gene McLatchy, ed., "From Wisconsin to Montana, 1863-1889: The Reminiscences of Robert Kirkpatrick," M.A. thesis, Montana State University, 1961, p. 84.

[17] Stuart, *Forty Years on the Frontier*, vol. 1, pp. 234-61.

Thomas Metcalf, July 10, 1863 — $5.50 — "This acc was Squared by his saying that he had paid it & refusing to 'fork out.' "

Charles Kinseller, July 8, 1863 — $15.00 — "This acc was Squared by his leaving in the night for parts unknown & forgetting to come back anymore."

J. M. Boseman, July 10, 1863 — $4.41 — "This acct was Squared by his being Killed by the Crow Indians on the Yellowstone in 1865 or 1866." [In different handwriting is added: "It was in 1867. G.S."]

Gold Tom & Brown, Dec. 14, 1863 — $9.95 — "Brown blew his brains out on the Prickly Pear Creek in 1863."

Hank Crawford, July 10, 1863 — $16.00 — "Squared by Henry Plummer & the other Road Agents trying to assassinate him & compelling him to fly the country to save his life."

Charles Reeves, July 10, 1863 — $69.20 — "This acct was Squared by the Vigilantes making it too hot for him. So he left forgetting to Settle his little balance."

E. Bostwick, Mar. 14, 1864 — $199.09 — "This acc was Squared by The Crow Indians who fired into the camp of James Stuart's party just below the Canon on the Big Horn River in the night of May 13th 1863 and Killed [Watkins] & Mortally wounded poor Bostwick who blew his brains out next day —"[18]

In June of 1863, Granville went back to Bannack to try to collect some of the outstanding debts owed the Stuarts. He was able to get only $300 and returned to Gold Creek on July 3.

The settlement on Grasshopper Creek grew rapidly. Before the end of 1862 a town was laid out, business houses were established, the diggings became known as Bannack, and an estimated 500 men were living there. In late May 1863, the discovery of even richer deposits in Alder Gulch sent an exodus of miners from Bannack in a wild scramble, and, by June, the new town of Virginia City was established. Spring brought with it ever-larger waves of emigrants, increasing the demand for mer-

---

[18] WCML, "James and Granville Stuart Account Book in 1862-63 at Bannack City, Montana (then in Dakota)."

chandise to meet the needs of the settlers and for better means of communication and transportation to America. During the winter, A. H. "Hod" Conover agreed that if he had a minimum of 250 letters he would take them to Salt Lake City. Within a few days he had enough letters to make the trip, and an express service of sorts was established.[19]

Traveling to the Mines

Determination and ingenuity seemed essential qualities for emigrants completing the long trek to Montana. All types of vehicles were used to carry the few precious possessions of those seeking their fortunes or a new home. The San Francisco *Alta Californian* noted "crowds of passengers travelling by Concord coach, on horse, mule, or jack back, per handcart express, and, in hundreds of instances, by shank's mare [are arriving in Montana]. There is a wild independence about this latter method which may captivate some, but for those who have 'been on the ground' it has few charms." [20]

Some of those who made the trip "on the ground" found walking extremely arduous. In September 1863, four men started on foot for Montana with bedding and provisions on their backs. The trip took them four months, and they were subjected to freezing winter temperatures known to reach 40⁰ below zero at times. Often the streams they crossed were not completely frozen over, so the men undressed, carried their clothes above their heads, and waded through the icy currents. At night they slept on blankets spread on the snowy ground around a campfire.[21]

R. C. Wallace fared better in 1869, however. He was told in Corinne, Utah, that the Montana country was played out and that

---

[19] W. A. Clark, "Centennial Address on Montana: Delivered October Eleventh 1876," in *Contributions to the Historical Society of Montana*, vol. 2, p. 47; Barzilla W. Clark, *Bonneville County in the Making*, p. 7; *Deseret News*, Jan. 14, 1863. Dakota Territory, created March 2, 1861, included former portions of Minnesota and Nebraska and extended north from the forty-third parallel to Canada and from the present boundary of Minnesota to the Continental Divide. Congress created Idaho Territory March 4, 1863, and Montana Territory in 1864.

[20] BL, "Bancroft Scraps, Montana Miscellany," vol. 90, p. 44.

[21] William R. Allen, *The Chequemegon*, p. 8.

As the handwritten caption states, en route to Montana in 1866. A. J. Fisk is in the foreground. *Courtesy of William D. Livingstone.*

wages were down to $6 a day. Being low on finances, Wallace concluded that a place where wages were as much as six dollars a day might be just the place for him. He arranged with a freighter to carry his "traps" to Helena for $20 and bought himself a coffee pot, frying pan, and fish hooks and lines. Then each day he would start out ahead of the train and fish in whatever streams he found until the wagons overtook him. The men enjoyed the fish, and he kept "in good trim" by walking most of the way and "enjoyed every mile of it." [22]

A variation on traveling by "shank's mare" was the system known as "ride and tie." Two men who had only one horse between them would take turns riding. The first would ride for some time, find a place to tie the horse, and continue on foot. When the second man reached the horse, he would ride until he had overtaken the first and had gone some distance ahead of him. Then he would tie the horse for the other to ride and take his own turn at walking again. Slow, but better than having no horse at all! [23]

Making the trip on horseback would seem to be a relatively convenient and inexpensive way to cover the miles between Salt Lake City and the mining areas in Montana. But while some made the journey with ease, others suffered severe hardships because of mishaps, lack of preparation, or poor judgment. Certainly these were the causes of the trouble that dogged Miles J. Cavanaugh and his two companions in early 1864. After wintering in Salt Lake City, the three men were a little too impatient for the coming of spring and by February had decided to risk the weather and start for Montana on horseback. It was a sad mistake. The first day out they had to walk to break trail for the horses. Next morning Cavanaugh's boots were frozen so hard he could not get them on, and he had to walk about three miles in his stocking feet before reaching a spot where the men could build a fire and thaw things out. They camped wherever the wind had blown the snow off the grass, but even so, on some nights it was so cold the horses would not feed. Crossing the Portneuf, their packhorse fell, and they had to get into the water to save him. In the melee, their cooking utensils

<hr />

[22] WCML, B. C. Wallace, "A Few Memories of a Long Life," p. 50.
[23] ISUA, Murdock M. McPherson, "Murdock M. McPherson's Recollections," p. 21.

were lost in the river, so at mealtime they made bread in the top of the sack of flour, baked the dough on a shovel, and held their bacon over the fire on a stick. When they came across a freight train that had been abandoned in the snow, they helped themselves to cooking utensils, hay, and food for the rest of the journey. Because the two young men knew nothing of the route and Cavanaugh was suffering from snowblindness by the time they reached the Snake River, they couldn't determine the location of a cabin where Cavanaugh had hoped to find aid. As darkness came on, they got down under the riverbank for shelter from the blowing snow and built a fire to cook their supper. Snow covered the sand by the stream and hid the ice crusted along its edge. Just as the "slapjacks" were about ready, the fire, supper, and all fell into the water through a hole melted in the ice. The men gave up and went to bed hungry. Next morning they discovered that the cabin they sought was just across the river. They rested there for three days and made the rest of the journey in fairly good order.[24]

More elaborate transportation was also to be found on the road. In 1864, Mr. and Mrs. W. H. Parkinson were nearing Virginia City in their carriage, which, according to Mrs. Parkinson, "was a grand affair, silver mounted, and its like was never seen before—nor possibly since—in Montana." Their horses had developed sore feet so the Parkinsons borrowed a team of oxen from a nearby camp and set out again. The spectacle of such a gorgeous vehicle being drawn by plodding oxen rather than by a handsome team of horses provoked derisive comments, jeers, and so much laughter from all the people they met as they neared town that poor Mrs. Parkinson hid on the floor of the carriage to avoid the humiliation. She could not endure the thought of making their first entrance into a strange town in such a ridiculous fashion. Her pride was saved when an understanding friend, whose coach was not so fine, offered to lend his horses to draw the Parkinson carriage. As they entered the town she was able to hold her head high after all! [25]

New Routes

Those who had managed to reach the Montana gold fields by

---

[24] MSUL, Miles J. Cavanaugh, Sr., "Autobiography, 1863."

[25] MSHS, Martha E. Plassman, "The Silver Mounted Carriage...."

the winter of 1862–63 were, for the most part, people already in the West seeking gold or a new way of life. It was not until early summer of 1863 that the first Easterners began to arrive at Bannack and Virginia City, and by the time they crossed the Snake River, the effects of the journey were apparent. Stock, weakened by overwork and scarcity of grass, slowed and faltered; wagons broke down more frequently; and the emigrants themselves regarded with dismay their dwindling supplies and daily search for grass, wood, or water. It is small wonder, then, that although the routes were fairly well established, there were those who couldn't help thinking, "There must be a shorter, faster way to get there."

Some adventurous souls did find cutoffs to shorten the journey, while others found nothing but trouble. When James Stuart arrived at Soda Springs with his Yellowstone Expedition of 1863,[26] he found two emigrant trains and one freight train breaking a new road directly to Eagle Rock Ferry on the Snake River. They were guided by one of the ferry owners, Harry Rickard. Although Stuart had misgivings about members of the train being able to hack their way through the sagebrush, he and his mounted expedition decided to try the new road themselves. They soon came upon the Rickard trains and some soldiers lost and mired in a swamp. He wrote in his diary, "Harry was very glad to see us, for the pilgrims were . . . talking about hanging him for bringing them on such a route. . . . it's plain that Harry don't know anything about the way there. It's such fun to hear the Pilgrims damning the new roads, Harry, and the soldiers. They even quarrel with each other about who was to blame for coming this way." Later, after three chains were broken trying to pull out a wagon stuck in a creek, Stuart noted that "it was a great mistake to come this way." [27]

In the summer of 1863, Colonel Samuel Word also tried a new route. He was with a group that had broken away from a train

---

[26] By the spring of 1863, the available placer ground on Grasshopper Creek at Bannack City had been claimed, and a number of the miners formed an organization to prospect for gold in the Yellowstone Valley. After choosing James Stuart as captain, the Yellowstone Expedition left on April 9, 1863, and returned to Bannack on June 12 having suffered several men killed and a loss of horses to the Crow Indians.

[27] B. Clark, *Bonneville County in the Making*, pp. 15, 17.

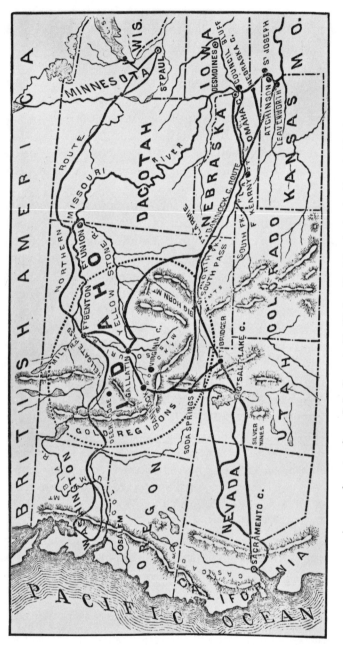

A map of routes from J. L. Campbell's *Idaho: Six Months in the New Gold Diggings. Rare Books, Marriott Library, University of Utah.*

near the Platte River to try a new cutoff to Bannack, later called
the Bozeman Trail, which promised to save 400 miles over the
usual route. At this time the Indians were determined not to allow
a road to be opened and forced the train to turn back. "It makes me
sick to think of it," Word told his diary, "loose a month and travel
300 miles for nothing." [28]

Impatience with established routes and procedures was
likely to exact a heavy toll in energy, health, and property. Those
less venturesome souls who depended largely on the experience of
others and on one of a rash of published emigrant guides often
finished their trek with fewer mishaps and less lost time. Several
guides became available to the public. The first one probably was
Jesse Fox's 1862 *Guide to Salmon River Gold Diggings*, which
included the following types of entries.

Localities and Remarks	Courses	Distance	From G.S.L.C.
**			
Head of Malad or Malad Springs	North 20 west	1.135	127.598
Here the Hudspeth cutoff, on the California road, crosses, which is a good place to camp; here the road turns to the left to go over on to Bannock Creek. There is also a good road on the east or right hand side of the Bannock mountain.			
Summit of Basin		5.820	133.418
This is the northern rim of Great Salt Lake basin. The road is smooth, and ascends gradually. The descent into Bannock valley is rapid, down a narrow spurridge....			
**			

---

[28] Samuel Word, "Diary of Colonel Samuel Word," in *Contributions to the Historical Society of Montana*, vol. 8, pp. 67, 83.

| Right Fork of Bannock | North 10 west | 9.564 | 164.862 |

This is better water than
the left fork.[29]

The next year, Captain James Fisk's guide offered greater
detail by naming four possible routes to Idaho, including a sea
voyage to San Francisco and up the Columbia; then he gave "a few
plain blunt words" to those who planned to travel to the gold fields:
"Take plenty of such staple items as flour, bacon or charside meat,
beans, mixed vegetables, groceries, etc.; and do not log along
chairs, bureaus or bedsteads. . . . The cheapest and best teams for
your freight wagons are well-broke, young, short-bodied, solid
cattle, with muscle and motion. . . . These teams will outlast horses
or mules and in any event will thrive so as to make good beef." [30]
They should start by May 15, move in parties of 100 or more, guard
their stock at night, and take along supplies to last nine months.
As J. L. Campbell explained in his guidebook: "You are . . . going
to a very new section where produce is scarce and high, and has to
be freighted many hundred miles; . . . the surplus of produce grown
in Utah the past season has already been freighted to this new Territory, and bears a high price. . . . We can but admonish all who go
to be sure and carry provisions enough to last until after another
crop shall have been grown in Utah." The 1865 edition by Campbell pointed out that it was cheaper to pay the high price of stagecoach fare and get there quickly than to travel by wagon and lose
valuable time at the mines—a concept that has a modern-day coun-
terpart in transportation advertising![31]

For $.25 the emigrant could purchase the handy, pocket-size
*Abridged Mormon Guide! Showing the Distances and Best Camping
Places over the North Platte Route from Omaha to Salt Lake City,
U., Thence to the Salmon River, Bannock and Virginia Gold
Fields.* This little book listed the landmarks from Omaha to Salt
Lake City and the mileages between them, and contained the

---

[29] Jesse W. Fox, *General Courses and Distances from G.S.L. City to Fort
Limhi and Gold Diggings on Salmon River*, pp. 4–5.
[30] Capt. James L. Fisk, *Idaho: Her Gold Fields, and the Routes to Them, A
Hand-Book for Emigrants*, pp. 20–21.
[31] John L. Campbell, *Idaho: Six Months in the New Gold Diggings. The
Emigrant's Guide Overland*, p. 36.

"cards" of eighteen Salt Lake City establishments that were ready
and eager to assist the traveler. Occasional brief comments, such
as "plenty of timber," "not bad to cross," "double teams," gave
incidental advice. Next came the "Route from Salt Lake City to
Bannock City," followed by routes to the Salmon River and Boise
mines. Advice to the emigrant was confined to a succinct statement on the first page:

> The publisher of this little work would here give the emigrant
> a word of friendly caution. 1st—It is better to keep an old and well-
> known route, rather than to risk the chances of disappointment on
> the many new roads, called "cutoffs," which is generally found to
> increase the distance.
>
> 2nd—Don't hurry your stock; take it slowly, and you will be
> through before those who "hurry up."
>
> 3rd—Don't miss the chance of camping where there is good
> feed and water for an uncertain camping-place, even though it is
> but the middle of the afternoon.
>
> 4th—Don't load too heavy at starting. Supplies are plenty at
> Salt Lake City and at prices much less than you can afford to haul,
> though, of course, higher than on the frontiers.
>
> 5th—At Salt Lake City can be had flour, butter, eggs, bacon,
> vegetables, meat and fresh teams, as well as every article needed by
> emigrants; reports along the road to the contrary, notwithstanding.
>
> 6th—Supply yourselves with a fair stock of vegetables, dried
> fruits, acids, pickles, &c., and use freely on the road. Let each wagon
> be supplied with some good cathartic, tonic and heating medicines.
>
> Lastly—Remember these cautions and watch your stock faith-
> fully at night, if you would go through safely.[32]

A latecomer to the field of guidebooks was John Mullan's
Miners' and Travelers' Guide of 1865. Drawing on his official
reports of assignments in Montana, Captain Mullan gave detailed
and experienced advice about the provisions needed, parts and
emergency repairs for wagons, pack train techniques, and preparations for going by steamboat. Although too late for the great
immigration of 1863, the guide was a boon to those who were
ignorant of the rigors of travel in the "great West." [33]

---

[32] *The Abridged Mormon Guide!* inside front cover.
[33] Captain John Mullan, *Miners' and Travelers' Guide to Oregon, Washington, Idaho, Montana, Wyoming and Colorado via the Missouri and Columbia
Rivers, passim.*

As the rush for gold gained impetus in the summer of 1863, many of those who had their own outfits followed the advice of most guidebooks and banded together to form trains before starting out. Some who had started alone formed into small groups or joined large trains that they encountered along the way. Traveling with a large group gave a reassuring sense of security against the possibility of being stranded far from civilization by a wagon breakdown, and also against the possibility of Indian attacks.

As winter approached in 1863, emigrants were still swarming the trail to Montana, and William Clayton, a prominent Utah Mormon, began to be a little pessimistic about prospects for winter supplies. As early as August he wrote: "The emigration through here for the gold mines has been immense and is still passing which has been a very heavy draw on our bread stuff." In October: "There are many strangers here, and constantly passing to and fro after the yellow god," and "If this immense drain continues there will be suffering for bread stuff before another harvest. Flour sells very fast and free at six dollars." Even the *Deseret News* managers worried about the flour market and asked to be paid for subscriptions with flour, saying that they had always been willing to take flour as payment when the price was low, and now that "it commands money" they wanted their share.[34]

Indian Troubles

Indian raids were reported frequently in 1862. Francis M. Thompson, who passed along the road in July, claimed that "the Snakes and Bannacks . . . between here and Salt Lake will attack any weak party they meet, when they think they will not get whipped. They have already killed some fifteen whites and destroyed several loaded wagons." [35] In August, in the vicinity of Fort Hall, Indians attacked twelve packers with twenty-five horses. Five men were wounded and twelve pack animals lost. At the same place another company was attacked the next day. Five men were killed, two were wounded, and "the Indians got two

    [34] BL, William Clayton, "Letter Books," Letters to George Q. Cannon, Aug. 6, Oct. 12, 1863; Letter to J. F. Kinney, Oct. 21, 1863; *Deseret News*, Nov. 25, 1863.
    [35] Thompson, "Reminiscences of Four Score Years," pp. 55–66.

wagons well stocked with groceries." [36]

Indians continued to badger travelers throughout the winter of 1862-63. On October 3, 1862, Chief Winnemucca and his "mixed band of Paiutes, Shoshones and Bannocks" appeared to be hostile as they passed Bannack City on their way to the Yellowstone for a winter's hunt, but "by a present of three beeves, a sack or two of beans, tobacco, pipes and matches, Winnimuck and his ... crowd simmered down to decent neighborship." [37] By December the people of Franklin, Idaho, had to ask for help from Camp Douglas at Salt Lake City, but the Indians eluded the soldiers by cutting the rope at Empey's Ferry on Bear River.[38] On January 14, 1863, A. H. Conover arrived with the news that George Clayton and Henry Bean had been killed by Indians on November 25 as they passed through Marsh Valley carrying the mail from Bannack. The Indians struck again on January 3 and January 21 killing eleven more miners.[39]

To protect the travel routes from the rising frequency and intensity of Shoshoni assaults, Colonel Patrick E. Connor had been sent from San Francisco to Camp Douglas with his company of California Volunteers in July 1862. Now he mounted an expedition "to chastize them [the Indians] if possible" for their campaign against travelers. At the Battle of Bear River on January 29, 1863, in what Utah Indian Superintendent James D. Doty termed "the severest and most bloody [battle] of any which has ever occurred with the Indians west of the Mississippi," the Indians were effectively subdued until well into the 1870's. A. H. Conover saw only a few Indians as he brought 500 letters to Salt Lake City in April;[40] N. P. Langford noted that "No longer in fear of attack by the Indians, immigrants had been steadily pouring into the

---

[36] *Deseret News*, Aug. 27, 1862.

[37] Meredith, *Bannock and Gallatin City*, editor's note; BL, "Bancroft Scraps, Utah Miscellany," vol. 109, p. 44.

[38] James Ira Young, "The History and Development of Franklin, Idaho, During the Period 1860-1900," M.A. thesis, Brigham Young University, 1949, p. 113.

[39] *Deseret News*, Jan. 14, 21, 28, 1863.

[40] *The War of the Rebellion: A Compilation of the Official Records of the Union and Confederate Armies*, pp. 185-87; Brigham D. Madsen, *The Bannock of Idaho*, pp. 134-40; *Deseret News*, Feb. 11, Apr. 22, 1863. General Connor reported 224 Indians killed in the battle. Utah Superintendent of Indian Affairs, James D. Doty, reported 255 deaths, while one local resident, James J. Hill, counted 368 bodies on the field.

Territory over the Salt Lake route during the month of June"; and Emily Meredith wrote to her father that Connor and the Battle of Bear River had made the trail safe from Indian attacks.[41]

Montana Pioneer Women

There were few white women in Montana before the gold strike, but many came with their husbands or fathers to make a home there and establish businesses. Among the early arrivals were Harriet Sanders, wife of Wilber Fisk Sanders, and Lucia Darling, niece of Sidney Edgerton, the first governor of Montana. The two women kept diaries, often recording the same incidents from differing points of view.

One day Harriet "Made sponge, at noon kneaded the bread and this evening baked nine loaves fried a half bushel of doughnuts and left a tin of biscuit to bake in the morning." The next night Lucia "Stood guard . . . myself last night all alone. . . . I sat up and watched the cattle and the stars all night with our indian pony for company." She had had to stay up until midnight anyway, to "get my fried cakes made as we wanted about a bushel." Lucia was amused at how "my friends would have laughed to see me going from one wagon to another with some bread and bacon for the hungry ones to eat, for we did not want to stop until we got to the fording place." When they had to be rescued on horseback from their wagon while fording the Snake River, Harriet recorded that "it was by far the richest experience we have had." [42]

These women had a servant who acted as nursemaid for the children and as cook's helper, but others were not so fortunate. The rigors of the journey seemed to engulf Katherine Dunlap with loneliness after leaving many of her friends at Lander's Cutoff. When some of the party turned back at Camas Creek, she wrote, "O, my dear friends, you can not appreciate the feelings of sorrow and lonliness . . . another 24 miles of desert without water and

---

[41] N. P. Langford, *Vigilante Days and Ways*, p. 171: MSHS, Meredith, "Experiences," p. 8.

[42] MSHS, Lucia Darling, "Journal of Trip Across the Plains in the Summer of 1863," pp. 44–45: MSHS, Harriet F. Sanders, "Diary of Harriet F. Sanders of a Journey from Omaha to East Bannack City, Idaho Territory, Summer of 1863, via Kearney, Laramie, South Pass, and Lower Snake Ferry," pp. 36–38.

grass lies before us." [43]

The women met emergencies with an aplomb acquired from long days on the road. When the Herndon's ox was poisoned by eating wild larkspur, the men bled it, but the treatment failed and the ox was dying. Sarah Herndon and her mother put on their big aprons and poured a quart of melted lard laced with bits of bacon on "Joe's" nose and down his throat. Next day, Sarah recorded that "Joe did not die . . . seemed as well as ever, except his nose, which looks as if it had been scalded." [44]

Getting the Gold Home

The people of Bannack and Virginia City felt that they had more than their share of another commodity—lawless, unruly men. Pete Albertson, a sixteen-year-old freighter, described the situation that developed through the first two winters of the gold rush.

> Highway Robers and murders Were plentyfull all over Montana . . in them Days it was not Safe for a man to Be alone any Where . . or have 25cts in his pockets for if a Rober would meete him . . and tell him to hold up his hands . . and onely find 25cts in his Pockets . . then the Rober would kill the Poor man for not having any more money than 25cts . . The Rober Would say you god D . . S . . O . . A . . B . . you ought to Die for not having any more money than that . .[45]

Getting "back to America" with their gold without being robbed or murdered came to be such a problem that those who were leaving had to plan their departure with as much stealth and cunning as if they were planning an escape. From November 1862, when Charles Guy was murdered while driving to Salt Lake City with several hundred dollars to buy supplies, the outlaws became bolder and bolder. Hugo Hoppe claimed that no one left Virginia City without being robbed, and if a man resisted he was murdered.[46]

---

[43] BL, Katherine Dunlap, "Overland Journal, May 15–August 16, 1864," p. 37.

[44] Sarah Raymond Herndon, *Days on the Road: Crossing the Plains in 1865,* pp. 245–46.

[45] ISUA, Pete S. Albertson, "Reminiscences," p. 16.

[46] Mable Ovitt, *Golden Treasure,* p. 49; Ida McPherren, *Imprints on Pioneer Trails,* p. 118.

A Mormon farmer nearly lost his gold by trying to hide it hurriedly as strangers approached. He had sold his merchandise and freight outfit in Montana and was returning to Utah with his profits of $2,500 in gold dust tied in a leather pouch. At a campsite in Beaver Canyon he saw ahead of him six pretty rough-looking men, and in desperation hid his pouch of gold in a mound of dirt beside a rodent's home. When the other men had gone the next morning, the teamster went to retrieve his "gold poke" but found the bag gone. After five hours of frantic shoveling along the twisting tunnel of the rodent hole, he finally found the spot to which the little animal had dragged the valuable piece of leather.[47]

The tide of emigration began to ebb in the summer of 1864, and many left the gold fields in disgust as fewer and fewer fortunes were made. The winter of 1864–65 was long and severe and discouraged travel, and by 1867 emigration could be counted by the number of trains. These few arrivals reported very little migration on the Plains.

The massive influx of new residents into Montana during these early years enormously increased the demand for food and Eastern and European industrial products. This expanding market was to generate businesses intent on transporting goods to satisfy the needs of the people. Packtrains and small freight trains had initially supplied the new settlements, but as new waves of settlers poured in, demand intensified until long lines of freight wagons were eventually making the air heavy with dust as they toiled north.

---

[47] Lee Martinson, "The Lost Gold Poke," *The Improvement Era*, vol. 61 (Nov. 1958), p. 815.

3

Bullwhackers and Mule Skinners

The greatly increased demand for goods that began with the rush for gold in 1863 brought about the rapid expansion of commercial freighting. Men on the road developed practices and policies to cope with the problems inherent in the long-distance transportation of a wide variety of merchandise—anything from a paper of needles to the latest and largest types of mining machinery or from a barrel of relatively stable molasses to a pound of perishable butter.

Packtrains

Perhaps the simplest and most reliable, but certainly the least economical, method of getting the goods to consumers was the packtrain. While wagons had frequently been used for freighting from Salt Lake City and Fort Hall to Montana before the discovery of gold in 1862, packtrains were much more common. Even after wagon freighting became established as the most efficient means of transportation between Utah and Montana, packtrains continued to be used to a surprising extent. With all kinds of goods in high demand, freighters frequently sent in packtrains early in the spring before their wagons could get through. In the fall, packtrains continued to travel for some time after the roads became impassable for wagons.

Included in a packtrain's three-score mules would be several riding mules for the teamsters and a bell mare to lead the mules. Army packtrains were regularly organized with fifty pack mules, fourteen riding mules, and the bell mare. The bell mare's mysterious charisma was well known to muleteers. She was usually a light-colored horse that the mules could see in the dark,

Photograph of pack animals with aparejos in 1874 by William H. Jackson. *Geological Survey, National Archives.*

and she wore a bell that tinkled reassuringly whenever she could not be seen. Nervous mules were calmed when the bell mare was near, and balky mules would relax and follow her for an entire day without stopping.[1]

Once a train started, it kept going until time to make camp for the night. Packing and unpacking the mules each morning and evening took quite a while, and the drivers felt that going through the process again at noon used too much precious time. If an adjustment had to be made to a pack or there was a problem with a particular mule on the trail, the train kept moving while the mule involved was stopped and the difficulty was remedied. The mule caught up with the train later. Packs had to be adjusted often; no matter how carefully the packer prepared the load in the morning, it settled as the mule jogged along, loosening the lashings until the pack had to be rearranged and the lashings tightened again. It took an expert to balance the load while placing the pack saddle and cargo on a mule, and blindfolds were often used to keep the mule from getting skittish. When camp was reached, the packs and saddles were removed and the mules were turned out to graze. Only the bell mare was hobbled or staked out since the mules would not stray very far from her.[2]

One mule could carry 250 to 300 pounds and travel about 25 miles a day. However, Harvey Riley warned that after mules traveled over 300 miles with such loads, the animals were "so reduced ... as to require at least four weeks to bring them into condition again." Grain was carried to supplement the meager forage found near mountain trails, thus reducing the actual amount of freight that could be carried. Wages for the minimum of four or five men that it took to handle a train of fifty mules were an additional expense. In 1860, John Owen was paying his packers $50 a month, with the head packers getting $75.[3] Considering the costs in time and money, with the payload of the entire

---

[1] Nick Eggenhofer, *Wagons, Mules, and Men: How the Frontier Moved West*, p. 17; Randolph B. Marcy, *The Prairie Traveler: A Hand-Book for Overland Expeditions*, p. 100.

[2] Marcy, *The Prairie Traveler*, p. 100; Eggenhofer, *Wagons, Mules, and Men*, pp. 18, 24.

[3] Harvey Riley, *The Mule: A Treatise on the Breeding, Training, and Uses to Which He May Be Put*, p. 50; John Owen, *The Journals and Letters of Major John Owen*, ed. Seymour Dunbar and Paul C. Phillips, vol. 2, p. 226.

train averaging not much more than two ordinary wagonloads,
freighting by pack mule was an excessively expensive method of
shipping goods and was used only when wagons could not get
through. Professional freighters en route to Montana from or
through Utah rarely used packtrains except in times of extreme
emergency or for a wintertime trip.[4]

Early Freighters

When gold was discovered, many of the professional freighters already in business in the Rockies merely turned their trains
toward Montana to dispose of their merchandise quickly and at a
high profit. There was no doubt that the man with the largest
trains who could make the most trips between the thaws of
spring and the storms of winter would in all probability garner
the greatest percentages of the season's business—if he could
finance such a venture in the first place. Few, if any, of the
large-scale operators relied entirely on their own resources for
capital. Those who tried it usually found themselves forced to
borrow or quit business in times of economic stress. Many of
them turned to the network of financial enterprises built up in
Montana by Samuel T. Hauser, who in turn was supported by
firms in the eastern United States and Canada.[5]

On the other hand, some Montana–Utah freighters were
affiliated with eastern firms from the start. John J. Roe & Co.,
for example, was a subsidiary of a Missouri mercantile company
of the same name. In the fall of 1863, Mr. Roe sent his son-in-law,
Captain Nick Wall, and a nineteen-year-old bookkeeper, Edgar
Gleim Maclay, to set up a branch office in Virginia City. The
young entrepreneurs tried their hands at anything that looked
profitable and in the process sometimes accepted freight wagons
or stock as payment for bills due them. Since there was no profit
in idle freighting equipment, Maclay suggested that it be put to
work. Their first venture was made in April 1864 when they

---

[4] Marcy, *The Prairie Traveler*, p. 100f.; Henry P. Walker, *The Wagonmasters*, p. 204.

[5] Paul F. Sharp, "Merchant Princes of the Plains," *Montana: The Magazine of Western History*, vol. 5 (Winter 1955), p. 18; Alexander Toponce, *Reminiscences of Alexander Toponce*, pp. 119–22.

hauled a load of hides to Helena, and from then on they were primarily a freighting concern. In 1865 they changed their name to The Diamond R Transfere Co. and soon managed to corner a large share of the Utah–Montana freighting business.[6]

In 1868, however, the firm changed hands, and Maclay, the former bookkeeper, became one of the new owners. His partners were George Steell and Matthew Carroll, both Fort Benton men who had been employees of the American Fur Company. Headquarters were moved to Helena, and, in 1869, a fourth partner, Colonel C. A. Broadwater, who had been wagon master for the Diamond R for four years, entered the firm. They retained the Diamond R insignia, even though they assumed a new name for the company—E. G. Maclay & Co.[7]

Wagons on the Road

The wagons these freighters used were, in general, the old reliables that had been seen for years in Plains freighting and in the mountains of California and Nevada. The huge Murphy wagons, the smaller Chicago wagons that Mormons liked to acquire for their farm work, the Studebaker, the Espenchied, the Bain, and the Schuttler were among those seen most frequently on the trails. Most of them were modifications of the old Conestoga wagon and its European prototype, the heavy wagon used in eighteenth-century Germany. Whether any of them could lay claim to being an entirely new design in wagons is doubtful; time, experience, technological advances, and the pressures of competition all contributed to frequent changes and improvements in the wagons being built. For example, the "prairie schooner" shape was retained for many years because its bed, bowed in the middle, and its ends, sloped outward and upward suggesting the shape of a boat, were thought to give stability to the huge loads by somewhat reducing the inevitable shifting of freight from end to end as the wagon rolled up and down the

---

[6] MSHS, Matt Carroll, "The Diamond R Transfere Co.," Diamond R file; MSHS, "Diamond R Papers," Diamond R file, Ms dated Sun River, Oct. 9, 1884; MSHS, Freighting Clip File; Joaquin Miller, *An Illustrated History of the State of Montana*, vol. 2, p. 792.

[7] BL, Colonel C. A. Broadwater, "Dictation"; MSHS, Freighting Clip File.

steep mountain grades. However, as more and more freighters adopted the practice of pulling wagons in tandem, the overhanging wagon ends proved to be a nuisance, so the back end of the lead wagon and the front end of the trail wagon were made straight to allow for a closer connection between the two. The shorter the connection between wagons, the easier they were to manage on the sharp turns on the mountain roads. Eventually all wagons were built with little or no flare at either sides or ends.[8]

The favorite of freighters was the great Murphy wagon with its sixteen-foot bed, six-foot high sides, and seven-foot high rear wheels. It could carry almost five tons and frequently did. Built by Joseph Murphy of St. Louis, the wagon contained only well-seasoned wood that did not shrink and fall apart on the trail, as did the wood of some other makes. In many other ways, too, it bore evidence of the craftsmanship of a master wagon builder. A second choice of freighters, especially those in the Utah–Montana trade, was the small Chicago wagon. It was useful as a trail wagon, but, more important, it was easier to sell at the end of the haul when freighters did not want to make the return trip with empty wagons. Its size made it useful as a farm wagon, and it was eagerly purchased by farmers and ranchers in Utah, Idaho, and Montana for as much as $500 after a trip from the East, where it had sold for approximately $120. The Chicago wagon's bed was twelve feet long, three-and-a-half feet wide, and one-and-a-half deep; it could carry 2,500 to 3,500 pounds.[9]

Early Plains freighters had already begun fastening two wagons together and pulling both with one team, thereby cutting their payroll expenses in half and substantially reducing the number of animals needed for a train. One driver and his helper could handle both wagons, and, while a single wagon might require a six-horse team to pull it, two together could be pulled by eight or ten horses at the most. This tandem arrangement was so successful that freighters were soon using three wagons to a team instead of two. The lead wagon usually carried about 9,000

---

[8] Walker, *The Wagonmasters*, pp. 95–98; Eggenhofer, *Wagons, Mules, and Men*, pp. 35–55; Merrill D. Beal and Merle W. Wells, *History of Idaho*, vol. 1, p. 399.

[9] Beal and Wells, *History of Idaho*, vol. 1, p. 399; Walker, *The Wagonmasters*, pp. 95–98; Eggenhofer, *Wagons, Mules, and Men*, pp. 35–55.

Eight-horse hitch for pulling two wagons in Virginia City Montana. *Montana Historical Society, Helena.*

pounds, the middle or swing wagon, about 6,000, and the trail wagon about 3,000. On steep grades or where mud or deep sand made the going heavy, wagons were often uncoupled and pulled over the difficult places one at a time.[10]

Oxen, Mules, or Horses?

To a man in the freighting business, his teams were no less important than his wagons, whether he drove oxen, mules, or horses. The relative merits of each as a draft animal was a subject for warm debates, for journalists as well as for men in the business. Randolph Marcy, in his handbook for prairie travelers, pointed out that mules were faster and could stand summer heat better than oxen, but that mules had to be used where grain could be bought en route or where there was an abundance of good grass, and that they also required good, firm roads and relatively short journeys (not over 1,000 miles). On the other hand, on a long journey of over 1,500 miles, oxen had more stamina and fared better on the scant grass found in many places. Some claimed that oxen were not subject to as many ailments as horses or mules. Others pointed out that oxen required very little night herding because they filled up on grass and lay down to chew their cuds, while horses and mules tended to wander some distance from camp as they grazed. Because of this, and because they were slow to stampede, oxen were less likely to be stolen by Indians. A final consideration was the comparative cost of a team of mules and a yoke of oxen; the initial purchase price for a mule was more than double that of a steer, and the steer could be used for beef at the end of the trip. Or as one old bullwhacker put it, "the hide and tallow of an old ox will buy a young steer." [11]

Training Oxen for the Trail

Lafe Rose, a bullwhacker, recalled selling oxen after the summer freighting season was over and mentioned some of the

[10] Eggenhoffer, *Wagons, Mules, and Men*, pp. 35-55; Walker, *The Wagonmasters*, pp. 95-98; Beal and Wells, *History of Idaho*, vol 1, p. 399.

[11] Marcy, *The Prairie Traveler*, p. 27; Charles S. Walgamott, *Six Decades Back*, p. 255; *The Banditti of the Rocky Mountains, and Vigilance Committee in Idaho*, p. 95.

other work that went on during the winter to prepare for the next season:

> The poorest oxen and those that had reached the age limit and were unfit for more work, were separated and fattened for the market. The others, after their shoes were taken off, were turned on pasture until severe weather made it necessary to feed and get them in shape for spring work.... During the winter we made from old wagon tires hundreds of ox or bull shoes, and from cottonwood trees found along the streams we made extra yokes. As spring approached we began breaking young steers to take the place of those worn out.... The steer was considered old enough to break when he was coming four years old, and was generally good for four or five seasons.... The young ox soon learned to lean against the yoke, and in three or four days was doing the service of the older ox.[12]

Breaking and training steers to work in harness was always an exciting time despite the claims of some bullwhackers that it was simply a matter of putting an untamed steer in the middle of an experienced team and letting the older oxen train him. The gentleness and the willingness to work so often praised by bullwhackers were not always present when the bulls, as steers were called in the trade, were first hitched to a wagon. It was only after several days' work with steers that a man could "leave a rope dragging when we turned them loose" and merely pick up the end of the rope when he wanted to catch them again.[13] From the time the rope was placed around the neck of a new steer, "until he was being reluctantly hauled along as one of the team, the fun was fast and furious." [14]

This, of course, depended on what one thought of as fun. Frequently a steer would fight the yoke so strenuously that he would break it loose from the wagon and run wildly around with the heavy yoke swinging from his neck. At such times the bullwhackers could be found under their wagons until the yoke broke and fell off.[15] Then the process started over again. Sometimes a steer would not manage to break free, but would fight until the yoke turned upside down; then the driver might find himself

---

[12] Walgamott, *Six Decades Back*, pp. 254-55.
[13] ISUA, Art T. Owens, "Interviewed by John F. Ryan, 1936, at the age of 82," Idaho Historical Records Survey Interviews, Ms 83.
[14] MSHS, Freighting Clip File.
[15] Ibid.

Oxteam with freight wagon fording a stream. *U.S. Signal Corps, National Archives.*

with a pair of oxen turned backward to the other pairs in the team. If this happened on the trail, it meant serious trouble and delay.[16]

Men got to know the bulls on their particular teams and —affectionately or not—gave them special nicknames, usually chosen because of some characteristic such as color, personality, or action. Or the bull might have had some attribute—flattering or otherwise—of someone the driver knew, in which case that person's name was bestowed on the bull. Pete Albertson had "two Very good lea[de]rs for my teem . . and two very good names for them . . it was Brigham and Generl . . " One bullwhacker recalled knowing "many hundred oxen . . . named Brigham in honor of Brigham Young. . . . We had three Brighams in our outfit, designated as Big Brigham, Little Brigham, and Brigham With The Big Horn." [17]

Driving North

On the trail, drivers tried not to overwork their teams, rarely forcing the animals out of a walk and resting them often, especially for a long period in the heat of the day and all day on Sundays. Their notorious bullwhip, with its "popper" that could "bite out a bunch of hair wherever it landed," was seldom used with enough force to draw blood.[18] If an individual bull became "balky and held back," the popper was whipped out with a swift undercut to the tender belly, where it "whacked the loafing animal almost into the next county." [19] The rest of the team depended on the leaders for direction, but the ever-ready whip of the driver helped to keep them in line and to keep them working. These whips were usually handmade, with a hardwood stock from three to six feet long and a lash of braided rawhide that could be anywhere from ten to thirty feet long, tapering from an

---

[16] Nimrod Good, "A Close-Up of the Oxen," *Rigby [Idaho] Star*, Mar. 7, 1963.

[17] ISUA, Pete S. Albertson, "Reminiscences," p. 21; Walgamott, *Six Decades Back*, pp. 255–56.

[18] Marcy, *The Prairie Traveler*, p. 40; MSHS, "Experienced Bullwhacker," told by Anne Hawkins.

[19] William Francis Hooker, *The Prairie Schooner*, p. 21; William H. Jackson, *Time Exposure: The Autobiography of William Henry Jackson*, p. 116.

inch thick to the size of a pencil. On the end of the lash was a "popper," a V-shaped piece of leather that cracked with the sound of a gunshot when snapped just right. Poppers were sometimes "round pieces of lead about the size of garden peas." Pete Albertson's whip had a two-foot stock of hickory and a lash that was "about 15 feet long and up at the Stock.. it was 2 inches thick." In addition to the whip, the driver sometimes carried a goad, a long stick with a nail or other point in the end of it.[20]

If there were difficult spots on the road, where extreme effort was required,

> almost like magic the wagon boss would appear on the scene ...and order the bull whacker to...whip them into a straight line...until every chain was tight and every yoke filled by the bull's neck until the bow rested against his shoulders.
> Then the bullwhacker and boss... began to yell and use their lashes, swinging the string of seven yokes back into the trail and keeping them clawing the dirt until their tongues protruded...and the yelling and lashing continued until the team was out of its bad place, or seemed ready to quit; then there was a rest, and the process repeated, maybee for hours.[21]

The leaders were trained to move to the left at the command of "Gee!" and to the right at "Haw!" Of this, William H. Jackson said: "Only the voice of a master can make twelve bulls gee or haw with a single word," but William F. Hooker thought the words had to be "uttered in the peculiar musical tone of the whacker" and indicated that there was other language to which the exasperated driver could resort. Profanity became almost an art form among bullwhackers. They were proud of their long strings of expletives and practiced them diligently. Pete Albertson "would Sling the old Whip at the Bulls.. and holler out as loud as I could.. Wo.. hee Buck and Jerry.. get up Brigham you god D.. old S.. of.. A.. B.. then you ought to see old Brigham get up in his yok.. " [22]

---

[20] Agnes W. Spring, *The Cheyenne and Black Hills Stage and Express Routes*, p. 174; Ida McPherren, *Imprints of Pioneer Trails*, p. 34; Hooker, *The Prairie Schooner*, pp. 38–39; ISUA, Albertson, "Reminiscences," pp. 18–19.
[21] MSHS, "Experienced Bullwhacker."
[22] Jackson, *Time Exposure*, p. 115; Hooker, *The Prairie Schooner*, p. 31; ISUA, Albertson, "Reminiscences," p. 21.

A driver was expected to know his team well enough to pick them out in the morning and quickly harness them to his wagons. He usually yoked them in pairs and tied them to the wagon until all were ready to be hitched. The wheelers, the first pair next to the wagon, were the heavyweights of the team, able to hold back the heavy load on a downgrade or counter their weight against unruly teammates. After the wheelers came the pointers, and, if there were more than three yoke of oxen in the team, ahead of the points were the first, second, and perhaps third swings. The wild or half-broken cattle were placed with the pointers or swings to be trained where the leaders could aid in managing them. The leaders were the lightweights of the team—always the best trained and quickest to respond to the driver's signals. They were usually Texas longhorns, lighter and quicker than the Mexican shorthorn. The wheelers were hitched to the wagon tongue; the rest of the oxen were connected to the wagon by means of a chain running from yoke to yoke in such a way that when the team "stretched out" and the oxen were pushing against their yokes, the taut chain pulled the wagon along.[23]

Hitching time was likely to be quite a scramble, especially in the spring when men and oxen were out of practice—or even more of a melee if greenhorns were involved. William H. Jackson, who signed on (with no experience) to drive in an ox train that was heading for Montana in the summer of 1866, heard that Alexander Majors had once timed his men on an early morning start and they were ready to pull out in sixteen minutes. Jackson's inexperienced crew, however, took eight hours in the "mass confusion" of the first day and never did get the time down to much less than forty minutes, even after weeks on the road.[24]

Many bullwhackers felt that the only drawback in driving oxen rather than mules was that the driver had to walk all the way—that is, unless he followed Pete Albertson's tactics: "I had to Walk all of the time . . as you was not alowed to Ride on the Wagon tung . . and that was the onely place you could Ride . . and lots of time I would Steel aride When the Wagon Boss Would be

---

[23] William H. Jackson, *Bullwhacking Across the Plains*, n.p.; Hooker, *The Prairie Schooner*, p. 30; Eggenhofer, *Wagons, Mules, and Men*, p. 110.
[24] Jackson, *Time Exposure*, p. 112.

ahead of the trane . . looking for a place to camp for Brakfast. ." [25]

Breakfast came late in the morning. At the first light of dawn, the night herder brought the bulls into camp, rudely awakening the sleeping men, and before sunup the teams were hitched, the men had swallowed some scalding coffee and snatched some bacon, and the train was ready to start. The wagon master kept them going until midmorning, then found a place to camp. Here they had a hearty breakfast, and men and animals rested until midafternoon. If there were repairs to be made on clothing or equipment, this was the time for it. By midafternoon the train was on its way again and traveled until a good place to camp for the night was reached—anytime from sundown to midnight. Depending on the terrain and whether there had been unexpected delays, the train would have covered from twelve to sixteen miles, sometimes more.[26] Circumstances, or individual wagon masters, might vary the pattern somewhat, although, as a general rule, this was the day-in and day-out routine as long as the freighting season lasted.

Rivalries on the Trail

A rivalry for status existed in the freighting world. The derogatory remarks exchanged as a mule team passed an ox team on the road could be heard from both sides; but somehow the lowly oxen, with their driver plodding through dust, just did not present a picture quite as glamorous as a team of mules with their driver riding in state on the back of his wheeler.[27]

Not only were mules more expensive than oxen, but so were their harnesses. In 1866 a good span of mules cost from $200 to $400, while a yoke of good oxen could be bought for $75 to $145, and unbroken steers were even cheaper. The big freighting concerns, to whom speed was important, usually used mules because they were faster.[28] While oxen averaged 12 to 15 miles a day, mules could do 15 to 20. On the 500-mile trip from Salt Lake City

---

[25] ISUA, Albertson, "Reminiscences," pp. 18–19.

[26] Jackson, *Time Exposure*, pp. 112–16; Jackson, *Bullwhacking Across the Plains*, n.p.; J. H. Beadle, *Life in Utah; or the Mysteries and Crimes of Mormonism*, p. 222; Spring, *The Cheyenne and Black Hills Stage*, p. 174.

[27] Marcy, *The Prairie Traveler*, p. 27.

[28] Ibid.; Walker, *The Wagonmasters*, pp. 106–7, 125.

to Helena, this could mean that a mule team would get there a whole week ahead of an ox team. And saving a week each way could mean an extra trip for the freighters before the season ended.

Mules were preferred over horses, also, since horses seemed more susceptible to disease and certainly required better forage and easier roads than were to be found in the West. Joe Hartmann used horses in his outfit, but all of his horses were grown on western ranges. "Eastern-bred horses weren't of any use. They just couldn't stand up to the cold weather and rough living," Hartmann said.[29] In addition, the mule had the longest average working life—eighteen years—and endured fatigue better, but only if it had good handling.[30] Harvey Riley said that on his trip West with a train bound for Camp Floyd, Utah, in 1868, many young mules were ruined because he could not get water for them. In fact, he claimed that "thousands of the best mules in the army . . . were ruined and made useless to the Government on account of the incompetency and ignorance of the wagon-masters and teamsters." [31]

The wagon master could make or break a freighting venture. He was the man who was responsible for getting the train through and for the welfare of the men and animals in his charge. He chose the campsites, determined the length of the day's drive, and organized the daily routine of the camps. He had to do the hiring and the firing and see to the training of greenhorn hands. William Hooker had nothing but praise for his own wagon boss, Nate Williams, who hired him and then taught him to drive. When Nate needed to hire more drivers, he perched himself on a stool across the street from a saloon and waited. Eventually, as he knew they would, men wandered out of the saloon penniless and jobless after having spent their entire wages from their last trip for a spree in town. They were ready to hire out again.[32]

Wagon trains usually consisted of about twenty-five wagons;

---

[29] MSHS, Clyde Reichelt, "Joe Hartmann," Freighting Clip File; Walker, *The Wagonmasters*, pp. 102-3.

[30] Eggenhofer, *Wagons, Mules, and Men*, p. 90.

[31] Riley, *The Mule*, pp. 19-35.

[32] William Francis Hooker, *The Bullwhacker*, p. 7.

more meant that feed at the campgrounds might be scarce for so many animals. If two trains traveled together for some reason, they always separated at camp time to give themselves adequate water, grass, and wood. On the larger trains, the wagon master might have an assistant who helped in the daily routine. But ultimately it was the wagon master himself who was responsible for the $25,000 to $250,000 worth of freight in his charge and for the expensive stock and equipment under his command.

Driving Mules on the Montana Road

Driving mules was somewhat different from driving oxen. The mule skinner rode the nigh (left wheel) mule and directed the team by means of a single line that passed through a turret ring on the harness of each span and ended at the bit of the nigh leader. A steady pull on this line turned the leaders to the left, and a few quick jerks turned them to the right. A jockey stick, or wooden rod, connected the bit of the right leader to the collar of the left, or line mule, in such a way that when the left leader turned, he pushed or pulled the right leader with him. In long teams, other lines went to the swing team directly in front of the wheelers. These two spans were the only ones controlled by the teamster; the rest of the team followed the direction of the leaders. Driving could be rather tricky on a sharp mountain turn where the first spans in the team might be going east while the last ones were still going west, with a ridge between that cut off the driver's view of his leaders.[33] On mountain curves, the swing spans also had to jump the heavy chain that served as an extension of the wagon tongue. The wheelers were harnessed to the tongue itself, but the doubletrees of the leaders and of each swing span were attached along the chain. As the leaders went around a bend in the road, the chain would pull out from the wagon at an angle, pressing against the mules on that side of the team. These mules would then jump over the chain to the opposite side where their mates were, releasing the chain to be pulled taut. Then, as the road straightened out, the chain would swing back to a

---

[33] BYUL, Ebenezer Crouch, "Autobiography of Ebenezer Crouch, September 12, 1923," p. 52; Merrill D. Beal, *A History of Southeastern Idaho*, p. 279.

straight line, and the mules would have to jump back again to their own side of the chain.[34]

The line that guided the mules, often made of rope rather than leather, was called the jerk line because of the way it was jerked to signal the leaders. Since it was not easy to train a mule to pull in a jerk line team, mules so trained were considered something special and were treated very carefully. The leaders were especially quick, sure-footed, and intelligent animals —sometimes the smallest in the team. It was among the middle members of a team, or swings, that a freighter would often place wild or partly broken stock to finish taming and training. Then there was plenty of excitement in camp and more on the road. It might take several days before the new mule would settle down enough to add his weight to the steady pull of the team. In the meantime there would be "some breakage, and hardly any mileage." The largest mules in the team were the wheelers, which, as with oxen, were placed next to the wagon where they could supply braking power on a downhill grade, thereby reducing the strain on the regular brake of the wagon.[35]

The wagon brake was operated in a manner similar to the jerk line. A line tied to the pommel of the saddle on the wheeler ran back to the brake handle of the lead wagon and from there to the brake handles of the following wagons. In this manner, the teamster could work the brakes on all three wagons at once; in fact, Hugo Hoppe claimed that when he rode with a jerk line outfit to Montana, he worked "the brakes more often than the lines." [36] Mule drivers, as well as oxen drivers, seemed to think that mules responded better to profanity than gentle persuasion. On one occasion, when a driver was having no success coaxing his mules to pull uphill, an expert stepped up and offered to help. "All of a sudden there was a shouting and many profane words, and a crack of the whip! and lo those mules came up that hill on high!" [37]

---

[34] Walker, *The Wagonmasters*, p. 105.

[35] Beal and Wells, *History of Idaho*, vol. 1, p. 399; MSHS, "R. L. 'Dick' Potter, as told to Rozetta Bailey Sylten," in *The Saco Independent*, Aug. 1, 1936, Clip file.

[36] McPherren, *Imprints of Pioneer Trails*, p. 113.

[37] MSUL, Fannie D. Ennis, "Early Days in Virginia City, etc."

Life on the Trail

On the trail, life was very much the same for either bull-whacker or mule skinner. It was a hard, rough life with few tangible rewards. Rates of pay varied greatly, but one thing was always sure—the wages were low enough for a man to quickly spend his earnings at the end of the trip. At the age of sixteen, Pete Albertson was paid $35 for his first trip in 1866 because "they thought I was Rather Small for that kind of Work .. they said they would try me .. But Would not give me a man's Wedges .." The following year, after gaining a little experience and a little growth, he received $45 as a bullwhacker for Wells Fargo. When William H. Jackson was hired in 1866 to drive freight from Missouri to Montana, his pay was $20 a month and "found"—that is, grub and perhaps a couple of blankets. Two years earlier, Heber McBride had received $40 a month in Montana, an amount that seemed to be accepted as fairly good pay for the job. Wagon masters earned a good deal more than the ordinary teamster—$100 to $150 a month was not uncommon.[38]

Food in the camps rarely varied unless someone happened to have shot some game or caught some fish during the day—an occasion to be celebrated. The mess wagon at the rear of the train usually carried such staples as flour, bacon, beans, sugar or syrup, coffee, and dried apples to be alternated occasionally with "spuds and onions." The mess wagon usually brought up the rear of a large wagon train on the theory that no one would think of letting this particular wagon fall behind if it had difficulty, and no other wagon ahead of it would be allowed to fall behind either. The longer trains were usually divided into three or more messes to facilitate feeding a large number of men in a short time. One man in each mess did the cooking; he might be a volunteer who did all the cooking the entire trip, or he might be taking his turn on a rotation system.[39] Frequently, there was a "swamper," or general handyman, who could be called upon to assist the cook between his other chores in camp, and he "usually paid well for

---

[38] ISUA, Albertson, "Reminiscences," p. 17; Jackson, *Time Exposure,* p. 104; BYUL, Heber R. McBride, "Autobiography," p. 24; Walker, *The Wagonmasters,* p. 78.

[39] ISUA, Albertson, "Reminiscences," p. 17; Jackson, *Bullwhacking Across the Plains,* n.p.

his passage." [40]

In well-run trains, the wagons were numbered and might take turns at leading, although in many the lineup of the first day was maintained throughout the trip. In other trains, it was the first driver out who was able to ride in dust-free comfort for the rest of the day. In a train where it was the custom for each driver to cook his own breakfast before the drive began, the daily contest to head the line could result in having to choose between food and dust. Not all teamsters had the initiative of one old hand who was just putting his biscuits in the Dutch oven when he saw his neighbor pulling out. Grabbing his coffee pot and oven, he got his team in motion just in time to get in the lead position. The biscuits continued to bake under the coals on the lid of the oven, and later were "gnawed in grim satisfaction" and washed down with hot coffee from the pot on the driver's seat as the driver breathed the dust-free air that only the lead outfit could enjoy. [41]

The only other meal of the day might be eaten after the train had camped for the night or during the rest before the final drive of the day. While the other men busied themselves gathering wood, unharnessing the teams, greasing wagons, carrying water, or any of the other numerous chores about camp, the cook prepared dinner of the inevitable beans, coffee, and biscuits, with perhaps some dried fruit sweetened with brown sugar for dessert—or maybe a molasses cake baked in the Dutch oven. The men were hungry enough that dinner was relished despite the monotony of the menu. [42] In fact, a man could get mighty hungry during the day, especially a growing boy. Pete Albertson, whose inexperience relegated him to driving the wagon at the "tale end of the train," which of course was the mess wagon, was able to relieve some of his hunger. "Some time in the Day .. I would get hungry .. and nothing cooked .. But Bread .. But I would have Some thig to eat any Way So I Would go up in the Wagon .. and get a pice of Bread and Some Raw Bacon .. and Walk along By my Bulls .. and Eat Raw Bacon and Bread .. the Sun Would be Very hot and Ever time I would take a Bit of off the Bacon .. the

[40] Arthur C. Saunders, *The History of Bannock County, Idaho*, p. 51.

[41] Barzilla W. Clark, *Bonneville County in the Making*, p. 20.

[42] BYUL, Crouch, "Autobiography," p. 41; BYUL, McBride, "Autobiography," p. 24.

Grice Would Run Down Between my fingers.. But I thought it was a squar meal.. I done this Very often." [43]

At the end of the day, when the men relaxed for a time before turning in, came the "amusements of the evening, swapping yarns, singing songs, resitations, etc., but the best of all was the stag dance. We had our fiddler and accordion player, and every few evenings they would be called into service. Then at the call of the floor manager 'to form' Bill would crave the pleasure of dancing with Jack, Bob would choose Joe and so on. Then all set, up the music started. Swing your partner, all promenade, and away we would go. Oh boy, what fun." [44] About ten o'clock the wagon boss would yell "Bed time!" and the men would roll up their blankets and tarpaulins and soon be fast asleep—except for the night herders and guards. At daybreak the routine started again.

Three items were a continuing problem to the freighter on the road: water, blankets, and lice. Men frequently remedied their lack of blankets by "snatching" some from others, a practice that could have serious consequences in the bitter cold of the high mountains. But not everyone accepted lice with the aplomb of Pete Albertson. The first night out, when Pete began to wonder about a place to sleep, a kindly freighter said,

> young man you have got your Blankets With you. if you havent you can Role in With me.. I thanked him Very much.. and we went to Bead in his Wagon ... Well I tell you I was a happy Boy.. Did not Sleepe any that Night.. [worried about being able to yoke up the cattle the next morning]... But that was not all together the Risan I Did not Sleepe.. I was fighting and killing lice as Big as limey Beans.. all night but it Was not Very long untill I got used to lice I got so Well used to them that I Could not live Without them.. I Did try to get Reid of them once.. Bit I faled do Do So.. But I thought I had the Dead Sinch on them.. I took off my Shirt and Layed it over one of these ant hills.. and left it there all Night.. and Went over in the morning to get my Shirt.. and to my surprise.. the lice had liked the ants.. and taken Position of the hill.. my Riders [readers].. NO [do] Not Bleve this unless you Wantto.. it looks Very Resenbilly to me as my lice out Numbered the ants.. [45]

[43] ISUA, Albertson, "Reminiscences," p. 21.
[44] BYUL, Crouch, "Autobiography," p. 41.
[45] ISUA, Albertson, "Reminiscences," pp. 17-18.

The following year, smug in his familiarity with lice, Albertson watched eleven new men who had slept in the wagons because they had no blankets. "It was not long Befor you could See them out in the Brush With their Shirt off . . aprospecting . . and make a Strike Ever Now and then." At another time, he referred to lice as "the life Stock of the plains." [46] Perhaps this is why teamsters frequently wore the same clothing the entire trip, never bothering to wash it and discarding it at the end of the journey to buy complete new outfits.

An adequate water supply was a much more serious problem. Sometimes the men had to shoulder kegs and walk two or three miles to get water. Other times, the train drove late into the night to reach water. Many watering places were more than a day's drive apart, so each wagon had to carry its own supply in large forty- to sixty-gallon barrels. Since the barrels had to be strong and well made so they would not spring a leak as they bounced along, empty whiskey barrels were highly prized. These were filled with water and soaked to get the taste of whiskey diluted enough so that the animals would drink water from the barrels.[47]

Goods Sent North

The loads of merchandise being shipped into Montana were likely to contain almost anything that was needed or wanted by the miners and settlers in the new territory. Joseph R. Walker and Brothers accounts showed a typical load in 1862:

1 keg nails	2 kegs nails
1 box no. 72	1 case cotton
16 boxes soap	1 box pepper
1 box no. 100	1 bale blankets
1 box no. 46	1 bale dry goods
1 iron shutter	coffee
bake kettles	sugar
candles[48]	

---

[46] Ibid., p. 46.

[47] Beal, *A History of Southeastern Idaho*, p. 278; Jennie B. Brown, *Fort Hall on the Oregon Trail*, p. 349.

[48] BYUL, Joseph R. Walker and Brothers, "Account Books, 1860-1862," Ms 228.

Teams in Helena in 1865. *Courtesy of William D. Livingstone.*

To the people of Montana, it seemed downright uneconomical to buy mediocre merchandise when they had to pay such high freight tariffs. For example, if a man had to pay a $25 freight charge to get a shovel, what did it matter if the shovel had cost $10 instead of $5 back in the States? By the time it reached Montana, the price differential would be minimized by the added cost of freight. Luxury items, too, could be had in Montana if one had the gold to pay the freight. When the W. F. Sanders and Sidney Edgertons sat down to an 1863 Thanksgiving dinner with their host, Sheriff Henry Plummer, they enjoyed every expensive mouthful of the Utah turkeys that had cost Plummer $50 apiece.[49]

Transporting whiskey was another matter. Occasionally the whiskey would arrive at its destination somewhat altered from its original state. A favorite method of sampling the merchandise en route was to move a barrel hoop, bore a hole where the hoop had been, then drink the whiskey directly from the hole, suck it out with a straw, or catch it in a tin cup. After all interested parties had quenched their thirst, enough water was added to the barrel to make up for the whiskey consumed, the hole was plugged, and the hoop driven back in place. Obviously, if the drivers became thirsty very often, the liquor arrived in a much less potent condition.[50]

Prices fluctuated remarkably in very short periods of time. If the freighter were "long on what the people were short on," he would be able to sell at high prices. On the other hand, if two or more freighters arrived in town simultaneously with the same kind of goods, their prices had to be reduced accordingly in order to dispose of the merchandise. Weather, too, had a great influence on prices. A man who sat out a storm in camp would have to take second place to a man who pushed on through, often at the expense of many of his animals. In November of 1862, Mr. C. H. Howard reported the following prices to the *Deseret News*; the list serves also as a sampling of the kinds of things that were brought into the camps that first winter in Montana:

---

[49] Col. A. C. McClure, "Wilbur Fisk Sanders," in *Contributions to the Historical Society of Montana*, vol. 8, p. 24.

[50] Federal Writers' Project of the WPA, *Montana: A State Guide Book*, p. 89.

flour, per cwt.	$25.00
beans, 90 lb. sack	25.00
salt, per cwt.	25.00
bacon, lb.	.50
fresh beef, lb. (local)	.15
butter, lb.	1.00
turnips, lb.	.20
sugar, lb.	.75
coffee, lb.	1.00
tea, lb.	3.00
saleratus, lb.	.50
Cream of tartar, lb.	2.50
Dried apples	.60
vinegar, per gal.	4.00
milk, per qt. (local)	.15
bar soap, lb.	1.00
powder, lb.	3.00
lead, lb.	1.00
gun caps, box	1.00
ax & helve	5.00
heavy boots, pr	10.00 or 15.00
woolen socks, pr	1.00
chewing tobacco, lb.	3.00
smoking tobacco, lb.	1.00 [51]

Emily Meredith wrote to her father that during the winter of 1862-63, flour rose to $40 per hundred pounds, then dropped to $8 for a short time in the early spring because the Mormons brought in such large quantities. On November 27 of the following year, 1863, the *Union Vedette* reported that flour was $45 per cwt. and coffee was $1 a pound.[52]

Despite the fact that large fortunes could more easily be lost than made on the turn of a wagon wheel, the freighting business continued to expand during the 1860's until sometimes it appeared to travelers that there was one continuous freight train between Salt Lake City and the gold fields. The kinds of goods being hauled changed through the years, however. Leonidas A. Mecham noticed that "at first we hauled canned goods and liquor, mostly

---

[51] *Deseret News*, Nov. 19, 1862; BL, "Bancroft Scraps, Utah Miscellany," vol. 109, pp. 44.

[52] MSHS, Mrs. Emily R. Meredith, "Experiences and Impressions of a Woman in Montana, 1862–1863," p. 13.

whiskey. The liquor made up the principal part of our load. Later on I remember one load that I took up my trail wagon had nothing on it but sawing machines piled high. Another trip I made, I remember hauling a big horse threshing machine." [53] Occasionally some freighters attempted to haul perishable goods. A few were successful and others were not. Eggs arrived in the wintertime in a solid state; in the summer their condition on arrival was even less satisfactory. The wheat in which they had been hand packed to prevent breakage sometimes arrived in a sticky mess fit only for stock feed. A few freighters even attempted to carry butter. Art T. Owens told how he and others managed to get to their destinations with the butter still edible.

> Some of the freighters hauled butter. They sometimes took a light load and made a quicker trip. . . . They usually put it down in a sack of flour or down in the bottom of the load and piled flour over it. When they got up into the mountains they would take it out in the night and let it get cold and then put it back again. I suppose that some of it got a little stale but the miners had to eat something.[54]

The development of well-organized freighting companies that could transport such delicacies to the rough miners of Montana did not occur immediately. Rather, early freighting followed a somewhat hit-or-miss pattern until the mining camps became permanent settlements and commercial freighting between Utah and Montana began to increase.

---

[53] ISUA, Leonidas A. Mecham, "Interviewed by John F. Ryan, 1936," Idaho Historical Records Survey Interviews, Ms 83.

[54] ISUA, Owens, "Interview."

4

Freighting Supplies to the Gold Fields

Utah rapidly became the chief source of merchandise for commercial freighting to Montana. Goods and produce so desperately needed at the mining camps were already on hand, and Utahns were well supplied with freighting equipment, acquired at next-to-nothing prices when the outbreak of the Civil War necessitated the abandonment of Camp Floyd.

Camp Floyd, thirty-six miles south of Salt Lake City in Cedar Valley, was established by Utah Expedition troops in 1858. In 1857, Colonel Albert Sidney Johnston's Army had been sent to protect the new territorial governor and other federal officials and to ensure the proper enforcement of federal laws in Mormon Utah. After a winter of negotiations, the federal government and the Mormon leaders agreed to settle the so-called Utah War by staging a demonstration march of the army directly through Salt Lake City and establishing Camp Floyd as a military base.

When the troops were returned to the East in 1861, the government disposed of approximately $4 million worth of stores for not much more than $100,000. Even before the final sale, wagons that had cost from $141 to $196 sold for $25 to $30; ox teams could be had for $50; and mules that had cost from $168 to $179 went for similarly low prices. Alexander Toponce, then an assistant wagon boss in the Johnston's Army supply trains, told of seeing wagons "complete with bows, covers, neck yoke, double trees, stretchers and chains for six mules sold at $6.50. One Payson [Utah] man bought a score of them at $6.50 a piece." [1]

---

[1] Hubert H. Bancroft, *History of Utah*, p. 575. U. S. Congress, "Utah Expedition Contracts, Feb. 10, 1858, Mar. 2, 1858," *House Exec. Doc. 99*; NA, "Office of the Quartermaster General, Consolidated Correspondence File, 1794–

Farmers and freighters throughout the region were drawn to the Camp Floyd auctions and purchased wagons and teams that a year or two later would be heading north to the gold fields of Montana. Livingston, Bell & Company traced the beginnings of their successful expansion to the purchase of merchandise and freighting equipment at Camp Floyd. Walker Brothers, too, freighted their merchandise from California, and later to Montana, with stock and wagons from Camp Floyd. And Ben Holladay was able to expand his stagecoach enterprise with stock purchased at the Camp Floyd auction.[2]

Utah Freighters

Salt Lake City merchants already freighting to the Idaho mines were very quickly joined by Mormon farmers fortunate enough to have sturdy wagons, good teams, and a surplus of produce—always in demand in the growing Montana settlements. The people of Utah realized immense benefits from their own

1915," Utah Expedition, 1857, Box 1174, Abstract of Quartermaster's Stores Furnished to Cheyenne & Utah Expeditions, at Fort Leavenworth, K.T., in 1857, Letter from D. D. Tompkins to Maj. Gen. Thomas S. Jesup, 1857, Letters from G. H. Crosman to Maj. Gen. Thomas S. Jesup, Mar. 2, Sept. 30, 1859; Alexander Toponce, *Reminiscences of Alexander Toponce*, p. 39.

Toponce also related his own purchase of some mules at a Camp Floyd auction. On instructions from the main wagon boss, Toponce matched a corral full of mules into spans so that they could be sold as teams. In the corral were about 100 "culls and scrubs—little mountain pack mules" mixed in with "a lot of big, rangy mules that they had bought in Missouri at fancy prices." As he paired them off, he gave each team an identifying number. At the auction, the little mules were led out first, and most of them were sold for $30 to $40 to Ben Holladay, the famous Stagecoach King. He was "about the only bidder, except a few Mormon farmers who soon got all they wanted of those little mules and led them away." However, Toponce made a discovery. "Every time a team of these little mules were sold to Ben Halliday, some one would take the number off . . . and change them for the numbers on two of the big Missouri mules. So all day long they sold little mules . . . [and] as fast as they were sold some one traded the numbers for the numbers on the big mules. . . . Some of these [little] mules he bought two or three times. Then I decided to buy some myself. Ben glared at me but he would not bid against me and I got most of my mules at around $30. I bought 12 altogether. But I noticed that when my mules were turned back into the corral no one changed the numbers, so after a while I just went in and changed them myself. . . . I picked out the best riding mules in the corral . . . [and] one pacing mule I sold in Kansas City for $500." Toponce, *Reminiscences*, pp. 25-26.

    [2] Andrew L. Neff, *History of Utah, 1847 to 1869*, pp. 775, 788; BL, "Biographical Sketch of the Walker Brothers."

freighting ventures and from their trade with others freighting to the mining areas. Residents of Salt Lake and northern Utah towns were encouraged by the Mormon church and Brigham Young to take advantage of this unexpected opportunity to obtain cash or much-needed commodities.

With or without special prodding, large numbers of men in Cache Valley, indeed in all of northern Utah, engaged in the freighting business to some degree. Even as far south as Spanish Fork, Joshua Hawkes turned to freighting after having "such bad luck" farming. Although he was able to finance his venture by trading some land, others, if they had no freighting outfits of their own, hired out to those who did. Some of them were not much more than boys; John Stilley Carpenter was only thirteen when he drove an ox team to Virginia City in 1862. Others were already experienced freighters; John Ward Christian of Beaver, Utah, for example, had been freighting for some time between Los Angeles and Salt Lake when he began to extend his route into Montana in 1862.[3]

The *Deseret News* did all it could to support and promote the new enterprises by publicizing prices and profits and recommending the most advantageous routes to Montana from the settlements. On December 10, 1862, the *News* announced that the best route north was a new one through Cache Valley and Franklin, Idaho, to the old road in Marsh Valley. Mr. J. Gammill had taken his 7,000 pounds of flour by that route and reported the road excellent and feed and water plentiful. This route, of course, would lead the freighters right past the doors of Cache Valley farmers and would be profitable for the farmers whether they were freighting themselves, selling to freighters, or trading with passing miners.

In fact there were many who agreed wholeheartedly with Hugo Hoppe, who had ridden to Montana with some Mormons:

> The next day my Mormon friends sold the supplies they had hauled down from Salt Lake, and I wondered that day whether freighting supplies was not a gold mine without a rival. They had

---

[3] ISUA, Joshua Hawkes, "Autobiography," p. 9; John Stilley Carpenter Papers, Letter from John Stilley Carpenter to Alene Smith, Glendale, Ut., Dec. 21, 1921; John Ward Christian, MLUU, "The Bancroft Collection of Mormon Papers," microfilm no. 68.

Main Street, Salt Lake City, 1867–68. *Utah State Historical Society, Salt Lake City.*

purchased the supplies in Salt Lake at normal prices and sold them in Virginia City at abnormal prices. They bought flour at six dollars a hundred pounds and sold it at forty dollars; sugar at sixty cents a pound and sold it at fourteen dollars a pound. Other commodities brought the same huge margin of profit.

It is not against their religion for all freighters did the same thing but freighting of supplies was like the finding of gold—an element of luck went with it. Freighters who struck it rich were the ones who knew what supplies the people were short on, that the cities were long on.[4]

Not all Mormons looked upon the boom trade as a bonanza, however. In December, special messengers were sent to Cache Valley with a warning from Brigham Young to stop selling wheat because it was becoming so scarce that Young was buying all he could get at $3 a bushel for the California Volunteers at Fort Douglas, who were out of bread and had appealed to the church to furnish them with wheat.[5]

Freighting from Montana

The miners and settlers at Grasshopper Creek did not rely entirely on merchants from the south to bring in their winter supplies. Some of the men from the Fisk Expedition had wagons and ox or mule teams and put them to work hauling provisions from Utah. Individual freighting ventures, too, were common and sometimes disappointing. Emily Meredith's family had been lured to speculative freighting in the late fall of 1862 and had sent a driver, their two yoke of oxen, a wagon, and $100 with a Mormon train bound for Salt Lake City. On the return trip the cattle were sick, so their driver paid other freighters to take the load. Emily Meredith told her father in a letter that "by the time the freight bill was settled, we had not near the worth of our cattle & wagon left. Flour is now only $10 a sack." As he drove from Salt Lake City to Montana, Samuel Word noted on September 13 that "every day we meet more or less wagons returning from Bannack for freight and the like." He calculated that he

[4] Ida McPherren, *Imprints on Pioneer Trails*, p. 116.
[5] Henry Ballard, "Journal, 1852-1885," in Joel E. Ricks, ed., *The History of a Valley: Cache Valley, Utah-Idaho*, p. 172

had met over a hundred wagons going to Salt Lake for provisions.[6]

Many of these impromptu trips to Salt Lake City were motivated by a fear of famine if winter storms should close the roads before enough goods had been brought into Montana to supply the emigrants until spring. Although a mild winter permitted freighting to continue, there still was not an abundance of goods. Flour rose to $40 a hundredweight, but fell to $8 in the spring; beef from Deer Lodge was plentiful and relatively cheap, and local vegetables were frequently brought in and sold for $.20 to $.52 per pound.[7]

Freighters from Other Areas

As spring turned to summer in 1863, freighters from farther away than Salt Lake City began to appear in Bannack. One of these was Matt Taylor, a Missouri freighter who had come from Denver with a large stock of tea—a valuable commodity that was not too heavy to carry in large quantities. As he passed through Salt Lake City, Taylor went from house to house trading his tea for farm and dairy products. The English women, who missed their traditional beverage, were especially glad to trade salt pork, eggs, and produce for it. One woman gave him thirty-four pounds of butter for one pound of tea![8]

Alexander Toponce arrived at the mines in May from Denver. He brought nails and whiskey, both in great demand, and set out with his profits in September to fetch another load from Utah. This time he brought flour, tea, shovels, picks, butter, and a hog. He had seen a hog hanging dressed and frozen outside a store in Brigham City and bought it for $.06 a pound. He "put it right up on the top of the wagon cover, all spread out on top of the wagon bows, with his snout pointing toward Montana." When Toponce arrived in Bannack the day before Christmas, the hog attracted more attention than all the rest of the train, and he sold it for a $1 a pound. After selling his entire freight outfit, Toponce

---

[6] Granville Stuart, *Forty Years on the Frontier*, vol. 1, p. 231; MSHS, Mrs. Emily R. Meredith, "Experiences and Impressions of a Woman in Montana, 1862-1863," p. 8; Samuel Word, "Diary of Colonel Samuel Word," in *Contributions to the Historical Society of Montana*, vol. 8, pp. 88, 91.

[7] Harrison R. Trexler, *Flour and Wheat in the Montana Gold Camps, 1862-1870*, p. 5.

[8] Barzilla W. Clark, *Bonneville County in the Making*, p. 24.

had $20,000 to finance his next trip.[9]

Road Agents

As freighters continued to bring in all they could of anything that would assure them a handsome return on their invest-
ment, the large amounts of money they carried became a target
for road agents. Early in November 1863, Samuel Hauser and
Nathaniel P. Langford, two Virginia City businessmen, found
themselves the targets of a plot designed by the notorious Plummer gang, headed by Sheriff Henry Plummer of Virginia City.
Hauser and Langford were carrying a large sum of money to the
East via Salt Lake City and were forced to travel with a wagon
train because the Bannack City Express Company, an early mail
and passenger line, had returned to the use of pack animals for
the winter season. Langford and Hauser were detained in town
when the train started, so they arranged to catch up with the
others that night at the evening campsite on Horse Prairie. So
sure were they of a robbery attempt that they rode with guns
cocked as they set out to overtake the freighters. One unforeseen
circumstance after another foiled the robbers, however, and they
were finally frightened off in the middle of the night when Langford, armed and ready for action, almost stumbled upon them
near the camp. No further incidents occurred on the trip south,
although when they arrived in Salt Lake City Hauser and Langford met with inquiries concerning a group of freighters who had
left Montana the week before and had disappeared somewhere
along the way without a trace.[10]

The road agents attempted to capture another "splendid
prize" three weeks later. This time the victims were a party of
Virginia City businessmen, a Mormon freighter, and a train of
packers who had joined forces for mutual protection and aid
during the winter journey. According to Charles Goodhart, a
recent employer called him into the back room of a store in Virginia City, and there some men offered him $200 to take the gold
out of the city by stealth and hide it. He loaded 100 pounds of gold
dust in an old aparejo and rode to Blacktail Deer Creek Canyon,

---

[9] Toponce, *Reminiscences*, pp. 56–73.
[10] Nathaniel P. Langford, *Vigilante Days and Ways*, pp. 198–208.

where he concealed the aparejo in some willows and waited for the train to catch up with him.

The packers, among whom were John McCormick, Billy Sloan, J. S. Rockfellow, J. M. Bozeman, and M. V. Jones, rode out of the city ahead of the freight train and soon encountered Goodhart. They waited, however, until the three-wagon train belonging to M. S. Moody arrived before they retrieved the gold dust. In the meantime, two of the road agents rode up while the company was at breakfast, and disconcerted at finding every man with a rifle across his knees and a few with handguns cocked, the robbers pretended to be looking for stock and departed.

The hidden gold dust was finally brought up and distributed throughout the train. Most of it was put in cantinas on the pack mules, and the rest was concealed in the wagons under some hay. Toward evening the packers rode on ahead to find a suitable campsite for the night, leaving only three or four men to bring up the wagons. Goodhart rode in the lead wagon with Mr. Moody to the crossing of Red Rock Creek in Junction Valley. There highwaymen George Ives and Dutch John "were sitting on their horses, one above the ford, the other below, hidden by the willows. They sprang out with . . . shotguns in their hands, shouting, 'Throw up your hands!' Milt and I were sitting on the front wagon, looking down that shotgun that old John had in his hands, and we thought it was the best thing for us to throw our hands up, and we did. . . . [The robbers lined up all the teamsters at the side of the road.] George Ives sat on his horse and held his shotgun on us and waved it back and forth and said that if we moved he would fill us full of buckshot." [11]

In their eagerness to find the treasure the robbers had overlooked two men in the rear wagon, where one lay ill and the other was looking after him. Lank Forbes, the nurse, was able to slip out unseen and climb onto the rear of the lead wagon, where Dutch John was throwing out the sacks of treasure. Forbes "put his fingers in a small slit in the wagon sheet, spread it apart, and laid his six-shooter between, trying to get an aim on John's head, but the slit was so high that it was impossible to see his head, so he shot him between the shoulders. At the sound of the gun,

---

[11] George W. Goodhart, *The Pioneer Life of George W. Goodhart*, pp. 283-84.

George Ives . . . whirled his horse, jumped into the creek, went down it, and was soon out of sight." [12]

Moody then drew a hidden gun from his boot and wounded the fleeing robber. Three of the packers, following Ives's tracks, found most of the stolen packages and letters, some of them stained with blood. The gold in the cantinas hadn't been disturbed. In the melee, Dutch John also escaped, but Goodhart later learned that he had been caught and hanged. [13]

The attack on the Moody train had all the characteristic elements of most of the holdups staged by the Plummer Gang. As sheriff of Virginia City, Henry Plummer usually knew in advance about most heavy shipments of gold to the States and would order his gang to ride out of town ahead of the load of treasure. Lurking in the darkness and following by stealth, the gang would wait until the opportune moment to strike—when the train had reached a particularly narrow and difficult point along the trail, or when most of the freighters were distracted and had relaxed their vigil. Then, making the most of the element of surprise, the bandits would rush the startled freighters. The gang continued to terrorize travelers until Plummer and three of his men were hanged by vigilantes in 1864.

The Hazards of Winter Travel

The weather often presented a more significant risk for freighting speculation than did the road agents. The winter of 1863-64 was quite a contrast to the previous mild winter; by the first of December, snow was a foot deep at Virginia City, and a heavy snowfall at Pleasant Valley stopped even stage travel for three days. [14] Freighters who risked traveling after that date were in danger of being stranded en route, having their stock freeze or starve, or finding low prices when their merchandise was delivered. If a train were stuck in the snow, the train master had three choices open to him: he could try to find a sheltered valley or large ravine where his stock would find forage and wait

---

[12] Ibid., p. 284.

[13] Ibid., pp. 272-84; Prof. Thomas J. Dimsdale, *The Vigilantes of Montana*, pp. 46-49; Langford, *Vigilante Days and Ways*, pp. 219-23.

[14] MSHS, Joseph T. Walker, "A Trip Across the Plains, 1863, 1865," p. 15.

for a break in the weather; he could put runners on some of the wagons and get the freight through on sleighs; or he could use his freighting teams to pack some of the merchandise through.

Despite all the risks involved, both financial and physical, many men tried to make just one more trip before winter closed the road entirely. Those who succeeded made fortunes; those who failed or were delayed faced financial disaster and possible death. One who succeeded was William Andrews Clark, the Montana copper king of later years. Clark persuaded some of his Bannack friends to pool their resources and each take a wagon to Salt Lake City to "buy something appropriate to the mining camp ... and thereby make expenses and possibly something more." They made the trip south in twelve days and started back almost immediately, disregarding warnings of the dangers of winter travel in the Rocky Mountains. During their struggles to get through the snow on the Continental Divide, Clark witnessed "what I had never dreamed of before—several cattle in the moving train freeze to death in the yoke and go right down upon the ground." After several delays and exhausting labor, the men managed to get back to Bannack where they disposed of their merchandise at a profit.[15]

Alexander Toponce, who had arrived in Bannack the day before Christmas with little difficulty, found the return trip not quite so trouble free. He started for Salt Lake City with his $20,000 in gold dust on January 2, 1864, in company with several others carrying large amounts of gold. On the second night out, their camp was visited twice by road agents who were recognized and forced to leave the camp and ride out of rifle range. The next day the train continued through the mountains in deep snow. After reaching the Snake River Valley, they were able to make twenty-five to thirty miles a day, overtaking and joining up with people who had lost their animals or who were out of food, until eventually there were twenty-three men and one woman in the party. By the time they crossed the Malad divide no food was left, and the animals that had not already frozen were dying. The nearest help was forty-five miles away at Call's Fort, and "the only way to get there was to walk." They buried the gold dust in

[15] C. B. Glasscock, *War of the Copper Kings*, pp. 46–55; Tom Stout, *Montana: Its Story and Biography*, pp. 332–35.

the snow, marked it with sagebrush, and at six o'clock in the morning started for Call's Fort through snow from two to four feet deep. Carrying blankets, they began to travel on their own; the first to reach the fort was to send back a rescue party. Toponce and Hawkins, the wagon boss, took turns breaking trail until Hawkins gave out on the second day. Toponce continued on alone on a nightmare journey of which he was able to recall very little. "A hundred times I stopped and sat down, or laid down in the snow. . . . when my strength came back a little I would start out again. I slept some, I remember, with my blankets wrapped around me and curled up in the snow. . . . I ate snow as I went along, but that was all I had to eat." [16]

About four o'clock in the morning on the fourth day, "when I routed them out of bed at Call's Fort, I could hardly stand and could not speak above a whisper." Toponce returned with the rescuers, sleeping in the sleigh all the way. He found that except for Hawkins and the lone woman of the party, the others had not traveled half the distance to the fort and two, who were crippled, had hardly made any progress at all. Some had frozen hands, feet, or ears, but all were alive and able to continue their journey in a few days.[17]

By the coming of spring in 1864, a pattern of freighting was established that continued with few alterations for more than ten years. As soon as the weather broke in the spring, there was a rush of freighters vying to be first on the road. As the summer wore on, their urgency decreased until the crisp air of autumn warned the freighter that one more trip was barely possible if he made haste to keep his train moving. By the last of November, only the very hardy or rash attempted another round trip with a freight train.

The experiences of William Clayton in the summer of 1864 are probably typical of many northern Utah businessmen who pinned their hopes for financial gain on a few quick trips to the mines. Worried about not being able to pay a debt he owed, and feeling that it was useless to send his freight train to buy goods in San Francisco when greenbacks were worth only $.52 or $.53 on a $1.00, he decided to "send the teams in some other

---

[16] Toponce, *Reminiscences*, pp. 73-76.
[17] Ibid., pp. 77-78.

direction. . . ." He observed that "every one who goes to the northern mines with things to sell, when they return here are in a great hurry to get back again; a proof that they are doing well in the operation." Unhappily for Clayton, while his train was still traveling to the mines, two steamboats arrived at Fort Benton loaded with 12,000 sacks of flour, and several other trains were en route overland to the mines. On July 28, the *Salt Lake Telegraph* announced that prices at Virginia City "are reported on the rapid decline," flour was quoted at $15.00 a hundredweight, and "whiskey was unsalable—there being a large supply." [18]

Alterations in Freighting Patterns

More and more the professional freighter had the advantage in the rapidly growing competition for Montana trade. The summer of 1864 saw a large influx of settlers, many of whom were aspiring merchants with enough to do tending their new establishments without actually freighting the merchandise into the territory themselves. They turned to such men as Howard Livingston of Salt Lake City, who would carry freight to Idaho and Montana for regular rates per pound and who could be held responsible for any losses or damages. On September 3 and 7, Livingston advertised in the *Salt Lake Telegraph* and the *Deseret News* that he was "prepared to furnish transportation for any amount of freight . . . either by mule or ox teams, . . . with safety and dispatch, and upon reasonable terms" to Virginia City, Idaho City, Bannack City, or other points. On September 10, the *Telegraph* reported that Livingston had sent out his third train for the north with ten wagons carrying provisions for Virginia City and six loaded with salt for Boise—a total of 35,000 pounds.[19]

Another change in the type of freighting could be attributed to the influx of settlers. Many had gone to Montana hoping to establish prosperous farms and ranches. They lost no time in planting crops and accumulating herds to provide income. No longer did the people of Montana have to depend entirely on farmers to the south for provisions. On the first of September

---

[18] BL, William Clayton, "Letter Books," pp. 475, 469, 480, 492; *Union Vedette*, July 22, 1864.

[19] *Deseret News*, Sept. 7, 1864; *Salt Lake Telegraph*, Sept. 3, 10, 1864.

1864, the editor of Fry's *Traveler's Guide* visited a seven-acre "garden" near Virginia City growing potatoes, turnips, onions, cabbages, lettuce, cucumbers, and other vegetables. To his astonishment, the estimated income, calculated at current prices in Virginia City, would be about $6,000 in gold.[20] In addition to commercial farming, many settlers planted their own vegetable gardens as soon as possible.

With the demand for Utah farm products decreasing, most Utah farmers found little profit in making the trip north with their excess crops. Instead, they sold what they could to the regular freighters willing to speculate on the sometimes unpredictable rise and fall of prices in Montana; or, if the farmer sold directly to someone in Montana, it was usually on order, with either the buyer or the seller paying the freight charges. Two Utah products, however, continued to find a ready market in Montana: fruit and flour.

The Flour Riots of 1864-65

Perishable delicacies such as fresh, ripe fruit, were sent north by express rather than being subjected to extensive bruising in a freight wagon. Transporting flour could present problems, too, especially when it had to be hauled through winter snows. It was not until 1869 that Montana was able to produce enough flour to satisfy local demands. Until then, flour was the chief commodity shipped from Utah and suffered radical price fluctuations determined largely by the seasonal nature of the freighting business. The winter of 1864-65 began in October and did not abate until April. Temperatures remained extremely low, and the snow on the Divide was eighteen feet deep.[21] As a result of the early storms, the worried editor of the *Montana Post* remarked that "flour went up four dollars the morning of the snow. If it continues to go up as the snow comes down, where will it stop." The wholesale price on October 29 was listed as $26.00

---

[20] F. Fry, *Fry's Travelers' Guide and Descriptive Journal*, p. 43.

[21] W. A. Clark, "Centennial Address on Montana: Delivered October Eleventh, 1876," in *Contributions to the Historical Society of Montana*, vol. 2, p. 54; Chief Justice Hezekiah L. Hosmer, *Montana. An Address Before Traveller's Club, New York City, January, 1866*, p. 17.

for St. Louis flour, $24.00 for flour from the states, and $22.50 for Salt Lake flour. By December 17, the *Montana Post* reported, "We hear of 500 loaded teams laying up between here and Salt Lake, on account of snow. If the weather continues fine for another week, most of these teams will come in and we may look for lively times in our market." [22]

Unknown to the editor, most of the freighters had not yet reached the pass near Pleasant Valley and they were irretrievably snowed in until spring. As the supply of flour in the towns began to dwindle, the price spiraled and so did the miner's resentment. They felt that they had too long been at the mercy of the merchants, who had probably hidden stocks of flour waiting for the price to be forced up. In Nevada City, the price rose in one day from $25 to $120; the miners responded by marching through town, confiscating the flour they needed, and paying the merchants $27 a sack for it. [23]

The citizens of Virginia City, trying to solve the problem in a more orderly fashion, appointed committees to ask the merchants to consider "the alleged destitution of the people." When the merchants refused to listen (probably because most of them had little flour on hand), a riot threatened but was quelled by a well-armed and determined sheriff. However, by April 18, the price had gone from $125 to $150 a sack, and the miners took control of affairs. Almost 500 armed men marched in file from Nevada City, divided into six companies, and searched stores, homes, and even haystacks with a military air. The 82 sacks they found were taken to Leviathan Hall and kept under guard, and each owner was promised reimbursement, although the mayor insisted that the price of any flour brought in by packtrain not exceed $50 a sack—unless the freighter could prove it had cost more than that. Notice was printed in the *Post* that in the future sales merchants were to honor prices set by the "Flour Committee." The next day the flour was distributed in lots of ten pounds per man; those with families were allowed double or triple portions. [24]

---

[22] *Montana Post*, Oct. 29, Dec. 17, 1864.

[23] A. M. Holter, "Pioneer Lumbering in Montana," in *Contributions to the Historical Society of Montana*, vol. 8, p. 258; *Union Vedette*, May 15, 1865.

[24] *Montana Post*, Apr. 8, 21, 1865; Cyrus Morton, *Autobiography*, p. 21; Toponce, *Reminiscences*, pp. 88-89; BL, William J. English, "Dictation."

Actual starvation did not become a problem but settlers and freighters alike were affected by the shortages. Supplies were so low that when Cyrus Morton undertook a trip to Fort Benton from Virginia City, his provisions consisted of dried apples and beans, and, though he tried, he "could not buy a potato in camp." He took with him his one remaining sack of flour, which he hid in a trunk, and sold half of it at a dollar a pound when he reached Helena. There he hired four drivers and went on to Fort Benton, hoping to get a load of freight for Helena. En route he used the last of his flour to make biscuits for breakfast, "one for each of the four drivers and one for myself." When they reached Fort Benton he bought flour, and they feasted on biscuits and "a mess of bacon grease and syrup (a dose that would almost turn my stomach the first time I ever saw any one eating it), but I had been initiated previous to this and did not allow myself to be badly beaten." [25]

Most speculators lost heavily that winter. The loss suffered by one was due indirectly to the sharp trading of Virginia City businessman and future copper king William A. Clark, of whom it was said he was always ready "to undertake any labor, danger or deal which promised a profit." Clark, anxiously awaiting news of one of his shipments from Salt Lake, finally met the owner of the ox train, who had come into town on snowshoes with a plan to obtain mules and sleds to fetch the freight from his marooned train. Most of the merchants having goods on that train readily fell in with the plan and advanced money for mules and feed. However, the wily Clark "had had an experience with mules the winter before . . . and found that when Mr. Mule got down in the snow he would not get up until he was dug out." Clark's counter offer, then, was for the freighter to buy Clark's merchandise himself and sell it when he got to town. The price was high enough to provide a neat profit for Clark, yet low enough for the freighter to hope he could make a tidy sum when he resold it. Borrowing money from the bank, the freighter bought out Clark's interest and set out with sixteen mules and high hopes. Unfortunately, by the time he had put sleigh runners on his wagons the weather had moderated, and enough bull teams were able to get

---

[25] Morton, *Autobiography*, pp. 22-23, 26.

through to drop prices below what the freighter had paid Clark.

A man had to be on his toes in dealing with some Montana merchants. In one case, alerted to the approach of a flour train from Salt Lake, a Virginia City merchant hurriedly stacked a few sacks of flour in front of his store with a price tag of $15 each. The unwary freighter sold his load for not much more than that per sack at a time when the price of flour was $75 in the stores.[26]

Alexander Toponce, the youthful enterpreneur who had flaunted the frozen hog atop his wagon bows the year before, bought another outfit in Utah to haul flour. It was the tenth of November 1864 before he could get it loaded. Once on his way, he found the traveling fine until he reached Dry Creek, where a storm dumped three feet of snow. Leaving his wagon master to guard the stalled train, Toponce took the stage to Virginia City and found that the price of flour had jumped to $125. He hired a packtrain of horses and mules, and in two trips hauled all his flour to town. To his dismay, enough flour had already been brought in to lower the price to $30 or $40 a hundredweight. Since he had paid $24 for the flour in Utah and had paid the packer $20 a sack to transport it to Virginia City, he probably would have fared better if he had left the flour at Dry Creek until spring. To make matters worse, Toponce lost all his cattle as well. He had taken them to winter on Big Island in the Snake River near present St. Anthony where they would have plenty of grass and water. When he returned for the cattle in April 1865, there was one lone survivor; the rest had frozen or starved because the snow had crusted so hard they could not get down to the grass underneath.[27]

Few other speculators fared better. Even though an occasional packtrain was able to get through with some goods, most of the freight remained in marooned wagons until spring. There were, in fact, almost daily notices of cattle, mules, wagons, or pack animals being sent from Montana to fetch one train or another that had wintered in Idaho. Flour was brought up in small lots, and with the arrival of sixty-four sacks on May 6, the price fell to $65 a hundredweight—probably a reasonable price to ask for flour that had been unloaded three times and carried

[26]Glasscock, *War of the Copper Kings*, pp. 46–55; *Deseret News*, Jan. 4, 1866.

[27] Toponce, *Reminiscences*, pp. 87–89.

on men's shoulders "over 200 yards at a stretch" because the Divide was impassable. Only the very "choice" freight could be worth paying the going rate of $.20 a pound for bringing it twenty-two miles over the Continental Divide! Warm May weather melted the hard snow crust the pack animals walked on. Now they sank almost out of sight; even the single mule used for the mail had to stop—the rider walked over the Divide carrying the mail. One week later the road was finally open, and the mail was the first to come through on wheels in six months.[28]

Flour Prices and Goods in 1865-66

The prices of flour and other commodities fluctuated wildly that spring not only because of changes in supply and demand, but also because of changes in the value of gold. A Virginia City merchant, writing to the editor of the *Montana Post* in June 1865, pointed out that "last season everyone counted an ounce of dust would pay for thirty-six dollars worth of goods, but now they cannot count it at more than eighteen, if that; consequently they will have to raise their price of goods or lower the price of gold. Which shall it be?" The writer complained, too, about the quality of dust in circulation. In order to avoid being shortchanged in a deal, a man needed to know the difference between Alder Gulch gold, Last Chance gold, and gold from other mining locations. Eastern valuation of both gold and greenbacks ("Lincoln skins," to the miners) was somewhat modified in Montana by the availability of either the gold or the greenbacks. One example of the difference in value between the two in 1864-65 was the price of flour: in gold, it was $28 a sack; in greenbacks, $56. At this time, gold was $18 an ounce in the camps; by June 10, however, the editor of the *Post* noted that the kind of dust currently acceptable in trade was "worth no more than Treasury Notes, dollar for dollar, and some of the gold is not an equivalent for the paper!" [29] The weather, the value of gold, the quality of dust, the acceptability of greenbacks, and the sudden variations in supply and

---

[28] *Montana Post*, May 6, 13, 1865.

[29] John Hakola, "Currency in Montana," in *Historical Essays on Montana and the Northwest*, ed. J. W. Smurr and K. Ross Toole, pp. 120-21; *Montana Post*, June 10, 1865.

demand all combined to alter prices at a moment's notice.

By September of 1865, merchants and freighters had commenced to supply Montana with a huge stock of flour for the winter. There were no buyers for 300 sacks of Utah flour offered for sale in Virginia City on September 7 at $17. The *Union Vedette* stated that "$16 is all it can be sold for and in 'small lots at that.' " Nevertheless, by September 29 the editor of the *Vedette* was moved to comment that "the road from Montana's capital to Salt Lake is one continued flour sack. That is to say, it is 'lined' with loads of flour, going north. The 'staff of life' will be cheap and plentiful there this winter." One merchant alone—Hermann, Schwab & Loeb—had stored 1,200 sacks by October 7.[30]

Despite the increased supplies of flour, the price advanced steadily until the editors of both Montana and Salt Lake papers began to take people to task from diametrically opposed points of view. The Montana editor wanted his people to produce more of their own goods to avoid high freighting costs, and the Salt Lake editor wanted his people to wake up and charge freighters more for produce to share in the huge profits being made in Montana. Using potatoes as an example, the *Montana Post* pointed out that a few thousand pounds of potatoes from Salt Lake City had been sold locally, but if the Montana farmers would only bestir themselves, by the next season "home production will meet every demand." On the other hand, the *Deseret News*, on November 30, 1865, and on January 4, 1866, advised its readers to band together and do their own freighting rather than to let "outsiders" get all the business. The *Deseret News* also urged farmers to compare prices they received with those in Montana and "ask yourselves if it pays you to let it go for the paltry price you receive in the pay you get, while you could handle the gold for it yourselves." [31]

The winter of 1865 brought fewer hardships to late freighters, and some freight was brought through all winter. Trains were sometimes stranded by snowstorms, but within a short time the weather would moderate enough so that the freight could be moved. Some speculators suffered real disasters, however. Colonel Alexander Majors had brought thirty wagons

---

[30] *Union Vedette*, Sept. 7, 1865; *Montana Post*, Oct. 7, 1865.
[31] *Montana Post*, Nov. 4, 11, Dec. 2, 1865.

of flour and groceries from Salt Lake nearly to their destination when a storm stopped him on Sage Creek. The severe cold killed seventy-five yoke (150) of his cattle. From Virginia City, Majors went on to Helena; by the time he reached there on January 13, 1866, he had lost "no less than three hundred head of cattle since starting, by cold storms and want of feed in consequence of deep snow." [32]

Salt was a new freight item in the summer of 1866. In June, Benjamin F. White and J. M. Stump established a salt works at Oneida, about eighty-five miles east of Eagle Rock Bridge on the Lander Emigrant Road. In the first year of operation, the Oneida Salt Works shipped 15,000 tons, much of it to Montana.[33]

Most trains passing through Salt Lake City to Montana were from the East, but some were from California. One train arrived in Virginia City about June 2, 1866, after eighty-four days over a 1,300-mile road from Los Angeles. Another had come in on May 5, having been on the road since February 10, and a third passed through Salt Lake City on May 17 headed for Helena.[34]

Competing for Trade

Since on-time deliveries were important to Montana buyers, getting the freight through as quickly as possible led to heavy competition between freighters. In one case especially, a matter of a few hours made a difference of several thousand dollars in the price of a load of flour. In the fall of 1865, one Virginia City merchant contracted with a freighter for a very large amount of flour to be delivered the next spring for $20 a sack. Spring came, and with it spring floods. The freighter got his train through in good time until he came to the "Eau de Cologne," or Stinkingwater River. Here a flood made crossing impossible, and the train stopped. The price of flour had gone down considerably after the contract was made, and the mer-

---

[32] BL, "Bancroft Scraps, Montana Miscellany," vol. 90, from the *Montana Radiator*, Jan 13, 1866, p. 103.

[33] Robert E. Strahorn, *To the Rockies and Beyond*, p. 130; Eugene H. Walker, "Oneida Salt," *Idaho Yesterdays*, vol. 6 (Fall 1962), p. 8; MLUU "Walker Family Correspondence," Acct. 53.

[34] *Montana Post*, May 5, June 2, 1866; *Deseret News*, May 17, 1866.

Camp on the Stinking Water River, photographed by William H. Jackson. *National Archives.*

chant no longer wanted his order, so he refused the freighter's offer to take less money for delivering the flour only to the Stinkingwater, hoping that if the freighter failed to reach Virginia City he would not have to accept the flour at all. The merchant did not count on the resourcefulness and determination of the freighter—the flour was loaded in boats, rowed across the stream, and delivered on time.[35]

Time became so important that several freighters traveled day and night. One of these was Colonel Major's Overland Dispatch; another was W. H. H. Thatcher's fast freight express. In May, Thatcher made the trip north in thirteen and a half days, beating his own time of fifteen days in December of 1865. Of course, the condition of the roads determined speed to a great extent. In the dead of winter it took Forbes's train two to three months to get to Helena from Salt Lake, but in the spring, even though the roads were described as "very deep and heavy," a Mr. Jackson got through to Virginia City in about five weeks—not much over the average for summer runs.[36]

The summer of 1866 was so quiet the Utah Produce Company had to advertise for business. Their May advertisement read: "We wish to engage freight to the Northern Mines—wheat and flour purchased." When their train was finally sent off on May 17, freight rates were down to $.10 per pound and were expected to fall as low as $.05 or $.06. In August, a few trains from Virginia City appeared in Logan to buy flour; the harvest there was very good, making the market attractive to speculators.[37] By September, the fall freighting season was in full swing, but Montana merchants were well stocked with such staples as salt and flour.

Supplies in 1866-67

According to a survey of the winter market of 1866-67 made by a correspondent to the San Francisco *Alta Californian*, flour

---

[35] *Montana Post,* June 2, 1866.

[36] Ibid., Dec. 30, 1865, Mar. 31, Apr. 7, May 5, 1866; *Deseret News,* Apr. 26, 1866.

[37] *Deseret News,* May 17, 24, 1866; *Montana Post,* Sept. 15, 1866; *Idaho, Statesman,* May 19, 1866; LDSHD, "Cache Stake Manuscript History, Logan, August 9, 1866."

was selling for $.05 a pound in Salt Lake City even though the summer low had been $.07 or $.08. Late in February, the *Montana Democrat* declared that thousands of bushels of local wheat were lying in storage without a market because Mormons had flooded the cities in Montana with flour and had "virtually crushed the farmers of Montana," and flour was selling at less than freight costs—$7.50 a sack. The writer thought that this should deter Mormons from sending flour to Montana and that since Mormons were refusing to trade with Utah Gentiles, perhaps Montana should refuse to trade with Salt Lake. The article needled the editor of the *Salt Lake Telegraph* into responding on February 26 that Montana had been happy to get Utah flour when its people were starving.[38]

An early arrival on the 1867 spring freighting scene was Alexander Toponce. Up until 1866, his Montana freighting ventures had netted him enough to maintain a magnificently equipped $40,000 freight train and have $75,000 left in capital to bid on government stores at Fort Union. In a series of catastrophes during the winter of 1865–66, he lost everything. He arrived in Helena owing $18 and owning only his mule, Molly. Riding back to Salt Lake on Molly, he came into town just in time to purchase a twenty-six-wagon train from local merchant Bill Jennings. Financing the venture on credit, Toponce then contracted to carry freight to Virginia City for $.12 a pound in gold. He reached Virginia City in thirty-five days and sold his teams and wagons for $550—a profit of $175 on each rig. Returning to Salt Lake in October 1866, he bought six more six-mule teams and drove them up through Cache Valley, buying every egg he could find, wrapping them in newspaper, and packing them in boxes of oats. He didn't reach Helena until March 1, 1867, but the eggs were still unfrozen, and he sold them at $2 a dozen. At Pleasant Valley, he was forced to make sleigh runners of split logs, take the wheels off the axles, and attach the runners. Later, he replaced the wheels in order to traverse a twenty-mile stretch of bare road, then put the runners on again to continue to Helena. After one more trip, Toponce arrived in Salt

[38] BL, "Bancroft Scraps, Montana Miscellany," vol. 90, from the *Alta Californian*, San Francisco, Feb. 23, 1867, written in Helena, Mont., Dec. 20, 1866, p. 14; *Salt Lake Telegraph*, Feb. 26, 1867; *Montana Post*, Oct. 27, 1866.

Lake City in July 1867, set his accounts in order, and discovered he had made over $100,000 on the three trips.[39]

Relying on their experience in 1865-66, the shippers had over-extended themselves in stockpiling goods, and by the summer of 1867 they were feeling the pinch. Now the market was "perfectly glutted"; merchants were forced to borrow money at usurious rates in order to pay their freight bills, then in turn were forced to sell the goods at a fifty to seventy-five percent loss in order to pay their debts. On July 6, the *Montana Post* noted that goods just in from California were being offered at "very low figures" in Virginia City. Even so, on the same day, thirty wagons of produce arrived from Salt Lake City. Writing from Cache Valley, Utah, W. H. Shearman saw a silver lining to the clouds of gloom. Freighters caught with too much flour were trading it off to the people of Cache Valley, as there was no profit in taking it to Montana; and now that the grass-hoppers had "done immense damage & destroyed some crops entirely," Shearman could see that the Lord had provided the sur-plus in order to protect Cache Valley residents from starvation the following winter.[40]

In spite of the unfavorable situation, by September several Salt Lake trains were on the road laden with flour and other prod-ucts. On October 31, 1867, four loads of onions from Utah were "rendering themselves odorous" in the streets of Helena. Although the *Post* chose to ignore most of the freighting from Utah, the *Hel-ena Gazette* urged its readers to buy only local flour now that they had nearly exhausted the heavy stocks of that "generally poor arti-cle brought to our markets from Salt Lake City." [41]

In the early days of freighting between Montana and Utah, the freighter had often had the choice of selling his wagons and teams in Montana or returning to Salt Lake with an empty, and unprofit-able, train. But times had changed. More often than not, the train now originated in Montana. In earlier years, a produce freighter from Utah might hope to get a load of ore to haul on the return trip; now an ore freighter from Montana might carry a load of produce

[39] Toponce, *Reminiscences*, pp. 137–45.

[40] A. K. McClure, *Three Thousand Miles Through the Rocky Mountains*, p. 216; *Deseret News*, July 31, 1867.

[41] *Montana Post*, Oct. 26, Nov. 9, Dec. 14, 1867; *Helena Herald*, Oct. 31, 1867; *Salt Lake Telegraph*, Oct. 30, 1867.

or Eastern manufactured goods on his return trip from Utah. Newspapers supported this reversal because they could see that if Montanans patronized their own freighters, money would remain in the territory.[42]

Freighting stagnated in the summer of 1868, and more freighters than ever were trying to sell out their equipment. The *Post* (now published in Helena) noted that "the city is full of wagons, many of which will undoubtedly be sold for the wood and old iron in them. This has been the fate of hundreds of wagons in the past. . . ." A Montana resident traveling through the northern Utah towns noticed signs of discouragement there, too. "We found a disposition to abandon the Montana market, owing to the narrower margin in produce than in former years, and the excessive tolls. It costs $25 to $30 for each wagon to Helena, and nearly as much to return. We find now that Malad is turning its attention to the Boise market, where, owing to the absence of toll-gates, produce can be delivered cheaper than in Helena, with a better profit." [43]

The slowly approaching transcontinental railroad sparked a note of optimism for discouraged freighters, most of whom had found their business very dull indeed for the past two years. With the railroad delivering all freight from both East and West to a single point 500 miles from Helena, shippers could expect a huge increase in the demand for their services. A few began to prepare for the business and competition that were sure to come. Progress would also prove a boon for Utah farmers who had previously shipped produce to Montana—they would leave their farms to the grasshoppers and crickets in the summertime to go to work for the railroad.[44]

While the freighters were busy winning rich rewards hauling merchandise along the road to Montana, other industrious entrepreneurs were making and losing their fortunes carrying passengers and negotiating postal contracts for the new settlements. They, too, looked to the implications the coming railroad would have for their lucrative enterprises.

---

[42] *Deseret News*, Apr. 15, 1868; *Salt Lake Telegraph*, Mar. 17, 1868.

[43] *Montana Post*, Apr. 25, Aug. 8, 1868; *Deseret News*, Apr. 15, 1868; *Salt Lake Telegraph*, Mar. 17, 1868.

[44] *Montana Post*, Apr. 25, June 26, 1868; *Salt Lake Telegraph*, June 20, Aug. 10, 1868.

5

When Jehus Ruled the Road

While freighters did carry occasional letters and a stray passenger or two to Montana gold camps, new residents soon demanded regular mail service and more comfortable and expeditious means of travel. An old gold seeker from California, Jack (Andrew Jackson) Oliver, arrived in Montana in late 1862 and decided there might be surer profits in transportation than in searching for the elusive nuggets. He and a partner established a miniature pony express line with Oliver riding out of Bannack City and his associate carrying letters from Salt Lake City. They met halfway and exchanged the mail—until his partner was scalped by Indians. Jack Oliver then organized an express company with three other men: Ed House, George Clayton, and A. J. Conover. By November 1862, the firm announced that it intended to run a monthly express during the winter and a weekly coach during the summer from Bannack to Salt Lake City. Oliver and Conover arrived in the City of the Saints on November 28 with a four-horse wagon, some mail, and one passenger, having made the trip in sixteen days.[1]

Oliver & Co.

In May 1863, by traveling day and night and relaying teams every sixty miles, Oliver & Co. was able to deliver 500 letters in Bannack only nine days after leaving Salt Lake City. The Oliver line continued in business throughout the summer and fall

---

[1] Charles Bovey Collection, Fairweather Hotel, Virginia City, Mont., notes provided by the son of A. J. Oliver, Virginia City, Mont., 1968, on back of a picture of A. J. Oliver; Letter from Salt Lake City, Nov. 20, 1862, BL, "Bancroft Scraps, Utah Miscellany," vol. 109, p. 44.

Andrew J. Oliver, owner of A. J. Oliver & Co. Stage Line, competed with Ben Holladay's Overland Stage Line for the Montana trade. *Montana Historical Society, Helena.*

of 1863, providing a much-needed service for Bannack and vicinity, although it was "a primitive affair. A covered wagon drawn by indian ponies." Passengers had to bring along their own provisions.[2]

Oliver & Co. operated independently without a mail contract from the United States government, which issued the first six-month contract between Salt Lake City and Bannack to Leonard I. Smith on November 2, 1863. Smith continued his mail contract to Bannack until the end of 1864 and was paid $1,000 per month for the service. Like all mail contractors of the time, he was expected to live up to the conditions in his agreement:

> 1st. To carry said mail with certainty, celerity, and security, using therefor such means as may be necessary to transport the whole of said mail, whatever may be its size, or weight, or increase. . . .

> 2nd. To carry said mail in a safe and secure manner, free from wet or other injury under a sufficient oilcloth or bearskin if carried on horse, in a boot under the driver's seat if carried in a coach or other vehicle, and in preference to passengers, and to their entire exclusion if its weight & bulk require it.[3]

This last often caused a loss of revenue for the operation and a wait for the next stage for the passengers, especially when snow clogged the roads.

By March of 1864, the road to Bannack was filled with every type of conveyance, and books for Smith's company and Oliver's line were "full of the names of travelers awaiting their turns." The fare was $50 in coin to Bannack or $60 to Virginia City, and, as one cynical correspondent put it, "all the turkey, roast chicken, sardines and oysters are to be taken at the expense of the *voyageurs* of course." [4] Two other stage companies, one operated by Peabody and the other by Caldwell, began to compete with Oliver's Virginia City line since Oliver's venture was no doubt one of the richest gold strikes in Montana. Ten passengers paying $150 apiece could be stuffed into a small Concord coach, and by offer-

---

[2] *Deseret News*, Apr. 22, 1863; Helen M. White, ed., *Ho! For the Gold Fields*, p. 94.

[3] NA, "Mail Contracts, Utah, 1858-1862."

[4] BL, "Bancroft Scraps, Utah Miscellany," vol. 109, Letter from "Liberal" at Salt Lake City, Mar. 31, 1864, pp. 668-69.

ing triweekly service each way, Oliver & Co. could reap a weekly harvest of $9,000 from the travelers alone. Letters went at $1 each, and with 500 to 600 letters in the boot of the coach, there was an added $3,000 or so in revenue.[5]

A correspondent for the *Sacramento Union* praised Oliver's company in print on April 1, 1864, but poked fun at Leonard Smith, who was so "anxious to serve Uncle Samuel" that when the Post Office Department asked if he would require any more compensation for traveling by way of Soda Springs, instead of by the more direct route via Portneuf Canyon, answered, "nothing extra." But, as the writer said, Smith "little knew the country" and in late March was "plodding somewhere in the snow between Soda Springs and Bannock." The letter ended by reporting a rumor that Ben Holladay was preparing to enter the Montana competition.

Ben Holladay Enters the Competition

Salt Lake City papers had already speculated that Ben Holladay, the "Napoleon of the West," was trying for a mail contract between Soda Springs and Bannack and Virginia City, and that he would better Oliver's time of seven days by doing the trip in only four. On March 21, Nat Stein, Holladay's agent, arrived in Salt Lake to hire employees and to dispatch James Bromley to lay out the route and choose sites for stage stations. Bromley was to determine whether the Soda Springs or Portneuf route was better for stage travel and finally settled on the latter as the more direct of the two.[6] Upon his return, the *Union Vedette* concluded on April 25, 1864, that he had chosen a "most practicable route. . . . Abundance of wood, water and grass, is found throughout its entire length, and Mr. Bromley speaks in the highest terms of its practicability. In fact, he says it is one of the best natural roads on the Continent, requiring but little work to render it a splendid stage route. The route will run nearly due North to Old Fort Hall

    [5] Ralph Moody, *Stagecoach West*, pp. 247–49; Larry Barsness, *Gold Camp: Alder Gulch and Virginia City, Montana*, p. 186.
    [6] *Union Vedette*, Mar. 15, 22, 1864; *Deseret News*, Mar. 30, 1864; Moody, *Stagecoach West*, p. 250–52; James V. Frederick, *Ben Holladay, The Stagecoach King*, pp. 144–46.

Ben Holladay's agent Nat Stein in 1869. *Wells Fargo Bank, History Room, San Francisco.*

on Snake river, and thence two roads will diverge, one to Boise bearing to the Northwest ... ; the other to Virginia City, Eastern Bannack on which it is proposed to commence running four horse coaches." The distances were estimated to be 407 miles to Bannack and 418 miles direct to Virginia City. As the *Vedette* editor said on March 22, 1864, Ben Holladay's plan to establish a stage line north was "the sure harbinger of civilization."

Holladay received a mail contract from the Post Office Department to cover the period July 1, 1864, to June 30, 1868, binding the company to carry the mail from Fort Hall to Virginia City, 213 miles, three times a week for eight months of the year and once a week for the remaining four months, at an annual subsidy of $13,271. Holladay eventually received $53,084 under this contract. The mail stations on the line were Fort Hall, Snake River Ferry, Bannack, and Virginia City.[7]

To meet the July 1 deadline, Holladay sent Bob Spotswood to the Kansas–Missouri area to buy 290 mules, thirty stages, and ten lumber wagons. By some speedy deliveries, the route was stocked, and the first stage pulled out of Salt Lake City on time. Six-horse wagons were used as far as Fort Hall, then four-horse wagons took over.

Oliver & Co. vs. Ben Holladay

Oliver & Co. met the challenge from Holladay's Overland Stage Line partly by intensive advertising: "The nearest road by seventy miles," "Have made trips within four days," and passengers allowed 25 lbs. "baggage in Treasure, or anything they may choose to carry." [8] Oliver held on at first and even added a third weekly coach to match Holladay's triweekly service. But Jack Oliver did not have the resources to compete with the "Stagecoach King," who announced that the fare to Virginia City would be $25 beginning August 15. Holladay also practiced a little psychology along with his rate war. It was announced that he had eighty new Concord coaches en route for his line and

---

[7] NA, "Mail Routes, Utah, 1862–1866," Contract #14621, p. 277.

[8] Frederick, *Ben Holladay*, pp. 144–46; *Salt Lake Telegraph*, July 12, Sept. 3, Oct. 24, 1864.

Announcement of the Overland Stage Line's service to Montana. *Montana Historical Society, Helena.*

intended to offer daily service to Virginia City by the following spring. Holladay was now running 2,700 miles of staging across the West, with a government subsidy of $600,000, "unquestionably the largest stage line in the world controlled by any one man, or any company." [9] On November 19, the *Montana Post* made the sad announcement that Jack Oliver intended to "draw off the Salt Lake route" the next day but would continue his line to Bannack City.

Holladay moved rapidly to consolidate 'his position. He negotiated with Idaho's Oneida County officials for land for his way stations. It had been rumored that Holladay was facing bankruptcy when he took over the lucrative Montana trade. Certainly his circumspect and popular agent at Virginia City, Nat Stein, could report excellent revenue for the week of October 1 to October 8, 1864—receipts, including the balance due from September, amounted to $6,288.29, with disbursements of $57.50 for office expenses.[10] Now, with Oliver out of the way, the fare to Virginia City began to rise: $50 on October 13, $75 on October 16, and $150 on February 17, where it remained until it was reduced to $100 on September 1, 1865. But on September 25, the rate rose again to $125. Throughout the fall and winter of 1864-65, an average of six to seven passengers traveled north on each trip.[11]

The Overland Stage Line's determination to deliver the mail was well demonstrated during the winter of 1864-65 when some trips to Virginia City required as many as twenty days. During February, soldiers from Camp Douglas were ordered out to shovel snow and clear the road as far as the Weber River, suffering frozen feet in the process; however, beyond the Snake River, and over the Continental Divide, at Pleasant Valley, the driver and his venturesome passengers were on their own.[12]

In June 1865, Holladay placed new six-horse, seventeen-

---

[9] *Salt Lake Telegraph*, Nov. 5, 1864; *Union Vedette*, Oct. 10, 1864.

[10] Territory of Idaho, "Miscellaneous Records," pp. 8-12; Charles Bovey Collection, Letterbook, Fairweather Hotel, Virginia City, Mont., Stein to Holladay, Oct. 8, 1864, pp. 189-90; MSHS, Dan R. Conway, "Story of the Old Concord Stage Coach...," in *The Ismay Journal*, Oct. 8, 1925, Clip file.

[11] *Union Vedette*, Sept. 25, 1865; BL, "Holladay Overland Mail and Express Company Papers," Passenger Register, Virginia City (Mont.), to Salt Lake City etc. Sept. 16, 1864-April 30, 1865.

[12] *Montana Post*, Mar. 11, 1865; *Union Vedette*, Feb. 28, 1865.

passenger Concord coaches on the line, at a cost of $1,500 each, to take care of the surge of business that was pushing the population of Montana far beyond the 15,822 people counted in September of 1864. Sometimes as many as thirty-two eager gold seekers were jammed into and attached onto a coach for the dusty, bumpy ride to Virginia City. Also in June, the junction to Boise was changed from Fort Hall to the Bear River Crossing (later Hampton's Crossing) at Collinston, Utah, which reduced the journey to Boise to 400 miles and three and a half days.[13]

Jack Oliver Pioneers a New Line

The discovery of gold at Last Chance Gulch enabled the spunky Jack Oliver to pioneer another line, and on February 11, 1865, his first Prickly Pear and Last Chance Express arrived in Virginia City. Oliver also inaugurated passenger and mail service to Deer Lodge and brought in his coaches from there through twelve feet of snow in early March. On May 20, he announced a regular delivery to Fort Benton "as long as steamboats arrive." [14] With these main lines, plus his route between Bannack and Virginia City, Oliver again began to mine profits along the road. By October 28, 1865, a *Montana Post* advertisement announced:

> A. J. Oliver & Co.'s Express ... Are Running a Daily Line of Four-horse Coaches between Virginia and Rhea Cities (Jefferson Gulch) via Boulder Valley, Beaver Town, Jefferson City, Montana City, Helena (Last Chance), Green Horn, Blackfoot City and Washington Gulch; A TRI-WEEKLY LINE between Virginia City and Blackfoot (Ophir) via Nevada and Junction Cities, Jefferson Bridge, Silver Bow City, German Gulch, French Gulch and Deer Lodge City: A DAILY LINE between Diamond City and Helena ...; and A WEEKLY LINE between Virginia City and Gallatin City.

Jack Oliver now made a successful bid for a mail contract between Virginia City and Helena, to run from August 25, 1865, to June 30, 1866, for $6,900 per year. He was to deliver the mail three times a week to Helena and return, or more frequently if

---

[13] Frederick, *Ben Holladay*, p. 150; *Montana Post*, Oct. 8, 1864; George A Bruffey, *Eighty-One Years in the West*, p. 84; *Union Vedette*, June 10, 1865.
[14] *Montana Post*, Feb. 11, Mar. 18, May 20, 1865.

his coaches ran at other times.[15] Delivering the mail over winter roads proved a costly error, because the firm's new Concord coaches were badly battered before the unusually severe weather ended in May 1866. Farther south, Holladay's Overland Line had even more difficult times. According to the *Montana Post* of January 27, 1866, on one midwinter trip the stage sleigh encountered drifts thirty feet deep on the Pleasant Valley Divide, and the driver and passengers had to shovel a passage about six feet deep to get the horses out with the mail. The sleigh was left in a snow drift.

Other Stagecoach Entrepreneurs

Stagecoach managers from California were attracted to the new northern diggings and started branch lines to out-of-the-way gulches the large operators ignored. The *Union Vedette* announced on April 23, 1866, that seven six-horse coaches loaded with passengers had arrived from California en route to Virginia City. A little later, Captain C. C. Huntley passed through Salt Lake City with two six-horse Concord coaches and twenty-three passengers, reaching Virginia City after a journey of about forty days from Marysville, California. Within two weeks he established a line between Helena and Fort Benton, and announced that he would soon add several more six-horse coaches. Huntley was one of the few to continue in business for several years. John Allman showed up on April 28 at Virginia City with four heavily-laden coaches and 25 horses, sixty-two days out of Sacramento, having "nearly shipwrecked the whole concern" at Bear River, where some "crazy grass" hay nearly drove the horses mad. In May six coaches, thirty-two passengers, and 155 horses came in from Virginia City, Nevada, to form the nucleus for yet another stage line.[16]

There were also small one-coach operators running an extended frontier taxi service from town to town picking up passengers wherever possible. Herman Francis Reinhart once corralled eight passengers at $9.40 each for a journey from Helena

---

[15] NA, "Mail Routes, Utah, 1862-1866," Contract #14624, 416, 466.
[16] *Union Vedette*, Apr. 16, 23, 1866; *Montana Post*, Apr. 28, May 5, 19, 26, 1866.

to Benton as "passenger freight was better than goods." He charged $13.25 for the return to Helena and netted a profit of $180. Finally, Oliver's company met a rival in the California Stage Company, when Al Guitwitz and Ben Stafford brought stock and coaches from California to run an opposition line on alternate days from Virginia City to Helena.[17]

Trade War on the Trail

The new "gold" run to Helena naturally attracted "the Overland Autocrat." By June 2, the *Union Vedette* reported the arrival of eight new Holladay coaches "all of 'em 17 passenger, double-deckers" for the Helena line, with six more on the way. The Overland Stage Company's first daily coach from Virginia City to Helena left on June 30 at the same time that Jack Oliver's and the California Stage Company's coaches pulled out. Thereafter, every morning three six-horse coaches would depart from Helena and three from Virginia City. E. M. "Gov" Pollinger, division agent for Holladay, recounted the trade war that ensued.

> The overland when it was strung out on the road cut the fare to two dollars & fifty cents — $2.50 from Va City to Helena. Red Hot time followed. I started on 16 hours time . . . then Later to 12 Hours time Still later to 10 Hours time from Va City to Helena Making 12 1/2 miles per hour in entire distance of 125 miles from Va City to Helena including all stops etc. which was the greatest time in the History of Staging in any country that ever laid out of doors.[18]

The break-neck pace meant making more frequent team changes, driving at a fast gallop every minute, and, before the hostilities ended, losing over 100 head of horses from the killing speed. The Overland line had the best stock and made the best time, to the enjoyment of numerous backers who were wagering up to $500 each on a single race.[19]

The result was inevitable. On July 14, Guitwitz's California Stage Company withdrew, and a month later Jack Oliver gave

[17] Doyce B. Nunis, Jr., ed., *The Golden Frontier*, p. 254; *Montana Post*, June 16, 1866.

[18] MSHS, "Stage War of '66," Clip file; MSHS, E. M. Pollinger, "Letter, Alaska Bench, Montana, Twin Bridges, May 28, 1904, to Col. J. E. Callaway."

[19] MSHS, "Stage War of '66," Clip file.

up. As soon as the last rival quit, Holladay raised the one-way
fare to $37.50, revised the road schedule to twenty hours, and
replaced his new Concord coaches with any four-wheeled conveyance passengers could cling to.[20] One traveler reported to the
Montana Post that on one trip six passengers plus mail and baggage were stacked on a "seatless" carriage and forced to "lock
hands and hang across the load saddle bag fashion.... If the ear-
nestness and deep sincerity with which the maledictions are
uttered could insure their taking affect, I would not stand in Ben
Holladay's shoes for *two* mail contracts." Holladay was not upset
by such attacks—revenue from the passenger and express business on all his lines often totaled $200,000 per month.[21] Despite
defeats in encounters with his more resourceful and aggressive
rival, Jack Oliver still maintained his lines to Bannack, Deer
Lodge, and Diamond City, and inaugurated a new line to Missoula Mills.

Wells, Fargo & Co.

Quite another competitor finally convinced the Stagecoach
King that the time had come to dispose of his business. On
November 1, 1866, Holladay retreated before the advancing
Union Pacific Railroad by selling out to Wells Fargo. As early as
March of 1860, Wells, Fargo & Co. had become dominant in the
affairs of the Overland Mail Company, and when Holladay sold
out, Wells Fargo consolidated the Overland Mail Company, the
Holladay interests, and other express companies into one great
concern controlling the transportation and mail business west of
the Missouri River. Wells, Fargo & Co. gambled that the transcontinental railroad would not be completed for several years
and paid for their mistake with $70,000 worth of new coaches
never used and later sold at a loss. Holladay's price was said to
have been $1,500,000 plus $300,000 in Wells Fargo stock.[22]

---

[20] *Montana Post*, July 14, Aug. 18, 1866; Moody, *Stagecoach West*, pp.
252–54.

[21] *Montana Post*, Oct. 20, 1866; Moody, *Stagecoach West*, pp. 252–54.

[22] W. Turrentine Jackson, "A New Look at Wells Fargo, Stagecoaches and
the Pony Express," *California Historical Society Quarterly*, vol. 45 (Dec. 1966),
pp. 301, 306; Hubert Howe Bancroft, *History of Utah*, p. 753; Alvin F. Harlow,
Old Waybills: The Romance of the Express Companies, p. 266.

As the gold disappeared from Virginia City gulches, residents had to face the prospect of only occasional mail and passenger service from Salt Lake City. During the two and a half years Wells, Fargo & Co. operated the Overland and Montana lines, the people of Montana received service at least as good as Ben Holladay's, although opinions differed. There were a few patrons who praised the clock-like regularity and excellent time made by Wells Fargo coaches, but others complained that the company advertised free meals and then charged $1.50 apiece for poor meals at their home stations.[23]

Despite complaints, Wells Fargo monopolized the main route from Salt Lake City as far north as Benton, leaving only branch lines for a few secondary companies. Oliver continued in business until November of 1867. The Helena-to-Missoula mail contract then shifted to Captain C. C. Huntley, who in turn sublet to Chamberlain and Merriam. Huntley sold his Helena–Fort Benton line, initiated in 1866, to Wells Fargo on July 1, 1867.[24]

In August 1869, Wells, Fargo & Co. joined the ghost of Ben Holladay by withdrawing from the stage business. J. T. Gilmer and Munroe Salisbury of Salt Lake City bought the Overland Stage and Express Line, and from then until the iron horse penetrated the north, it was Gilmer & Salisbury on the Montana Trail.[25]

Moving the Mail

The principal mail stations on the Salt Lake City to Brigham City route in the early 1860's were Centerville, Farmington, Kaysville, Ogden, and Brigham City. A second contract was awarded by the Post Office Department in 1868 to Wells, Fargo & Co. for the 302-mile road from Bear River Crossing to Virginia City for an annual sum of $47,500. In the same year, the route from Virginia City to Bannack was awarded to L. H. Hersch-

---

[23] *Salt Lake Telegraph*, Sept. 14, 1868, Jan. 15, 1867; *Montana Post*, Aug. 28, 1868.

[24] MSHS, "A Thousand Miles of Road," in *West Shore*, n.d., Clip file.

[25] WCML, "Overland Stage Co., Passenger Register, Wells, Fargo & Co., Mails, 1868," p. 95; Harlow, *Old Waybills*, p. 286; MSHS, E. M. Pollinger, "Letter, Alaska Bench, Montana, Twin Bridges, May 28, 1904, to Col. J. E. Callaway."

field. The Virginia City-Helena contract was awarded to Wells Fargo in 1868 for $8,540 for triweekly service. Two years later the pay was doubled for service six times a week. There were other mail contracts in Montana—Virginia City to Fort Owen via Deer Lodge, Helena to Blackfoot City, and many more. In Utah, recommendations were made to the Post Office Department that Mormons be excluded from carrying contracts to avoid the "anomaly" of the government paying ten percent of the profits on the contracts as tithes to the Mormon church.[26]

The early postmasters on the mail routes occasionally demonstrated a frontier independence. One representative at Rattlesnake Creek, or Mountain Home, on the Boise route, Commodore Jackson, finally resigned over some trouble with Washington, D.C., about his postal reports. He asked to be relieved immediately. When the government was slow to act, Commodore Jackson crammed all his stamps and supplies into a postal sack and sent them to Washington with a note, "Here's your damned old postoffice." [27]

The Post Office Department instructions to mail carriers were quite explicit: seven minutes allowed at each intermediate station to open and examine the mail; no pay for trips not made, and if three such omissions occurred that could not be explained satisfactorily the pay would be deducted; and one-fourth pay deducted for arrivals too late to make connections.

The Telegraph

When the Creighton Brothers undertook construction of a telegraph line from Salt Lake City to Virginia City and Helena for Western Union, the constant delays in mail service became less important. On July 17, 1866, John A. Creighton started a crew digging holes for poles furnished at the southern end by Brigham Young and at the northern end by another entrepreneur from William's Gulch. By early October crews were "putting up the line on a trot," and the Helena–Virginia City segment

---

[26] NA, "Mail Routes, Montana, 1866-1870," pp. 182, 370-71, 380; U. S. Congress, "Affairs in Utah and the Territories," by James F. Rusling, *House Misc. Doc. 153*, p. 25.
[27] *Times-News*, Hailey, Idaho, Mar. 25, 1954.

opened for business on October 12. The cost of a telegram was $1.50 for the first ten words and $.10 for each additional word.[28] Edward Creighton sent the first telegram into Montana on November 2, 1866.

The military authorities at Forts Hall, Ellis, and Shaw were to maintain the line, much to their exasperation. The operator at Fort Shaw, for example, made a typical report in 1874 that the line was working at 8:30 A.M., but ceased to function at 10:00 A.M.— probably, he said, because the line was wet. As soon as it dried out, he believed it would be operable again. In 1875, a new line was built from Franklin, Idaho, to Marsh Valley, to avoid the worst portions of the old line to Corinne, Utah. At the same time, civilian contractors were employed to elevate the wires "so that no injury can be done by wagons."[29]

Riding the Coach

While the telegraph might transmit news to Montana with speed and dispatch, passengers found the trip slow and exhausting because of the stage equipment used and the perils and physical torture endured during the journey. As Washington Irving had noted, "There is a certain relief in change, even though it be from bad to worse; as I have found in traveling in a stage coach, that it is often a comfort to shift one's position and be bruised in a new place."

Abbot, Downing Company of Concord, New Hampshire, were suppliers of the famous heavy Western Concord coach used on the road between Salt Lake City and Montana. The firm also built numerous "mud wagons," plus some models known as Passenger Wagons, Passenger Hacks, and Overland Wagons. The Mail Jerkey, a short, two-seated wagon, and the Yellowstone Wagon, a three-seated conveyance with roll-down curtains, also saw service in Montana. All of these models were built with leather straps supporting the body of the carriage, called thor-

---

[28] Merril G. Burlingame and K. Ross Toole, *A History of Montana*, vol. 2, p. 66; *Montana Post*, Sept. 22, Oct. 12, 1866.

[29] NA, "Records of United States Army Commands, 1784-1821," RG 98, Letter from A. Christian, Telegraph Operator to Post Adjutant, Ft. Shaw, Mont. T., May 14, 1874. *Montanian*, June 10, July 29, 1875.

Stagecoach in Montana. *Montana Historical Society, Helena.*

oughbrace suspension. Mountain "dead axe" wagons, with iron springs rather than thoroughbraces, were also used occasionally; and some of these had tops, although many dispensed with such luxuries and gave their passengers an excellent and unobstructed look at the Big Sky of Montana.

The Western Concord rolled on front wheels 3 feet 10 inches high and rear wheels measuring 5 feet 1 inch, with tires 2½ to 3 inches wide. The coach was 8 feet 6 inches tall, and the body of the vehicle rested on thoroughbraces, fastened to the upper ends of S-shaped iron standards. The brake was an iron rod connected to a brake shoe that pressed against the wheel. There was a front boot under the driver's seat to hold tools, the treasure box, a pouch of mail, a water bucket, and, in bad weather, a buffalo robe. The rear boot was for trunks and luggage. Two riders could sit on the cushioned seat beside the driver if he so honored them, and there was space for three additional passengers on the hurricane deck above and behind the driver. Heavy leather curtains were used on the Western Concord instead of glass because of the rough roads.[30]

The most important feature of the Concord coach, as far as the passengers and drivers were concerned, was the thorough-brace construction, which gave a fore-and-aft as well as lateral motion to the coach body that resembled somewhat the gentle roll of a ship on the ocean. Riding in a Concord was considered to be the most comfortable way to travel. But, as Captain William Banning explained, "the most important function of Concord thorough-braces . . . [is that] by allowing the heavy body to rock fore and aft, they enable the force of inertia to supply the timely boost to relieve the team of strain due to obstacles of the road. The horse was the vital consideration. The less taxed, the more he could pull and the faster he could go. The coach that could run the easiest with the greatest load was the best for the horse. And the Concord was that coach." [31]

Inside the coach were three seats, one at each end, with the forward seat facing the rear. The center seat had three sections,

[30] Nick Eggenhofer, *Wagons, Mules, and Men: How the Frontier Moved West,* pp. 151–52, 160–68.
[31] Merrill D. Beal and Merle W. Wells, *History of Idaho,* p. 408; Captain William Banning and George H. Banning, *Six Horses,* p. 359.

with the two outer sections hinged to allow passengers access to the rear seat. A broad leather band, which detached to let riders get in or out, was suspended from the roof and hooked to brackets on the side panel to provide a backrest for center-seat riders.[32]

Coaches were pulled by two to eight horses, depending on the weight of the coach and the road conditions. Eight horses were used on particularly bad stretches. When a second team was used, the doubletree of the lead pair was fastened to the end of the tongue and slipped over a long iron hook. In a six-horse hitch, an extra pole was hooked on, and similarly with an eight-horse hitch. All teams were thus hooked to doubletrees.

A lighter stage, or mud wagon as it was usually called, was simpler, with just a roof and curtains of heavy canvas. The chief difference in the undercarriage was in the thoroughbraces, which were placed directly over the axle instead of being hung on S braces; these features, according to most passengers, made the mud wagon a less comfortable vehicle. Even worse was the light two-seated jerkey, fitted with a top and side curtains and the same type of thoroughbraces as the mud wagon. Disgruntled customers by the score have left grim accounts of the utter misery endured while riding in a jerkey, including Episcopal Bishop Daniel S. Tuttle:

> [A Jerkey] was a small canvas-covered affair, seating four inside and one outside with the driver, and drawn usually by only two horses. This, when the wheels struck obstacles, did not have the easy roll and swing of the coach, but, as the name imparts, jerked the passenger unmercifully on, or oftener off, his seat. To be alone in a jerker was to be in the extreme of discomfort. The vehicle not being steadied by a good load, and the passenger not being supported by contact with other passengers, the ceaseless unsteadiness drove away sleep, and wore one out in frantic efforts to secure some tolerable sort of bodily equilibrium. During the last fifty miles of that Boise trip I was more used up physically than at any other time I can think of in my life. I was past the point of grinning and bearing, or shutting the teeth and enduring. All the forces of resistance seemed to be beaten down and disintegrated. I was ready to groan and cry, and would have offered not a jot of opposition if the driver had dumped me down upon the roadside and left me behind under a sage brush. That experience made me under-

---

[32] Eggenhofer, *Wagons, Mules, and Men,* pp. 168, 172.

stand the stories I had heard of the stage passengers who could not
sleep, coming in after long journeys downright sick and even actually demented.[33]

Jehus

Running a stage line required the services of many people
from a variety of trades. Wells Fargo employed a general superintendent and three divisional superintendents on the road between Salt Lake City and Helena. In addition, there were paymas-
ters, station agents, stock tenders, buyers, messengers, harness
makers, blacksmiths, carpenters, and general roustabouts. To
the coach passenger, all of these people seemed to exist only to
support that central figure of every stagecoach ride, the driver,
the individual whose skill with the horses meant either a safe,
relatively comfortable journey or an uneasy, dangerous passage.
He was usually called the Jehu, after the Old Testament verse
found in 2 Kings 9:20: "and the driving is like the driving of Jehu
the son of Nimshi: for he driveth furiously."

Captain William Banning described two types of Jehus: one,
who drove a "tight-laced" team whose wheel and swing horses
were so rigidly fastened to the tongue that their traces were
never slack; and the other, a true "reinsman," whose six horses
were harnessed rather loosely, with the breast straps "swinging
liberally." The former, less able driver, sacrificed

> along with certain elements of grace and certain practice in the
> most delicate sort of fingering and brake work, a great deal of
> efficiency to include power, speed [and] endurance. . . . Where the
> mountains in America were loftiest and most rugged, where the
> roads were most narrow and threatening, there, above all places,
> was the greatest demand for the whip who had learned to "rein,"
> the driver who had mastered the most difficult of modes of driv-
> ing. His was a strictly triplex power plant of duplex units operat-
> ing on twenty-four hoofs; and if, by means of his six lines and his
> brake and whip, he could exact from all of its parts and potentiali-
> ties a maximum degree of efficiency at all times, then he was a
> master of masters. He was a reinsman indeed.[34]

---

[33] Daniel S. Tuttle, *Reminiscences of a Missionary Bishop*, pp. 91–92.
[34] Beal and Wells, *History of Idaho*, p. 408; Banning and Banning, *Six Horses*, pp. 361, 364.

A Jehu and his team. *Courtesy of William D. Livingstone.*

Such an expert looked with disdain on the more mediocre driver who often resorted to filling the front boot with small rocks with which to pelt the leaders at crucial moments. The swing, or middle span, was often vigorously motivated with a long-handled whip, while the wheelers were lashed with a chain whip. Thus did a novice driver "worry" his six-horse team over the road. A Jehu usually drove the fifty or sixty miles between home stations, stopping only long enough to change teams at the swing stations, spaced ten to twelve miles apart. A. K. McClure described a typical driver who very carefully checked the traces, harnesses, etc., of his six-horse team, then, with proper dignity and responsibility, gathered the lines in his hands, and "with the majesty of a legislative presiding officer," called out "all aboard" and was off in a cloud of dust. McClure's admiration for a skilled driver was shared by all those whose good fortune it was to be assigned to a coach driven by an expert Jehu. "I . . . was charmed with the caution and precision they display in the narrow, steep, and sharply curved roads of the mountains. With a single hand they will sweep their horses around a short turn, or pass another team, with a grace and elegance that are perfectly artistic; and, while they almost fly down the steep mountain declivities, they insure safety by never losing for a moment the complete control of a single horse in the team." [35]

One occupational hazard of stage drivers was frozen fingers and hands. The Jehus wore silk gloves next to the skin and buckskin over these, but it was still quite common to read in the *Montana Post* of January 18, 1869, that Tom Caldwell, "the well known overland driver," had one of his frozen fingers amputated. This rather casual attitude toward the hazards of travel was somewhat helped by a rough western humor. On one trip from Helena to Blackfoot City, a passenger recounted how the driver had forgotten the mail, so he dumped the passengers out and went back to get it. At the first station, the driver was told that there was "nary cayuse" around for a change of teams and that the best thing he could do would be to put the wheelers on the lead because this maneuver would delude the horses into imagin-

[35] Henry A. Boller, *Among the Indians: Eight Years in the Far West: 1858–1866*, p. 414; James K. P. Miller, *The Road to Virginia City*, p. 112; A. K. McClure, *Three Thousand Miles Through the Rocky Mountains*, pp. 103–4.

ing they were fresh. The arrangememt apparently worked, as the horses pulled the stage through two feet of snow.[36]

The constant companion of the stage driver was the shotgun messenger, at least when there was heavy treasure aboard. On March 19, 1878, the *Idaho World* commended the bravery of one, Mike Burke, for his gallant defense of the stage from robbers, although there had been one bad feature: "Mike was on the hind seat and used the driver for breastworks." Wells Fargo instructions to messengers required that they be obliging to all persons, especially passengers, and that there would be no excuse accepted for "incommoding a stage passenger." [37]

But while the shotgun artists were given due respect, public attention tended to focus on the driver. Most Jehus liked to wear white, Stetson-type hats, wide decorated belts, and in other ways contrived to display a certain dash. The H. K. Knight whip was a favorite, and was usually decorated to suit the driver's taste. Winter tended to destroy their bright appearance, as most drivers donned first a suit of woolen underclothing, then a suit of buckskin, the whole being surrounded by the ever-present buffalo robe and cap.[38]

For such careful handling of the lines a driver received from $150 to $250 a month depending on his tenure and ability as a "reinsman," but this salary did not give adequate recognition to another aspect of his work—that of news dispenser. Drivers usually exchanged the latest gossip during their short stops at the stations while they were engaged in greasing the axles of the coaches with "dope" as they called the axle grease. The expression "dope telegraph" therefore came to be attached to this type of news, which often found its way into the columns of the frontier newspapers.[39]

The Arduous Journey

The swing and home stations along the road to Montana

---

[36] BL, "Bancroft Scraps, Montana Miscellany," vol. 90, Letter from Montana, Helena, Dec. 3, 1867, in *San Francisco Alta Californian*, Dec. 5, 1867, p. 95.

[37] Wells, Fargo and Company, *California and Oregon Express Rules, Instructions and Tariffs*, p. 43.

[38] MSHS, "R. L. 'Dick' Potter, as told to Rozetta Bailey Sylten," in *The Saco Independent*, Aug. 1, 1936, Clip file; A. K. McClure, *Three Thousand Miles*, pp. 431–32.

[39] John W. Clampitt, *Echoes from the Rocky Mountains*, p. 77; Bruffey, *Eighty-One Years in the West*, p. 78.

were real havens to the weary travelers who dared the rough and seemingly interminable journey. Ben Holladay established the first ones, rather crude adobe or log huts, which gradually improved, depending on the tastes and ambitions of the agents. When Katherine Dunlap and her husband traveled the road in 1864, the agent at Pleasant Valley offered Red Rock Station, forty miles farther on, to Mr. Dunlap, with a contract calling for $800 to build the station house and $30 a month to "board his hands." After a week's consideration, the Dunlaps decided against the venture because "it would soon eat us up," having to supply fifty pounds of flour per man for a month "would not pay." George A. Bruffey was station keeper on the Jefferson stage line at Fish Creek during part of the 1870's and described his duties, which included seeing that all the horses were properly fed, checking the harnesses, replacing lame or otherwise incapacitated horses, examining all the waybills, making sure the passengers were properly billed, supplying drivers for the stages, and sometimes having to secure hay and oats during a shortage. He, of course, also handled the mail and on the side developed a general supply store. Bruffey traded in clothing, dry goods, wagons and buggies, hides, ores, gold dust, cattle, horses, and food supplies but sold no whiskey and allowed no card playing.[40]

The stage stations between Salt Lake City and Helena varied in the degree to which passengers' needs were met. Small adobe hotels were available at Brigham City for the convenience of travelers, and one of the finest way stations on the line was built in the summer of 1867 by the firm of Godbe and Hampton at Bear River Crossing at the junction of the Boise, Montana, and Cache Valley roads. The hotel was a nineteen-room, two-story affair built of local sandstone at a cost of $150,000. It remains in excellent condition and is now used as a private dwelling. After Hampton's Crossing, as it came to be called, the northbound traveler next passed the small mud-hut village of Malad, after which he continued through the wastelands of Idaho. Ranches were nonexistent beyond the Snake River, and the small station houses were the only signs of habitation. Past the Pleasant Valley Divide,

---

[40] BL, Katherine Dunlap, "Overland Journal, May 15–August 16, 1864," pp. 39–40; Bruffey, *Eighty-One Years*, pp. 80, 84, 88.

Bear River Crossing and the Bear River Hotel photographed by William H. Jackson in 1872. *National Archives.*

scattered ranches began to appear along the river valleys of western Montana.[41]

During the early period of the gold rush, Holladay issued orders to his station agents to feed no one but the passengers and employees of his line and hired spies to see that his orders were obeyed. Along the route to Boise, seasoned travelers warned others to take along their own rations. A few along the Montana route found the "stations magnificent," but most coach passengers wondered why Ben Holladay had to hire spies to stop inroads on his bad fare. Meals cost from $1.25 to $2.00; the menu apparently rarely varied from bacon, beef, and baking powder biscuits. One traveler decried the terrible cooking and wished Ben Holladay might "be unfortunate enough to be snowed in for a couple of weeks at old 'Brogans,' in Pleasant Valley, and be compelled to feed and pay $2 per meal for cold bacon, cold beans and cold bread." On a trip made by A. K. McClure, he described a miserable time at Moose Creek Station near Big Hole Valley on the road to Deer Lodge. He made his bed on the floor, along with the other passengers and the family of the station agent. Bedbugs in the dirty ticking kept him awake most of the night. When morning came, the landlady began making biscuits, and McClure had a good view of her bare feet, which he decided she had not washed since spring. The cook captured a couple of bugs running around in the biscuit dough and flung them into the stove, whereupon McClure decided he didn't want any breakfast.[42]

Not only was a passenger uncertain of the kind of meals that awaited him, but payment of his fare did not insure a ride the whole distance in a comfortable Concord coach. At any time he might be shifted to a jerkey, a lumber wagon, a sleigh, or any other nondescript kind of hack, or he might have the pleasure of walking. When Mrs. W. F. Sanders traveled from Virginia City to Salt Lake City in February 1866, she rode in the following

---

[41] Daughters of Utah Pioneers, Box Elder County, *History of Box Elder County*, pp. 22–23; *Salt Lake Telegraph*, Nov. 15, 1867.

[42] ISUA, Murdock M. McPherson, "Murdock M. McPherson's Recollections," p. 23; "Protection Across the Continent, 1866," by D. B. Sackett, U.S. Congress, *House Exec. Doc. 23*, p. 54; MSHS, "Those Early Days were Tough for Greenhorns," Oct. 1, 1942, Clip file; BL, "Bancroft Scraps, Montana Miscellany," vol. 90, J. B. B. letter in *Sacramento Union*, Mar. 22, 1866, p. 1; A. K. McClure *Three Thousand Miles*, pp. 305.

conveyances: coach to Bannack, sleigh to Market Lake, coach to Ross Fork, lumber wagon to Bear River Crossing, coach to Box Elder, lumber wagon for another distance, then a sleigh again to Salt Lake.[43]

Sleep was a stranger to most passengers, even though the *Montana Post* took pride in describing Superintendent Taylor's private sleeping coach, "the Northern Light," drawn by "eight magnificent greys." Wells Fargo had provided the novel wagon with seats arranged so that they could be made into a comfortable bed. For the hoi polloi, a feather pillow could be taken along, the passenger attempting to sleep "sitting bolt upright. . . . The first night is hard and trying; afterward, with the head resting against his pillow . . . one's repose is ample and refreshing." At least, so wrote one satisfied customer.[44]

The early stage lines did not even allow this kind of sleep. The first Oliver stage between Bannack and Alder Gulch was a "dead-axe" wagon hooked to four unbroken broncos. A half dozen men held the wild horses down until the "last tug was hitched, and when they were turned loose they struck a dead run and kept it up to the next station." Or Morpheus might be betrayed by the custom of stage companies stuffing as many as ten people inside and three on top of a rickety hack built to hold six. Gurdon P. Lester had such an experience at Bear River Crossing on his way to Virginia City, noting that while "our suffering had already been great, . . . now they were ten fold greater. . . . I can think of nothing only the misery we are in and the manner in which we are knocked and jamed about." [45]

Summer coach travel was uncomfortable, but a winter journey between Utah and Montana could be dangerous, if not impossible. Joseph T. Walker, for example, recorded that he and four others left Virginia City on December 1, 1863, on a stage company wagon after waiting nine days for a seat on the regular

[43] MSHS, "Those Early Days were Tough for Greenhorns," Oct. 1, 1942, Clip file; MSHS, Harriet F. Sanders, "Diary, Virginia City to St. Louis, February 21–March 17, 1866," Feb. 21, 1866.

[44] *Montana Post*, June 26, 1868; BL, "Bancroft Scraps, Utah Miscellany," vol. 109, clip from *New York Herald Tribune*, p. 434.

[45] MSHS, "A Thousand Miles of Road," *West Shore*, n.d., Clip file; Gurdon P. Lester, "A Round Trip to the Montana Mines," *Nebraska History Quarterly*, vol. 46 (Dec. 1965), p. 293.

coach. When the wagon became stuck in the snow, the five passengers were employed breaking trails for the mules near Pine Butte Station. Near the summit, the passengers tramped a road for the mules, then went back to pick up nine sacks of mail and some gold dust to carry out to the spot where the mules were. The passengers, two drivers, and one messenger then took the wagon bed from the running gear, and part by part carried the dead-axe wagon forward to the mules.

After putting everything together, the snow-bitten crew started out again but soon had to stop and repeat the entire process. Exhaustion had set in by this time. Night came, and the men dug holes in the deep snow for resting places. The mules had no feed and spent the night eating up the harness, the wagon box, and a coat off one man as he lay asleep. The next morning, after going only a short distance, what remained of the wagon settled down in the snow, and the men decided to abandon it. A relief party of five men and fourteen horses came in sight from Pleasant Valley Station, just five miles away, and everyone reached safety "just at Sun Sett, a hungry and fagged party."

After resting at the station three days and paying $1.50 in gold or $3.00 in greenbacks for each meal, the drivers started out, each riding a mule, and allowed the five passengers the two other mules. By alternately riding and walking, they finally reached Dry Creek Station having "walked or rather waded snow for over thirty miles and paid the Stage Company 37 cents per mile for the privilege of doing it. . . . " The party reached Salt Lake City on December 13.[46]

Few complained when the mail was delayed by such conditions as the Walker party encountered. The *Idaho Statesman* on March 30, 1865, did comment on the "basket full of mush" that the staff received from the post office and added that "it must have encountered great dangers by land and sea, but principally by sea. . . . The addition of a little more liquid would have made porridge." Little wonder that most Montana residents hoped for roads as "hard as a road-agents heart" when alternate thaws and freezes turned thoroughfares into bottomless pits. James Knox Polk Miller, for one, soon discovered why the stage companies

[46] MSHS, Joseph T. Walker, "A Trip Across the Plains, 1863, 1865," pp. 59–71.

had a custom of carrying a shovel for each passenger. Upon reaching any mud hole, the Jehu would sing out, "Now gentlemen if you will be so kind as to give me a lift for only 20 steps," which usually meant a slithering walk through the mud from two to four miles each time. Stagecoach riders of the 1860s on the road to Montana could appreciate the cryptic comment of the *Montana Post*, "The passengers on one of Oliver & Co's coaches which left this town on the 17th inst., had a break down, got mad, and burnt up the coach on Snake river." [47]

Most of the experienced miners and those who had spent time in the West took the rough stage journeys with little grumbling and were freer from the quarrels and disagreements which seemed to be commoner in more civilized climes. The revolver at every man's belt kept in "every one's mind a clear perception of the bounds of meum and tuum." The *Omaha Herald* summed up the proper decorum for passengers on overland stages:

TIPS FOR STAGECOACH TRAVELERS

The best seat inside a stage is the one next to the driver. Even if you have a tendency to seasickness when riding backwards--you'll get over it and will get less jolts and jostling. Don't let any 'sly elph' trade you his mid-seat.

In cold weather don't ride with tight-fitting boots, shoes, or gloves. When the driver asks you to get off and walk do so without grumbling, he won't request it unless absolutely necessary. If the team runs away--sit still and take your chances. If you jump, nine out of ten times you will get hurt.

In very cold weather abstain entirely from liquor when on the road; because you will freeze twice as quickly when under its influence. Don't growl at the food received at the station; stage companies generally provide the best they can get.

Don't keep the stage waiting. Don't smoke a strong pipe inside the coach--spit on the leeward side. If you have anything to drink in a bottle pass it around. Procure your stimulants before starting as "ranch" (Stage Depot) whiskey is not "nectar."

Don't swear or lop over neighbors when sleeping. Take small change to pay expenses. Never shoot on the road as the noise might

---

[47] *Montana Post*, Oct. 29, 1864, Jan. 20, 1866; BL, James Knox Polk Miller, "James Knox Polk Miller Diaries," May 28, 1867.

frighten the horses. Don't discuss politics or religion. Don't point out where murders have been committed especially if there are women passengers.

Don't lag at the wash basin. Don't grease your hair, because travel is dusty. Don't imagine for a moment that you are going on a picnic. Expect annoyances, discomfort, and some hardship.

Most people understood and followed these precepts. For everyone who complained there were probably ten who took their journeys philosophically and stoically. As the *Montana Post* of March 10, 1866, pointed out, it should be remembered that life's "water-spouts and geysers" make the news, not its "calm rivers and quiet springs." [48]

Not unexpectedly, the high speeds of up to ten to twelve miles per hour over rough mountain roads led to many stage accidents. Most injuries to passengers occurred when they were thrown out of the coaches. In one near upset, the driver righted the stage, but not before a man fell out. Ice and slippery roads caused many upsets, and during a trip to Deer Lodge from Virginia City a stage overturned, with two men suffering broken legs. Perhaps the best commentary on the casual attitude of passengers toward the dangers of mountain staging came when a driver was tossed from his coach while going down the long hill from Prickly Pear to Boulder. The stage passed over the body of the Jehu, and the driverless horses continued down the slope at a breakneck pace. The driver of the rival Oliver stage finally stopped the team at the base of the mountain, and, as the *Montana Post* editor remarked, "What is stranger than all is that the inside passengers, seven in number, knew nothing of the accident." [49]

Vigilantes Strike Back

The chief terror for drivers and passengers, however, was not stage accidents, but the sudden appearance of masked men

---

[48] Edward B. Nealley, "A Year in Montana," *Atlantic* (Aug. 1866), p. 236; *Omaha Herald*, Oct. 3, 1877.

[49] *Montana Post*, July 21, 1866.

crying out "Halt! Throw up your hands, you sons of b——s!" The first stagecoach robbery on the road from Montana to Salt Lake probably occurred in November 1863 when George Ives, Whiskey Bill Graves, and Bob Zachary stopped the stage outside of Bannack. The three relived the passengers of $500 and a bag of gold dust. Finally, exasperated citizens in Bannack and Virginia City followed a California example and on December 23, 1863, formed a vigilante group in reaction to the numerous robberies and murders. According to one version, the twenty-five original signers swore each other to secrecy and agreed that the only punishment the group would mete out would be death.[50]

On February 5, 1864, the *Union Vedette* correspondent wrote that when Sheriff Henry Plummer was arrested, he had on his person a list of eighty-five members of his robber band. The vigilante group hanged Henry Plummer, Ned Ray, Buck Stinson, and Dutch John Wagner at Bannack City; Jack Gallagher, George (Clubfoot) Lane, Haze Lyons, Boone H. Helm, and Frank Parrish were hanged at Virginia City; and Reed (Erastus "Red") Yager and Brown were hanged at Laurin. It was added that the committee was just starting the trials of seventy more suspected robbers and murderers, and he expected that their appearance in court would be conducted by the same "sober, quiet [and] ... determined assemblage of citizens" that had tried the first men.

Montana vigilantes did not confine themselves to the area between Bannack and Virginia City, but searched for road agents along the route to Salt Lake City. When James Kelley held up a stage and committed other indiscretions, the vigilantes formed a posse and left Virginia City August 8, 1864, determined to catch him. At Oliver's Station in Portneuf Canyon, the posse learned that a party of California prospectors had caught Kelley hiding in a haystack. After a trial, Kelley was hanged September 5, 1864.[51]

The most famous holdup along the Montana Road was the

---

[50] M. A. Leeson, ed., *History of Montana*, p. 276; Prof. Thomas J. Dimsdale, *The Vigilantes of Montana or Popular Justice in the Rocky Mountains*, p. 156; *Madison County Mentor*, Mar. 2, 1900.

[51] Dimsdale, *The Vigilantes of Montana*, pp. 156–59; Hoffman Birney, *Vigilantes*, p. 341; *Salt Lake Telegraph*, Sept. 10, 1864; *Union Vedette*, Sept. 10, 15, 1864.

Vigilante Headquarters in Virginia City. *Merrill Beal Collection, Virginia City.*

Boot Hill in Virginia City where members of the Plummer Gang were buried. *Merrill Beal Collection, Virginia City.*

Great Portneuf Stage Robbery on July 13, 1865. According to one report, as a coach from the north was passing through Portneuf Canyon, one of the passengers yelled "Boys, here they are!" A. S. Parker, sitting on the box beside the driver, fired first; instantly, the road agents riddled the coach with broadsides of buckshot. Examination later revealed that seventy-five charges had been fired into the stage body. Seven robbers made the actual attack, but several others were hiding in the brush holding the horses. When the gunfire ceased, four men lay dead and three were dying inside the coach. Under their bodies lay L. F. Carpenter, wounded but alive. Charley, the messenger, had had both feet shot off and would later have a leg amputated at the thigh. One passenger was unhurt and escaped into the brush. After rifling the bodies and treasure box of $65,000 in gold the road agents prepared to leave, when one realized that Carpenter was not dead and decided to finish him off. Carpenter pleaded that he was dying anyway and asked that he not be disfigured. His wish was granted. Another ruffian came up to shoot the driver, but was stopped by Jim Locket, leader of the gang—"Hold on; a driver never has a d——d cent. He's of no account any way." So the driver, Frank Williams, was also spared. Within a few days, however, Williams, who had never had a cent in his life, showed up in Salt Lake and began to spend money in prodigious amounts. He immediately came under suspicion, was followed to Colorado, confessed to being in league with the robbers, and was hanged at Cherry Creek. A few others were finally caught and executed. By this time the forbidding Portneuf Canyon was coming to be knows as the "road agent's play ground." [52]

Community leaders kept asking for military escorts for coaches carrying treasure, and Governor Thomas F. Meagher of Montana made a formal request to the Commander of the Military district of Nebraska for army assistance to halt the bloody

---

[52] For varied accounts of this robbery see: Helen F. Sanders, ed., *X. Beidler, Vigilante*, pp. 103–6; N. P. Langford, *Vigilante Days and Ways*, pp. 432–34; Dimsdale, *The Vigilantes of Montana*, p. 183; J. K. P. Miller, *The Road to Virginia City*, p. 79; Leeson, ed., *History of Montana*, p. 302; MSHS, Joseph T. Walker, "Diary," p. 60; MSHS, "Portneuf Canyon... Danger for Stage...," in *Stage Coach and Covered Wagon*, Sept. 11, 1941, Clip file; *Union Vedette*, July 17, 21, 22, 1865; *Idaho Statesman*, July 20, 1865; *Montana Post*, July 22, 1865, Mar. 31, 1866.

assassinations.[53] But by July 27, 1867, the *Montana Post* remarked that on two different occasions coaches were stopped near Divide Creek, but the robbers, "evidently unfitted for their business for want of ordinary pluck," ran away before getting anything. It appeared that the wild frontier was disappearing under the onslaught of civilization.

[53] NA, "General Records of the Department of State, October 14, 1864–July 16, 1872," RG 59, Meagher to Wheaton, Oct. 20, 1865.

6

The High Cost of Tolls

Eager miners rushing pell-mell toward the gold awaiting them
in the gulches of western Montana found their way barred by
numerous swift streams and difficult passages through ravines
and over mountain divides. Most of them were happy to pay a
small toll to get their wagons and animals through safely. The
early territorial governments were virtually bereft of funds for
road improvements and granted almost unlimited ferry, bridge,
and road charters.

Toll Roads in Utah

The Utah Territorial Legislature, in its first annual session
in September 1851, attempted to meet the needs of its citizens
and other travelers for better ways to cross the large rivers of
Utah. A comprehensive act was passed establishing a road tax of
one percent on all taxable property, to be applied on the public
roads. In addition, every able-bodied man over eighteen years
was expected to pay a poll tax of "one day's labor yearly" upon the
roads of the territory. Moreover, a charter was granted to James
Brown giving him the right to take tolls on the road between the
Weber and Ogden rivers, provided he improve the road and
maintain the bridges already spanning the two streams. The
final section of the law stated that any person building any other
bridge, ferry, or road across the rivers was to be fined not less
than $3,000 nor more than $5,000.[1]

The legislature also issued a three-year charter to Joseph

---

[1] Territory of Utah, *Acts, Resolutions and Memorials Passed by First
Annual and Special Sessions of Legislative Assembly of Territory of Utah, Sept.
22, 1851*, pp. 111–12.

Young, David Fulmer, and William Empey to establish a ferry across the Bear River (an important junction of the two roads to Montana and Boise before completion of the railroad), with ten percent of the toll to be paid to the territorial treasurer. Any other person establishing a ferry along this stretch of the river was to be fined $1,000, but this was not to be construed "to prevent any person from ferrying themselves with their effects." The same four men were also required to build a bridge over the Malad River, "about two miles north of the ferry on Bear river." [2]

To avoid the tolls, travelers frequently crossed streams at established fording points. On the Malad, there was a crossing at Rocky Ford a few miles north of the bridge, and there were at least three fords across the Bear River that could be used at low water. One of these, located between present Honeyville and Deweyville, was often used by emigrants going to western Idaho and was known as the Boise Ford.[3]

The acts of the first legislature of Utah were bravely worded and gave some promise to weary travelers, but many receiving charters failed to construct adequate bridges. The meager improvements made by James Brown were sad precursors to other toll road operations in Idaho and Montana. Brown's first bridge over the Ogden River, built for $200, contained mud, wet brush, and willows as fill between the logs. The right of Brown to operate bridges across the Weber and Ogden Rivers was reaffirmed in 1853 but more specific instructions were given for the building of the structures including four-inch by eight-inch planks to be used as decking.[4]

---

[2] Ibid., pp. 164–69. In 1855, Brigham Young, Sr., and Joseph Young, Sr., were given the right to operate and control the ferry across the Bear River and a bridge over the Malad. Governor Young finally left the ferry business and turned the Bear River Ferry and Malad Toll Bridge over to Joseph Young, Sr., for a five-year contract. In 1866, Alvin Nichols and William S. Godbe were authorized to build a toll bridge across the Bear River and, except when, occasionally, the bridge was out, travelers no longer risked the dangers of ferrying across this stream. Territory of Utah, *Acts, Resolutions and Memorials Passed at the Several Annual Sessions of the Legislative Assembly of the Territory of Utah, Jan. 19, 1866*, p. 211; Territory of Utah, *Acts, Resolutions—Legislative Assembly of the Territory of Utah*, Eighth Annual Session—for the Years 1858–59. p. 24.

[3] L. A. Fleming and A. R. Standing, "The Road to Fortune: The Salt Lake Cutoff," *Utah Historical Quarterly*, vol. 33 (Mar. 1965), pp. 260, 266.

[4] James V. Barber, "The History of Highways in Utah from 1847 to 1869," M.A. thesis, University of Utah, 1949, p. 43; Territory of Utah, *Acts and Resolutions Passed at the Adjourned Session of the Territory of Utah, June, 1853*, pp. 155–56.

Because of the constant bridge failures, public sentiment began to swing toward tax support of bridges to ensure uninterrupted travel and get rid of bothersome tolls. The 1859 legislature signified its willingness to pay three-fourths of the expense of building a bridge across the Weber River as soon as the county would vote enough money for one-fourth the expense. The territory finally appropriated $1,503 for the structure and six years later voted $3,000 to assist in building a bridge over the Ogden River. In Cache County, where there had been agitation for a bridge across the Bear River above Bear River Canyon, the legislature granted five Cache County citizens the right to sell stock to raise enough money for construction. It was understood that as soon as the net profits amounted to one hundred percent above the primary cost of the bridge, the span was to be turned over to the county and thereafter would be "free to the traveling community." [5]

The roads north from Salt Lake City were not much better than the bridges. The *Deseret News* opined on November 23, 1859, that the road would be in good condition "if there was not so much mud everywhere." There were some attempts to improve the road north of Salt Lake City. In 1862, the legislature directed the Territorial Road Commissioners to "locate" a road from Layton, Utah, to Willow Creek in Box Elder County, Utah, and to facilitate completion of the road as well as to raise money for other road purposes. The act also provided for a poll tax of two days' labor for every able-bodied male inhabitant over sixteen. [6]

Five years later the Kaysville Wagon Road Company was incorporated by the legislature to operate a toll road from Kay's Creek to Haight's Creek in the same county. [7] Apparently, the road was not successful because a correspondent of the *Deseret*

---

[5] Territory of Utah, *Acts, Resolutions and Memorials Passed by the Legislative Assembly of the Territory of Utah During Ninth Annual Session for Years 1859-60*, pp. 31-32; Territory of Utah, *Acts, Resolutions and Memorials Passed by the Legislative Assembly of the Territory of Utah, Fourteenth Annual Session, 1864-65*, p. 8.

[6] Territory of Utah, *Acts, Resolutions and Memorials Passed by the Legislative Assembly of the Territory of Utah During the Eleventh Annual Session for the Years 1861-62*, pp. 5-9.

[7] Territory of Utah, *Acts, Resolutions and Memorials Passed and Adopted During the Sixteenth Annual Session of the Legislative Assembly of the Territory of Utah, Jan. 18, 1867*, p. 19.

News reported on March 31, 1869, that as he traveled along through fifteen inches of mud he was informed about a "defunct toll road through Kaysville, which encouraged" him until he found the ex-toll road, that is "the top of the road but no human being could find the bottom—it was like that well-arranged hereafter for the wicked—bottomless."

Keeping the roads in some kind of passable condition was difficult enough with meager tax resources and incompetent toll road operators, but there were other problems as well. Irresponsible citizens paid little attention to road upkeep until the legislature decreed that persons damaging public thoroughfares would be fined $500 and jailed for six months. In addition, any teamsters or wagon masters who camped on the roads or caused any delays for other travelers could be fined $100 and costs. This became law in February 1869.[8]

Traveling Through Idaho

Moving north through Idaho, wagon travelers came first to the small Portneuf River, which ordinarily presented no serious obstacle. Occasionally the stream would overflow its banks, causing some anxiety and delay, as James Knox Polk Miller discovered on a trip to Montana—high water had prompted a man and a woman to erect a rickety bridge covered with willow sticks, and they were charging $4 for passage for a man and a horse.[9]

After the Portneuf, Montana-bound emigrants reached the Blackfoot River. Sarah Herndon's party, already exasperated by toll bridges built at places that could easily have been forded "if let alone," came to the Blackfoot bridge and noted that although the levy was only $1 per wagon, an excellent ford just below the bridge, which they could have taken, had been spoiled by the toll operators' digging ditches along both banks. The captain of the Herndon party tried the ford anyway, found it could be used, and took his wagons through despite the imprecations of the toll collectors.[10]

---

[8] Territory of Utah, *Acts, Resolutions and Memorials Passed and Adopted by the Legislative Assembly of the Territory of Utah, Eighteenth Annual Session, 1869,* p. 19.

[9] James Knox Polk Miller, *The Road to Virginia City: The Diary of James Knox Polk Miller,* pp. 66–67.

[10] Sarah R. Herndon, *Days on the Road: Crossing the Plains in 1865,* pp. 234-40.

Prior to gold discoveries in Idaho and Montana, crossing the broad, turbulent Snake River called for considerable ingenuity. Ferries, when they existed at all, ran irregularly. B. F. Cummings, on a trip to the Mormon Lemhi mission in 1856, noted that he had to repair "the old ferry boat which was in very bad condition." Following the gold strikes and before the coming of the railroad, ferries operating along the river proliferated. Lewis F. Crawford recorded that, in 1863, a ferry was being constructed on the river at the site of Old Fort Hall, and he hired out to help build the boat and then operate it. Apparently the increasing traffic on the road convinced him that this old crossing point should be revived.[11]

Traveling upstream, the emigrant next reached Meeks' and Gibson's Ferry, which, by July 6, 1864, was being advertised in the *Deseret News* and elsewhere as the "Best, Safest, and Cheapest Ferry on Snake River.... Other ferrymen and their runners say to the contrary notwithstanding." It was located just below the mouth of the Blackfoot River but was often abandoned by Jacob Meeks when he took off on a hunting or trading expedition. Jacob Meeks' and John P. Gibson's ferry was legalized by an act of the first session of the Idaho Territorial Legislature in 1864. The language was specific. The boat was "to be run in the proper season, by a rope stretched across said river of sufficient size, and blocks upon the same of strength sufficient to sustain ... the pressure of the current of said stream." Tolls were assessed at the rate of $4 for each wagon carrying under 2,000 pounds with another $1 for each additional 1,000 pounds.[12]

By the late 1870's, the Central Ferry, about eight miles above the Gibson and Meeks location, was being operated by T. T. Danilson for travelers to the Salmon River Mines. A final well-known ferry crossing was that built in 1863 by Harry Rickard and William A. Hickman, a former scout for Colonel Patrick E. Connor. When F. E. W. Patten reached this crossing on August 5, 1863, he noted that the ferry seemed to be "considerably under the control of Colonel Connor," because ten soldiers of his com-

---

[11] HL, B. F. Cummings, "Journal—Salmon River Mission," p. 30; Lewis F. Crawford, *Rekindling Camp Fires: Exploits of Ben Arnold (Connor)*, p. 81.

[12] Territory of Idaho, "General Laws of the Territory of Idaho, First Session, 1864," pp. 441, 645.

Crossing at Stubbs Ferry near Helena. *Courtesy of William D. Livingstone.*

Harry Rickard's Ferry at Eagle Rock on the Snake River. *From J. L. Campbell's* Idaho: Six Months in the New Gold Diggings, *Rare Books, Marriott Library, University of Utah.*

mand were operating the boat at the location on the Snake River, which marked the end of "Connor's cutoff." The whole operation was "doubtless a private enterprise in connection with his military employment." The river at this point was about 400 feet wide and quite deep. Patten's group paid $6.00 and $7.00 per wagon and $.50 for each span of animals.[13]

Many travelers refused to pay a toll to cross the Snake River and found other means to get to the west bank. George A. Bruffey found an old boatman, a Mr. Leonard, who offered "to row our wagons across." This was in November of 1863. Heber R. McBride came to the river in the early winter of 1864 and "saw something that pleased us all over." A large freight outfit had dug into the riverbank and graveled the ice, so McBride's party proceeded across and went "on our way rejoicing." Arriving at the crossing, the Edgerton party was told by the ferryman that the wind was blowing too hard to maneuver the boat. The impatient travelers, also upset at the high toll charges, went ten miles above to cross at an old ford. The current was quite swift, and one of the wagons was carried downstream almost into a set of rapids. It was necessary to take the passengers off the wagon in midstream and get them to shore by horseback.[14]

It soon became evident that ferries could not handle the increasing traffic across the Snake River and that a bridge would have to be built. A freighter, James Madison (Matt) Taylor, reached that decision one evening while at Eagle Rock chasm, where he and his fellow teamsters had pitched camp because of the relative lack of mosquitoes. He is said to have tied a stone to a coil of light string, hurled it across the narrow defile in the black lava, and, when it caught on the other bank, tied a knot in the string, pulled it back, and measured it. The distance was eighty-three feet. In the fall of 1864, he had timbers hauled from Beaver Canyon, and, in January, when the ice was thick enough, he took his crew of men out onto the ice and in six days

[13] *Salt Lake Tribune*, Aug. 8, Dec. 27, 1878; Barzilla W. Clark, *Bonneville County in the Making*, pp. 14–21; John L. Campbell, *Idaho: Six Months in the New Gold Diggings*, p. 12; MSUL, David J. Bailey, "Diary and Reminiscences," pp. 60–62; MSUL, F. E. W. Patten, "Journal of Travels . . . 1863," pp. 22–23.

[14] George A. Bruffey, *Eighty-One Years in the West*, p. 33; BYUL, Heber R. McBride, "Autobiography," pp. 24–26; MSHS, Lucia Darling, "Journal of a Trip Across the Plains in the Summer of 1863," pp. 36–38.

had the bridge trusses in place. By spring, the structure was almost completed, and Omaha newspapers carried the story that the Snake River had finally been bridged. Taylor advertised in the *Salt Lake Telegraph* of April 12, 1865, that his bridge would soon be ready for the spring rush of travelers.[15]

The Eagle Rock bridge was the first step in a much larger attempt to control the road from the Malad Divide to the Montana line. The second session of the Idaho legislature had granted Taylor, Edgar M. Morgan, and William F. Bartlett the right to incorporate their business under the name Oneida Road, Bridge and Ferry Company. After building the Eagle Rock bridge, which was an immediate money-maker, the concern failed to construct the road.

As early as 1864, the Oliver and Conover pioneer stage line abandoned the old Bannock Mountain Road, so praised by Captain Stansbury, for the more rugged but more direct route through Portneuf Canyon but were forced off the route by Ben Holladay. When Taylor and his partners failed to take advantage of their road charter, Ben Holladay undertook to improve the way along the Portneuf River with the help of his banking associate, William F. Halsey. The venture was incorporated as the Oneida Wagon Road Company by an act of the territorial legislature on January 5, 1866. On the same day, the Oneida county seat was moved from Soda Springs to Malad, and because the county extended from the Utah line to the Montana line, taking in all of eastern Idaho, the county officers became very interested in the potential profits from traffic over the main thoroughfare to Montana. The legislature helped them out by decreeing that county commissioners could issue toll road franchises for five-year periods and could revoke the licenses of operators who neglected the upkeep of their roads.[16]

Prior to their move to Malad, the county commissioners had ordered all parties having toll roads, bridges, or ferries to appear and show cause why the county should not take possession of

---

[15] B. W. Clark, *Bonneville County in the Making*, pp. 25, 44–45.

[16] Territory of Idaho, "General Laws of the Territory of Idaho, Second Session," Dec. 10, 1864, p. 477; Donald N. Wells and Merle W. Wells, "The Oneida Toll Road Controversy, 1864–1880," *Oregon Historical Quarterly*, vol. 58 (June 1957), pp. 113–16.

Taylor's Bridge at Eagle Rock, Idaho. *Idaho State Historical Society.*

these properties. A month later the sheriff was ordered to take possession of all unchartered and unlicensed toll ferries, bridges, and roads. The "Hon Board" at Malad then began to issue charters right and left, including a license to Telford Kutch to keep a toll ferry across the Snake River. As one of the three county commissioners, Mr. Kutch saw no impropriety in voting to award himself such a franchise and also saw to it that he was allowed to acquire the defunct Portneuf Canyon toll road charter originally issued to Taylor, Morgan, and Bartlett. A month later, the legislature granted the same route to the Holladay–Halsey Oneida Wagon Road Company. Undeterred by territorial action at Boise, County Commissioner Kutch sold his road franchise to County Recorder Murray A. Carter for the modest sum of $700. Carter, using his official position, now forced the Holladay–Halsey interests to consolidate the two franchises and agreed to get the charter of the consolidated Oneida Wagon Road Company confirmed at the next legislative session. As part of the agreement, Carter acquired a one-third interest in the new concern but immediately sold it to the Holladay–Halsey concern for $5,000—a profit of 700 percent in two and a half months.[17]

Controlling the Road through Idaho

When Ben Holladay bowed out and sold his interest to Wells, Fargo & Co., William Murphy gained control of the Portneuf Canyon toll road. The year before, Murphy had hired Murray A. Carter as his attorney to gain a franchise for a toll road along another section of the Montana Road from "Cammas Creek and running in a northeasterly direction to the northeast boundary line of Oneida County," an artery commonly known as the Beaver Canyon road. Murphy, with the aid of his lawyer, next outmaneuvered his rival, Telford Kutch, and acquired an exclusive fifteen-year franchise covering the old Bannock Mountain road, which effectively eliminated the only free road that could have competed with the Portneuf route. Murphy was now in control of the

---

[17] Territory of Idaho, "Proceedings of County Commissioners, Soda Springs, Idaho Territory 'Book A,' County Records," Oneida County, Aug. 3, 1865, p. 2, Sept. 5, 1865, pp. 6, 7; Wells and Wells, "The Oneida Toll Road Controversy," p. 117.

two important segments of the freighter's road to Montana, having a virtual monopoly in the collection of tolls over the sections in Idaho.[18]

Operating a toll road frequently lead to litigation and trouble; but with the contentious Mr. Murphy in charge, it was almost a foregone conclusion. In June of 1869, for example, he brought suit against freighter O. W. Simpson for driving six yoke of oxen and a wagon, plus a mule team and a wagon, through the ford near Portneuf Canyon to avoid paying tolls to cross over the bridge. The judge ordered Simpson to pay the toll road company $15 plus $47 in court costs, but when the local constable, with Murphy along, attempted to arrest Simpson at his camp in Marsh Valley, Murphy called his antagonist "a lying son of a bitch, which [said Simpson later] were abusive and hurtful to my feelings." Simpson then preferred charges against Murphy before Justice of the Peace P. G. Evans, whose record shows that Murphy testified he had no intention of hurting Simpson's feelings, and "that such expressions have become so familiar to him by a course of habit in Mountain life" that he was not always careful enough in his use of language. Murphy was fined $1.[19]

The editor of the *Corinne Reporter*, and the citizens of that town generally, did not like William Murphy and the tolls he levied on Corinne freighters. Interested parties continually agitated for a reduction in Murphy's toll rates, and these actions finally resulted in a hearing before the county commissioner's court. There seems to be some confusion in the records about what happened; but apparently Murphy began to abuse the commissioners and others present, threatening to shoot Judge Dennis Toohy of Corinne. B. F. White objected to being called a thief and a liar and "approached Murphy. Murphy drew and cocked a navy revolver and was aiming at White when Sheriff M. Morgan rushed between them and was shot in the leg. The sheriff chased Murphy out the front door, caught him as he was trying to shoot again, took his gun 'and before he could draw another arm' shot

---

[18] Wells and Wells, "The Oneida Toll Road Controversy," pp. 118-19; Territory of Idaho, "Proceedings of County Commissioners," Oneida County, Dec. 13, 1865, p. 12, July 2, 1866, pp. 26-27; NA, "Territorial Papers, Idaho, July 11, 1863—Dec. 1, 1872."

[19] Territory of Idaho, "Justice Court Records, 1869-1873," June 1, 3, 1869, Oneida County, pp. 33, 35.

him through the heart 'producing instant death.'" A later investigation cleared Sheriff Morgan, who had acted "in discharge of his duty." [20]

The widow, Catherine Murphy, continued to operate the Oneida Wagon Road Company, occasionally suing such large freighting outfits as Garrison and Wyatt, who claimed that they had traveled the road in 1863 when it was "considered a highway" and, therefore, toll free. Catherine Murphy ended her widowhood by marrying Henry O. Harkness at her residence at Portneuf Canyon toll gate on August 17, 1871. H. O. Harkness had been Murphy's manager on the Beaver Canyon toll road, knew the business well, and operated the two roads profitably enough to bring in $20,000 annually until the coming of the Utah and Northern Railroad in 1879-80.[21]

Reducing Tolls

Teamsters and stage companies fought constantly for toll reductions. On July 11, 1870, the rates were reduced to $1.00 for each team of one span with one wagon, with an increase up to $3.00 for five or six wagons. A county order of January 11, 1871, exempted all Oneida citizens from paying the tolls and lowered the rates again, although two years later the exemption was annulled, with the proviso that the low rates could not be changed by the county commissioners for a period of six years. Each team with a loaded wagon was to be charged only $.50.[22]

H. O. Harkness soon encountered further trouble. In a few cases, the courts began to find in favor of freighters who refused to pay tolls on the grounds that no improvements had been made on the road. In *H. O. Harkness* v. *Jordan Hyde* in July of 1873,

---

[20] *Corinne Reporter*, Feb. 8, 1870; *Idaho Statesman*, Mar. 10, 1870; Wells and Wells, "The Oneida Toll Road Controversy," pp. 123-24; *Corinne Reporter*, Apr. 14, 1870; Territory of Idaho, "Justice Court Records," Apr. 11, 1870, Oneida County, p. 46.

[21] Territory of Idaho, "Justice Court Records," Oct. 15, 1870, Deep Creek Precinct, n.p.; *Corinne Reporter*, Aug. 19, 1871; *Helena Herald*, May 27, 1875.

[22] Territory of Idaho, "Proceedings of the County Commissioners," July 11, 1870, Oneida County, p. 46; Wells and Wells, "The Oneida Toll Road Controversy," pp. 124-26; ISUA, Ray J. Davis, "Toll Fares," p. 1; Territory of Idaho, "General Laws of Idaho, Sixth Session, Dec. 1870-Jan. 1871," p. 88.

one witness declared that he did not travel on "said road, but on each side of the road, most of the time on the right side of it," and that it was a mere track, too narrow for trail teams. The jury found in favor of the defendant, and Harkness was forced to pay $87.80 to the defendant plus all the property attached in the action. The *Helena Herald*, on May 27, 1875, complained that wagons were so deep in the mud and mire at Portneuf Canyon that twenty span of mules were unable to move them. As if these attacks were not enough, the Bureau of Indian Affairs now claimed that exacting tolls for passage across the Fort Hall Indian Reservation was illegal and was "making enemies to the reservation and profits to Harkness." By July 29, 1879, people were agreeing with a *Salt Lake Tribune* correspondent that "the toll road system ... is in fact ... nothing but grants to private individuals to rob people on the highways." The Harkness clan members finally lost their lucrative business when Associate Justice Henry E. Prichett decreed, January 3, 1882, that Congress had invalidated Idaho toll road franchises when it banned such special legislation on March 2, 1867. All Idaho toll road concessions were thus abolished, much to the relief of the public.[23]

Roads in Montana

An early map, prepared by Colonel George Thom for army use in 1864, showed two main routes over the Continental Divide into western Montana. One was the old Fort Owen route by way of Medicine Lodge Creek, across Horse Prairie Creek, down the Big Hole River, over Big Hole Mountain to the headwaters of the Bitterroot River. The other route led down "Red Butte Creek" (Red Rock Creek) to Horse Prairie Creek. Here there was a junction, one road leading left to Bannack City then north to the Big Hole River, up that stream to its bend to the south and over the divide to Deer Lodge Creek, thence down the Hellgate (Clark Fork) River to its junction with the Bitterroot River. The right-

---

[23] Territory of Idaho, "Justice Court Records," July 7, 1863, Oneida County, pp. 64–67; U.S. Congress, "Report on Agreement with Indians in Idaho, Feb. 3, 1874, Salt Lake City, Utah Terr., Nov. 17, 1873," *House Exec. Doc. 129*, p. 3; Territory of Idaho, "Miscellaneous Records," Oneida County, June 23, 1876, pp. 69–71; Wells and Wells, "The Oneida Toll Road Controversy," p. 126.

hand fork led to the headwaters of Black Tail Deer Creek, down that stream and across the Beaverhead River to join up with the road from Bannack City and so over to Deer Lodge. Virginia City was located on the map but there were no roads shown to that gold camp.[24]

The W. W. deLacy map, prepared for the Montana Territorial Legislature for January 1, 1865, marked out a new road from the headwaters of Red Rock Creek to the head of Black Tail Deer Creek. Here the road branched to the right down the Stinking Water River (Ruby River) to Virginia City. The left road continued on down Black Tail Deer Creek, then right, down the Beaverhead River to connect with a road from Virginia City along the Stinking Water. Another road was shown leading north from Virginia City along the west foothills of the Tobacco Root Mountains to a crossing of the Jefferson River at its junction with White Tail Deer Creek, then over the divide at Boulder and down the Prickly Pear Canyon to Helena. The way north to Benton was then via Mullan's Road, down Little Prickly Pear Canyon, across the Dearborn and Sun rivers, and so to Fort Benton. In this map, the only segment missing of the later most-traveled road from Monida to Helena and Fort Benton was from a point above the confluence of the Ruby and Beaverhead rivers down the Jefferson Fork of the Missouri to its junction with White Tail Deer Creek at Whitehall.[25]

W. W. deLacy's map only confirmed what the early residents of Montana already knew—that they were faced with a very difficult terrain across which some main arteries and branch roads had to be built to establish communication between the isolated gold camps and civilization. Little wonder that the gold-miners-turned-legislators of the First Legislative Assembly of Montana should be chiefly concerned with road franchises. One correspondent wrote that the legislature "had many members of ability and intelligence—equal to any you could find on the woolsacks of the west. Charters were the strong suits, and divorces next in order. All the streams and roads through the Territory were spanned with charters for a ferry or a toll gate. . . . Every

---

[24] Colonel George Thom, "Map of Idaho and Montana."
[25] W. W. deLacy, "Map of the Territory of Montana."

stream (except a sluice head) that was large enough for a trout to turn in was bridged 'with a charter of incorporation.' " [26]

Governor Thomas F. Meagher began to veto some of the road franchise bills during the second session of the legislature in 1866, but his recalcitrant legislators passed many of them over his veto. One such bill authorized the Beaverhead Wagon & Road Company, owned by James M. Ryan and William Sturgis, to build a road from the Idaho border down Red Rock Creek, across Black Tail Deer Creek, and through Beaverhead Canyon to a point on the Stinking Water River at or near Laurin's ranch, which was about ten miles northeast of Virginia City. There were to be two toll gates: one at the mouth of Beaverhead Canyon and one at the Idaho boundary line. The toll was to be $3.00 for each wagon with one span of horses or mules or yoke of oxen and $.50 for each additional span. Governor Meagher wished to stop the road at Junction—where the Bannack City and Virginia City roads met—wanted one toll gate only, and urged a $2.00 fee. The council passed the bill over his veto by a vote of five to two in April 1866.[27]

James Ryan immediately started work on the Beaverhead Canyon portion, which at that time was impassable for wagons. In answer to criticism from the backers of the governor, Ryan defended the route for its "easy grades and comparative freedom from snow drifts." Moreover, he was able to produce affidavits from several people that his partner, Sturgis, was working seven men along the route to get the bridges built and the blasting out of the way. The *Montana Post* heartily approved the Ryan-Stur-

[26] BL, "Bancroft Scraps, Montana Miscellany," vol. 90, "Montana As It Is," from *Goldrick*, Aug. 22, 1866, p. 75. A partial list of charter acts introduced may give some idea of the legislative prodigality which only underscored the critical problem of transportation in a primitive area: toll bridges over the Beaverhead, Big Hole, and Jefferson rivers; toll roads: Bannock to Beaverhead Valley, Bannack City and Montana Wagon Road, Grasshopper Canon Road Company, Helena Wagon Road Company, Idaho and Montana Wagon Road Company, Junction and Black Tail Deer Creek Wagon Road Company, Nevada and Red Rock Wagon Road Company, Rams Horn Toll Road, Virginia City and Summit City Wagon Road Company, Virginia City and Camas Creek Wagon Road Company, Beaver Head Wagon Road Company, Prickly Pear and Virginia City Wagon Road Company, Little Blackfoot River to Ten Mile and Helena Road, Helena to Butte, and the Little Prickly Pear Canyon Road.

[27] Territory of Montana, *Council Journal of Second Legislative Session of Territory of Montana, March 5, 1866, to April 14, 1866, at Virginia City*, pp. 101-2, 182-85; NA, Territorial Papers, Montana, "Acts and Resolutions—2nd Session of Montana Legislative Assembly, 1866," vol. 2.

gis venture and estimated the improvements on the road had cost the firm up to $15,000. The new route was supposedly thirty miles shorter than the older "Parson Road," and, as Ryan said, his thoroughfare had "sounded the death-knell of an oppressive monopoly." The *Montana Post* believed that the route of the new Beaverhead Wagon & Road Company "eventually must accomodate the principal part of the travel . . . especially as it will be a good winter road." The Black Tail Deer route was still used by a few, but most preferred the Ryan line of travel. Sturgis quit after one year, and in March 1870, M. Henneberry bought out Ryan, with an announcement that he would issue a round-trip pass to freighters for $2.50. In July 1875, T. M. Barrett and Company took over the charter until the coming of the railroad in the fall of 1880. The Beaverhead Road became the main artery for freight and passenger travel from Utah and Idaho into western Montana, and despite some complaints, most freighters looked forward to smooth travel as soon as they reached the head of Red Rock Creek.[28]

Neither Bannack City nor Virginia City residents were satisfied with having the main road bypass them by shooting straight down Red Rock Creek and the Beaverhead and Jefferson rivers. There were occasional attempts to put Bannack City on the line to Helena by building a public road via Medicine Lodge Pass. In 1865 a group of promoters had tried to secure a charter for a road from Virginia City to Salt Lake City. A year later, B. F. Price and others were attempting to get a franchise to construct a road from Nevada City to the Snake River. But the most persistent efforts from Virginia City residents were aimed at providing a road from the Snake River by way of Henry Lake, which would supposedly shorten the distance to Salt Lake City by eighty miles and would "afford a solid and level roadway, instead of the sandy plains and high mountains which now impede the passage to the railroad." [29]

---

[28] *Montana Post*, Apr. 7, 27, July 7, 21, 1866; *Rocky Mountain Gazette*, Oct. 29, 1870; *Helena Herald*, Mar. 22, 1870, July 1, 1875, Sept. 5, 1878; MSHS. Thomas J. Hosford, C. O. Trask, and George D. French, Affadavits on Work by Wm. Sturgis on Red Rock and Beaverhead Canon Road, March 12, 1866, "The Great Beaverhead Wagon Road."

[29] *Montana Post*, Jan. 7, 1865, Jan. 5, 1867; Territory of Montana, *House Journal of Third Session of Legislative Assembly of Territory of Montana, Nov. 5–Dec. 15, 1866*, p. 310; *New Northwest*, Feb. 25, 1870; *Montana Democrat*, Feb. 13, 1869; *Helena Herald*, July 15, 1870.

Taking Tolls

As more and more roads were cut through the Montana wilderness, travelers had to face interminable tolls. Herman Reinhart, who spent two years in almost constant travel as a freighter and stagecoach operator, on one trip from Helena to Virginia City wrote, "I had so many toll roads and ferries to cross... that it took off a good deal of the profits of the trip." When he finally left for Salt Lake City to work on the Union Pacific Railroad, he paid a $6 toll into Weber Canyon, "and we had toll roads, and toll bridges, and toll ferries until I was sick of them." A few travelers were more fortunate. When a span over the Big Hole River disappeared with a flood, a correspondent of the *Helena Herald* wrote on July 31, 1879, that he had to detour by way of Brown's bridge. Mr. Brown "was very kind and charged no toll, saying that 'preachers, paupers and printers had a free pass over his bridge at all seasons.'" [30]

Whenever a freighter reached a toll gate, he had to turn over hard-earned profits at high rates. One mail contractor paid out $173 in tolls over the Madison Bridge and Sterling Toll Road during ten months of deliveries. Colonel S. G. Brackett warned his superiors that if more troops were to be sent to Montana the quartermaster should be supplied with "*two* or *three* hundred dollars" for toll charges.[31]

On August 6, 1869, the *New Northwest* ran a lead article expostulating against the high charges for getting supplies to Montana. For a wagon loaded with 4,500 pounds, the editor listed the following tolls:

Bear River Bridge, Corinne, Utah	$5.00
Bear River Bridge, Upper Crossing, Utah	5.00
Port Neuf Canyon road, Idaho	8.00
Eagle Rock Bridge, Snake River, Idaho	8.00
Beaver Tail Canyon Road	5.00
Beaverhead Junction Road, Montana	5.00
Big Hole Bridge	4.00
Parson's Bridge and road	$5.00 or 8.00
Total for each wagon	$48.00

[30] Doyce B. Nunis, Jr., ed., *The Golden Frontier*, pp. 248-92; *Helena Herald*, July 31, 1879.

[31] NA, "Mail Routes, Utah, 1862-1866," p. 355; NA, "Records of United States Army Commands, 1784-1821," RG 98, Letters Sent: Fort Ellis, Montana, Brackett to Ruggles, Oct. 4, 1869.

The editor explained that these toll charges added $.01½ to the cost of every pound of freight, meaning an additional annual cost of $150,000 to the consumers of the territory.

The Territorial Legislature of Montana was not unaware of the complaints from its constituents about "the extortions of toll keepers" and, by 1870, began to agree that if tolls "should eventually reach zero... the public would not suffer from the effects." The Montana legislature had already adopted some safeguards to protect travelers: fords could not be blocked by ferry or bridge operators, illegal tolls could not be collected, obstructions across highways were to be removed, taxes were assessed on toll corporations, and proper signs were to be placed on bridges and near other toll gates. But in complete exasperation, the members decreed during the 1869–70 session that a long list of toll franchises, filling two printed pages, be "hereby repealed, and declared void and of no effect." The register included such important franchises as the Beaverhead River bridge, the Helena Wagon Road Company, and the Great Beaverhead Wagon & Road Company. The governor allowed the bill to become law without his signature; but, eventually, some of the companies were reinstated as legal entities. Two years later, the legislature commanded that "from and after the passage of this act no corporation shall be formed... for the purpose of establishing ferries, toll bridges, or toll roads," and established road districts and a tax structure to support this end.[32]

The legislative action, the continued protests of the public, and the imminent approach of the railroad combined to reduce the number of chartered concerns still operating toll roads. The editor of the *Missoulian* summed up the feelings of most Montanans on March 16, 1877, when he stated that toll roads had been "abhorrent" to the residents of the territory from the earliest times. He advocated fighting "such enemies of the public good until the lower regions freeze over and then fight them on the ice." Within four years the Utah and Northern Railroad reached southern Montana, and the great controversy over toll roads became an argument of the past.

---

[32] *Montana Post*, Dec. 25, 1868; *Helena Herald*, Sept. 29, 1870; *Montanian*, Nov. 2, 1871; NA, "Territorial Papers, Montana, Fourth Session, Nov. 4–Dec. 13, 1867," pp. 89, 247; "Fifth Session, Dec. 7, 1868–Jan. 15, 1869," p. 97; "Sixth Session, Dec. 6, 1869–Jan. 7, 1870," pp. 49, 54, 71; "Seventh Session, Dec. 4, 1871–Jan. 12, 1872," p. 542.

7

Rivalry from the Missouri River Trade

Freighters using the Montana Trail often found themselves in competition with freighters arriving in the territory from other directions along other routes. One alternative was the Mullan Road stretching across 624 miles of wilderness from Walla Walla to Fort Benton. For years, goods had been brought from San Francisco up the Columbia River by steamboat then carried to Idaho mines by packtrain. By extending their journey another 150 miles along the Mullan Road, these packers could also supply the mining camps of western Montana. The Mullan Road, however, was impassable for wheeled vehicles over the 450 miles between Walla Walla and Helena, so merchandise had to be restricted to lightweight goods of high value that could be carried on the back of mules. In a peak year, 1865, an estimated 750 tons of freight were moved along this road to Helena by an estimated 1,500 to 4,000 mules at a cost of $.18 per pound. By 1868, however, the route was in "horrible condition," and trade across it had diminished to insignificance by the time the transcontinental railroad was completed.[1]

Another route of considerable importance between 1864 and 1866 was the Bozeman Trail leading from the Missouri River across the Plains and through Wyoming to Montana. In 1867, however, Indian attacks became so fierce that wagon trains began to seek other routes.[2] A third alternative was the road opened by the government in 1864 that led from Sioux City via

---

[1] Henry P. Walker, *The Wagonmasters*, pp. 202–5; Hubert H. Bancroft, *History of Washington, Idaho, and Montana*, p. 426; Alton Oviatt, "Pacific Coast Competition for the Gold Camp Trade of Montana," *Pacific Northwest Quarterly*, vol. 56 (Oct. 1965), pp. 169–75; *The Dalles Weekly Mountaineer*, Sept. 15, 1865, Aug. 17, 1866.

[2] Walker, *The Wagonmasters*, pp. 209–10.

the Niobrara River and the Black Hills to Virginia City—100 miles shorter than the emigrant road through South Pass. Despite urging from the citizens, the government failed to guard the Niobrara road, and Indian hostilities effectively blocked travel. Not to be outdone, Californians, too, entered the competition for the Montana trade by proposing alternate routes from the Columbia to Helena and by claiming that a wagon train had been driven 1,300 miles from Los Angeles in eighty-four days, even though it had broken down three times between Salt Lake City and Virginia City.[3]

Emigrants and freight traveled from Oregon, from California, and up the Missouri River by steamboat, but it was this last rival that posed the greatest threat to stagecoachers and freighters on the Salt Lake–Montana route. Missouri River freighters were in an enviable position to outbid their Salt Lake rivals for the Montana trade. To equal the 150 tons of cargo a steamboat could carry, a wagon freighter would have had to assemble a train of sixty or seventy wagons pulled by 700 to 800 mules or oxen.

Early River Navigation

Low water on the river and poor organization gave steamboat transportation a slow start, but during the 1860's competition from this route rapidly increased. Many hoped that the coming of the railroad in the 1870's would undermine river transportation profits, but freight rates generally remained slightly higher for transportation from the railhead at Corinne, Utah, to points in Montana. During months when water was low and river travel difficult, the railroad maintained the advantage. Throughout the 1870's competition remained fierce between the two rivals, but with extension of the rail line into Montana, railroad shippers became the main suppliers to the northern markets.

The first steamboat to reach Fort Benton, the *Chippewa*, captained by John La Barge, arrived on July 17, 1860. The follow-

[3] BL, Wilbur Fisk Sanders, "Notes, Helena, Montana, Feb. 6, 1885"; Bancroft, *History of Washington*, p. 729; BL, "Bancroft Scraps, Montana Miscellany," vol. 90, article in Stockton *Independent*, 1866, p. 14.

ing year the *Chippewa* and a sister boat, the *Key West*, started out with more goods for the Indian trade. The *Key West* reached its destination, but the *Chippewa* burned to the water when a deckhand bored a gimlet hole in a barrel of alcohol and it ignited. In the subsequent fire, twenty-five kegs of powder blew up. A band of Crow Indians spent some time retrieving calico and blankets along the riverbanks. Despite this loss, La Barge's boats beat three American Fur Company steamboats from St. Louis to Fort Benton by three days in 1862 and delivered 300 passengers and 400 tons of cargo.[4]

St. Louis shipping firms quickly determined that there were more profits to be made from transporting goods to the new mines than from the Indian trade, but 1863 was a year of disappointment. An "extraordinary drouth" caused low waters on the river and held back four boats en route to Fort Benton. When the steamer *Shreveport* ran aground 180 miles below Benton, the captain posted notices stating that those remaining aboard would be charged $2 a day for food, so passengers picked up their baggage and walked to Fort Benton. In 1864, four steamers attempted the rapids-filled journey to Fort Benton, but only two made it all the way with, among other things, 12,000 sacks of flour.[5]

Edward H. Hall, in his emigrant guidebook for 1864, advised that the best route to Bannack, Virginia City, and other Montana gold camps was by way of the Missouri River. He said that boats drawing not more than four feet of water were capable of carrying up to 150 tons of freight and provided easy and safe passage to Fort Benton, from whence coaches traveled the 140 miles to Helena. Other writers were not so optimistic. Gad E. Upson wrote that the steamboat *Yellowstone* could only get as far as Cow Island, 175 miles by water and 125 miles by land below Fort Benton. Discharging its freight and passengers on the

---

[4] Joel F. Overholser, *Centenary History of Fort Benton, Montana, 1846–1946*, n.p.; "Steamboat Arrivals at Fort Benton, Montana, and Vicinity, 1859–1874," in *Contributions to the Historical Society of Montana*, vol. 1, p. 317.

[5] U. S. Congress, "Expedition of Captain James L. Fisk to the Rocky Mountains," *House Exec. Doc. 45*, p. 22; BL, "Bancroft Scraps, Montana Miscellany," vol. 90, Letter from Fort Benton and Beaver Head, Aug. 1, 1863, p. 28; Bancroft, *History of Washington*, pp. 729–33; Overholser, *Centenary History*, p. 318.

riverbank, the boat turned around on July 1 and departed downstream. Upson, Indian agent for this region and in need of the annuity goods now stranded in a desolate spot, exploded to the commissioner in Washington, D. C.: "These repeated failures to deliver goods to their point of destination on the Missouri by steamer as per contract is getting to be a nuisance unbearable, and might be easily avoided were a less grasping disposition shown by steamboat men; the want of water certainly cannot be put forward this year in extenuation of this failure." [6] Nevertheless, in 1868 most Montana businessmen agreed that until a transcontinental railroad was completed, there was no doubt of the superiority of river travel over wagon transport from any direction. This fact was well expressed by the *Montana Post* on June 16, 1868. "One thing is certain, pack trains, or other land travel, cannot compete with water navigation."

Transporting Goods on the Missouri River

After the first three years of fumbling starts and low water on the river, the St. Louis merchants were determined to get their wares to Fort Benton in 1865 and take home the lion's share of trade profits. Some twenty to twenty-five boats left for the north in time to catch the "June rise" on the Missouri, but only four made it all the way to Fort Benton. The common practice when a steamer grounded downriver was to send a messenger to Fort Benton asking the waiting freighters to come downstream and pick up the cargo. Many of the boats couldn't get within several hundred miles of their destination; three of them sank; and the balance discharged their cargoes "promiscuously along the river at nearly every trading post." One train of over 250 wagons was dispatched to Milk River to pick up the goods from two boats stranded there. It was impossible to get all the abandoned freight to the Montana towns that year, since many of the steamships were forced to unload much farther downstream than

---

[6] Edward H. Hall, *The Great West: Emigrants, Settlers and Traveler's Guide and Hand-Book*, p. 17; U. S. Congress, "Report of Commissioner of Indian Affairs, Upson to Dole, Sept. 1, 1864," *House Exec. Doc. 1*, pp. 439-40.

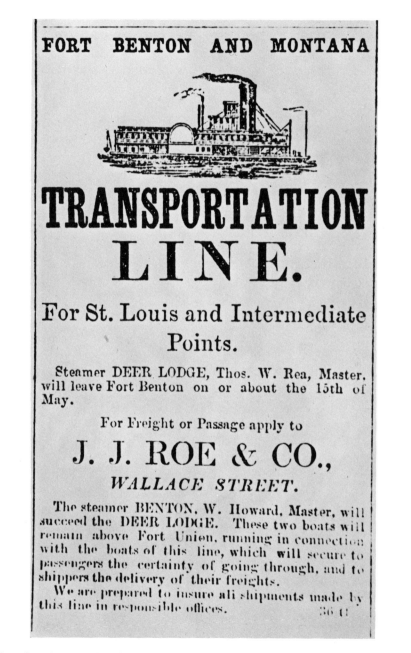

An advertisement for the steamer *Deer Lodge. Courtesy of William D. Living-stone.*

Fort Union. Also, merchants had to pay additional charges of from $.14 to $.20 per pound for the extra wagon trip.[7]

The *Montana Post* noted on November 18, 1865, that McGrew and Company's train of twenty-seven wagons was near town after seven months on the trail from the Missouri River. The impatient freighters, waiting at Benton for boats that never came, fought over the cargoes that did show up. Cyrus Morton recorded that there were so many wagons and such strong competition that he had to wait several days before he could get a load. On June 16, 1866, the *Montana Radiator* berated the St. Louis steamboat owners. "No one is prepared to say that navigation of the Missouri River is impracticable, but that as it is at present conducted, it is not worth the patronage of the business community. The boats used in the trade were none of them built for it, but are old mud tubs grown gray in creeping up and down the sluggish rivers of the Western States. . . . As well might the Overland stage line attempt to send one of its coaches through with one team, and send the passengers out in the sand hills for feed, as to attempt to run steamboats in this way."

High water on the Missouri River after heavy winter snows in 1865 made 1866 a banner year for steamboat traffic to Montana. As a result, the obscure fort below Great Falls became an important inland freight depot. Thirty-one steamboats brought 2,000 passengers and 6,000 tons of merchandise valued at $6,000,000. Freight charges averaged $.12½ a pound for a total of $2,000,000. One "old tub," the *Peter Balen*, brought up 400 tons, which returned $65,000 in profits for the owners. The *Luella* took 2½ tons of gold dust worth $1,250,000 back down the river and cleared $25,000. The *Deer Lodge* made two complete trips, the first in fifty-eight days upstream and ten days downstream, and earned $45,000 on one trip alone. It required 2,500 men, 3,000 teams, and 20,000 mules and oxen to transport the goods to the various mining camps at $.06 a pound to Helena and $.10 a pound to other towns. One observer counted 1,500 teams on the road at one time between Benton and Helena. The people of the two towns relished these juicy statistics, which cast a pall over the Salt Lake freighters struggling over the Pleasant Valley Divide trying to bring their cargoes to market.[8]

The first boat on the Missouri to reach Fort Benton in 1867 was the *Waverly*, arriving in fifty-five days from St. Louis with 170 tons of freight. Thirty-nine more steamers eventually landed 8,061 tons of freight and about 10,000 passengers—at an average fare of $150 apiece. As many as 1,000 oxen were hitched along the streets of Benton at one time waiting their turn to load. It is difficult to determine the rates charged, but nearly everyone agreed that the river trade forced costs down to an average of $.08 per pound from St. Louis to Benton plus an additional $.02½ a pound to Helena. Some steamers demanded as much as $.12 plus insurance charges of $.06½ on side-wheel craft and $.08 for stern-wheelers. The *Helena Herald* thought these rates extortionate and at the same time complained that the sudden arrival of so many boats the year before had overstocked the country. Helena now had more goods than the balance of the territory combined—and this was in January before another forty steamers had reached Benton![9]

Traveling by Steamboat

In 1867 it cost $305 to journey by stage from Boise to Omaha City, traveling via Salt Lake. Going by stagecoach from Boise to Benton and down the Missouri River to Omaha cost $245. River travel, although cheaper, was often less reliable than the stage. When Cryus Morton booked river passage on September 1, late in the season for river travel, since the water was at a low level, cabin rates were $100 and deck passage was $50. The trip required 60 days, and every day the boat became stuck on a sandbar. Passengers had to go ashore and help pull it free and

---

[8] *Montana Post*, Sept. 29, 1866; *Helena Herald*, Mar. 14, 1867; Bancroft, *History of Washington*, p. 729; Hiram M. Chittenden, *History of Early Steamboat Navigation on the Missouri River*, p. 275; Overholser, *Centenary History*, n.p.; *Tri-Weekly Republican*, Oct. 12, 1866.

[9] *Montana Post*, June 1, 1867; Overholser, *Centenary History*, n.p.; Bancroft, *History of Washington*, p. 729; Chittenden, *History*, p. 275; *Salt Lake Telegraph*, July 28, 1867; *Helena Herald*, Jan. 24, March 21, April 4, 1867; MSHS, T. J. Kertula, "Early Montana Days Marked by Freighters' Rate Wars," Clip file.

Cattle team in Fort Benton, 1884. *Montana Historical Society, Helena.*

Freight team beside the First National Bank of Fort Benton. *Montana Historical Society, Helena.*

gather firewood for the steamer's boilers. Food cost the passengers $100 apiece before they arrived at Omaha. Another steamer leaving Benton on September 18 with 400 passengers and fifteen day's provisions fared even worse. With the river rapidly falling, the steamer made only twenty miles in one week. When food ran out, the passengers starved for three days, then provided for themselves by hunting. The ship finally froze in the river, and passengers had to get to St. Louis or Omaha as best they could.[10]

Railroad Competition

The *Salt Lake Telegraph* optimistically forecast on March 17, 1868, that the Missouri River was "certain to be very low," and that the approach of the Union Pacific Railroad meant lower rates and more certain deliveries on the Salt Lake–Montana route. However, thirty-five boats reached Benton with 4,823 tons of freight, and five boats discharged freight below the fort between May 13 and August 4, 1868. The grand total delivered at Benton probably reached 6,000 tons.[11]

Many of the 500 to 600 teams that carried the 1868 river merchandise from Benton to other mining towns were controlled by the large freighting companies—E. G. Maclay & Co. (agents for the Diamond R freighting firm), Baker & Bros., Henry A. Schodde, W. S. Bullard, M. H. Bird, and Hugh Kirkendall. At least three—Maclay, Schodde, and Kirkendall—became prominent in the later trade to the north from Corinne, Utah.[12]

Steamboat traffic in 1869 saw twenty-four boats reaching Benton between May 19 and June 21, with eighteen of them having to "double-trip" to the Dauphine Rapids to pick up part of their cargo left on the first journey. Nearly every wagon train from Benton to Helena was attacked by the Blackfeet Indians

---

[10] *Idaho Statesman*, June 25, 1867; Morton, *Autobiography*, p. 34; Bancroft, *History of Washington*, p. 729.

[11] "Effects at Fort Benton of Gold Excitement in Montana," in *Contributions to the Historical Society of Montana*, vol. 8, p. 129; U. S. Congress, "West of the Rocky Mountains, Resources of the States and Territories," *House Exec. Doc. 58*, p. 138; Bancroft, *History of Washington*, p. 729.

[12] Overholser, *Centenary History*, n.p.; "Effects at Fort Benton," p. 129; *Montana Weekly Democrat*, June 13, 1868; *Salt Lake Telegraph*, Mar. 17, 1868.

this year, and at least fifty-six people were killed. The advent of the railroad forced river rates from St. Louis down to $.08 per pound.[13]

Expectations were high that at least half of the estimated 25,000 tons of goods that were to be shipped to Montana would depart from Corinne, Utah, the new railroad town on the Central Pacific at the mouth of the Bear River.

With the entry into the Montana trade of a new steamboat line, the Northwestern Transportation Company of Chicago, St. Louis merchants were forced to drop their rates to $.06 per pound for that year, a move that effectively stopped any competition from the Columbia River routes. Montana newspapers as well as Utah journals expected that now the old river route would be abandoned and the giant Diamond R firm, which had dominated land freight from Benton, would now shift its base of operations to Corinne. The only nagging worry was that river rates for 1869 averaged only $.10½ cents, while those by the railroad were $.12½. The *New Northwest* on August 6, 1869, blamed the excessive tolls on roads and bridges for this state of things. Good news came to Corinne that the Northwestern Transporation Company planned to maintain its steamboat line from St. Louis and also join with the Union Pacific in a fast express to Montana. The most exhilarating news in Corinne was the announcement that the Eastern firm of Graham, Maurice and Co. expected to establish a terminus in Utah for forwarding goods to Montana. Forty-three of the leading Helena merchants sent the company the following telegram:

> Gentlemen: Learning that you intend establishing a fast freight line from New York and other cities to this and other points in the Territory, *via* railroad to Corinne, thence by wagon train, we desire to tender you our support, with a view to the success of the enterprise. Navigation on the Missouri river is so precarious that we are anxious to avail ourselves of a route which offers a guarantee for the prompt delivery of our consignments. This we feel you can give by the means of transportation which you propose to employ.[14]

---

[13] Bancroft, *History of Washington*, p. 729; "Steamboat Arrivals at Fort Benton," p. 322.

[14] USLC, John Hanson Beadle, "Scrapbook," Feb. 21, 1869; *New Northwest*, Dec. 3, 1869; *Utah Reporter*, Nov. 11, Dec. 25, 1869; *Montana Post*, May 14, 1869.

The action of Helena merchants in seeking delivery of goods via the Union Pacific, plus the undoubted optimism which a railroad brought to any new territory in those days, so discouraged the river merchants that only eight steamboats traveled to Fort Benton in 1870. The *Helena Herald* concluded that there were now only two possible trade routes to Montana—by wagon from Corinne and by boat up the Missouri—the latter to be used only for "heavy goods." Although encouragement came with the news that the railroad had concluded an agreement with the Far West Fast Freight Line that would reduce rates by that route, the *Herald* acknowledged that the expense would be a "trifle more" than by the river. The chief quartermaster of the army made a thorough study of the two routes and concluded that despite the greater cost by land from the railroad the uncertainty of river transport indicated Corinne as the choice for a depot from which to send military and Indian supplies to the northern posts. He cited comparative figures to Fort Shaw as follows:

Rail to Corinne	$ 730.00
Wagon to Ft. Shaw (500 miles)	$1,600.00
Rail and Wagon	$2,330.00
River to Ft. Benton	$1,100.00
Wagon to Ft. Shaw (61 miles)	$ 195.20
River and Wagon	$1,295.20

Fort Ellis and Sun River Crossing showed parallel statistics. The general did advise that the river could be depended upon for the delivery of articles which were not urgently needed, if they were forwarded during "the proper" season of river navigation.[15]

Despite the gloom the transcontinental railroad brought to the Missouri River trade, there was a perceptible increase in river traffic again in 1871. Six boats reached Benton that year, while four others got as far as Cow Island, and one made it to Fort Peck. In 1872, twelve steamboats arrived at Benton, the *Far*

---

[15] Bancroft, *History of Washington*, p. 729; "Steamboat Arrivals at Fort Benton," p. 323; *Helena Herald*, Mar. 5, 11, 26, 1870; *Utah Reporter*, Dec. 5, 1870; NA, "Records of the Office of the Quartermaster General," RG 92, Letter from Chief Quartermaster, Omaha, Neb., Dept. of the Platte to Maj. Gen. D. H. Rucker, Chicago, Ill., May 18, 1870.

West making the quickest trip on record from Sioux City—seventeen days, twenty hours. During the winter of 1871-72, snow blockades on the Union Pacific line caused some concern for Corinne merchants and created as much as a three-month delay in getting goods from Chicago. The *Corinne Reporter* feared that the result would be a loss of thousands of tons of freight to the river trade. But Bentonites took heart at these developments, and one wrote the *Helena Herald* on January 11, 1872, that "the snow that kills the 'bulls' makes the river, and Benton is but one hundred and forty miles from Helena, while Corinne is four hundred and eight-two, so, by a loose calculation, what three trains will transport from Corinne, *one* will bring from Benton." [16]

The next two years, however, brought only greater depression to Benton. Only seven steamboats arrived in 1873, and just six in 1874. By this time, the rates were identical from Benton and from Corinne to the same towns in Montana, but since the Missouri River steamboats only operated for a few months each summer, the Union Pacific had no competition the rest of the year. The *Montanian* took the railroad to task for imposing a rate of only $1.60 per 100 pounds during the summer season but immediately advancing charges to $3.93 per 100 pounds as soon as the last steamboat departed downstream. "We are at the mercy of the U. P. road.... Railroads are all robbers; this is an established fact." [17]

The Pattern of River Travel

A significant alteration in the pattern of Missouri River steamboat operations occurred in September 1873 when Diamond R agents, E. G. Maclay & Co., signed an agreement with the Northern Pacific Railroad. With completion of the Northern Pacific to Bismarck, North Dakota, steamboats could now save

---

[16] Bancroft, *History of Washington*, p. 729; Overholser, *Centenary History*, n.p.; *Corinne Reporter*, Apr. 27, 1871, Mar. 4, Apr. 24, 29, 1872; *Helena Herald* Jan. 11, 1872; "Steamboat Arrivals at Fort Benton," p. 324.

[17] U. S. Congress, "Report on Reconnaissance of Northwestern Wyoming, 1873," *House Exec. Doc. 285*, p. 56; *Montanian*, Aug. 28, 1873; Bancroft, *History of Washington*, p. 729; "Steamboat Arrivals at Fort Benton," p. 325.

the 400 miles of river travel from St. Louis to Bismark and could make four round trips a year from Bismark to Fort Benton. Maclay agreed to construct a road from Helena to the mouth of the Musselshell River, to be ready when navigation on the Missouri began in 1874. He further agreed to furnish wagons and trains to transport goods delivered to the Diamond R by Northern Pacific Railroad boats. Maclay also promised to withdraw his business and teams from the Corinne route and to use his company's influence to favor the Northern Pacific Railroad. In return, the railroad company agreed to pay Maclay $40,000 in three equal payments during 1874 as a bonus for constructing the road to the Musselshell River. The Northern Pacific also promised to use its influence to obtain a mail contract for the Diamond R from Bismarck to Helena via the Musselshell. Maclay would refund the $40,000 bonus if the postal contract were accepted and establish a line of stagecoaches between Helena and the Musselshell for passenger and mail service. To complete the agreement, Maclay had to obtain a release from a prior contract with the Utah Northern Railroad and sell his warehouse in Corinne.[18]

The *Montanian* thought that Virginia City merchants would immediately shift to the new Musselshell route. The *Corinne Mail* was apprehensive about the Maclay-Northern Pacific contract, but rejoiced when it learned that the fall shipments of goods for Helena merchants had reached Bismarck and would have to remain there until the spring boats could carry the merchandise to the Musselshell. The *Mail* concluded that the Musselshell road was a "dead letter." [19]

Freighting Costs

Montanans eagerly looked forward to the time when the Northern Pacific would cross the territory. An 1876 meeting was called in Helena to discuss the possibility of a $3,000,000 loan to

---

[18] MSHS, "Diamond R Papers," Memorandum of Agreement, E. G. Maclay and Co. and Northern Pacific Railroad, Sept. 3, 1873, and Release of E. G. Maclay and Co. by Utah Northern Railroad Company, Nov. 21, 1873; MSHS, Walker, *The Wagonmasters*, p. 211.

[19] *Deseret News*, May 20, 1874; *Corinne Mail*, Nov. 4, Dec. 18, 21, 1874.

aid the Northern Pacific. One of the arguments in favor of the grant was the high cost of freight rates to get goods into Montana—$1,000,000 for supplies via the Union Pacific and the Salt Lake wagon road and $500,000 from the Missouri River and Benton.[20]

It was estimated that 25,000 tons would be shipped to Montana in 1877, but a year-end report in the *New Northwest* on January 4, 1878, indicated that only 21,200 tons had arrived. Of note in the following statistics was the large amount of goods shipped via the Yellowstone River, a route that had not received much newspaper comment up to this time.

Incoming Merchandise		
Missouri River, via Yellowstone		9,500 tons
Missouri River,		
via Benton & Cow Island		6,700 tons
U.P. & C.P.R.R.		
via Corinne & Franklin, Idaho		5,000 tons
	Total	21,200 tons
Outgoing Merchandise		
River & Wagon Shipments*		7,000 tons
Beef cattle,		
on hoof, live weight		9,000 tons
	Total	16,000 tons

*Exports included ores, crude and refined bullion, robes, furs, peltries, dressed skins, hides, and wool.

The Missouri River steamers enjoyed a banner year in 1878. Anywhere from forty-six to sixty boats reached Benton, and one craft made six trips in the season. Final statistics for the year indicated a large increase in freight traveling via the river—9,680 tons valued at $2,410,000—with a total tonnage by all routes of 22,000 tons.[21]

As the *Deseret News* of July 16, 1879, noted, a much larger business was conducted with Montana by way of the Missouri River than was "generally understood." Fort Benton received

[20] Bancroft, *History of Washington*, p. 729; *Helena Herald*, June 28, July 19, 1877.

[21] "Steamboat Arrivals at Fort Benton," p. 325; *Helena Herald*, Nov. 28, 1878; Frank W. Warner, *Montana Territory: History and Business*, p. 84.

9,499 tons of freight in 1879, deposited by twenty-one steamers. It became essential to advance the narrow-gauge Utah Northern Railroad, first laid in 1871 between Brigham City and Cache Valley, far enough into western Montana to turn the tide of business away from the river and to the Union Pacific. Early in 1879, the managers of the railroad tried to direct all of the eastern freight to the train by offering ridiculously low rates to Montana merchants. Still, the Missouri steamers received much more than fifty percent of the Montana trade. A correspondent to the *San Francisco Bulletin* was of the opinion that even when the Utah Northern reached Helena, merchants of that city would still order goods by the river, wishing to keep some competition alive. Passengers could still travel first class by the river for $68 to Benton and $83 to Helena, while travelers from the Utah Northern terminus had a choice of first-class passage on Concord stages, second class in covered mail wagons, or third class as emigrants in freight wagons.[22]

In 1880 the sharp contest between the railroad and the Missouri river route continued, with steamboats still having the advantage. At the end of 1880, total rail shipments to western Montana were 19,444,137 pounds and 13,459,598 pounds to eastern Montana. Freight on the Missouri and Yellowstone rivers amounted to 28,029,610 pounds. When the Northern Pacific Railroad reached Helena in 1883, Fort Benton received a death blow as a freight forwarding point. From then on, the Utah Northern and Northern Pacific railroads usurped the transportation of goods and supplies to Montana residents.[23]

---

[22] "Steamboat Arrivals at Fort Benton," p. 325; BL, "Bancroft Scraps, Idaho Miscellany," vol. 111, p. 230; *Helena Herald*, Apr. 24, 1880.

[23] *Idaho Statesman*, Feb. 3, 1880; *Salt Lake Tribune*, Oct. 20, 1880; "Steamboat Arrivals at Fort Benton," p. 325; Walker, *The Wagonmasters*, p. 211.

8

Corinne the Fair:
Gateway to Montana

During the 1870's, when Fort Benton served as the northern depot for goods and passengers to Montana, its southern rival was a would-be metropolis located a few miles west of Brigham City, Utah, on the new transcontinental railroad. The town was the last to be established on the long line of the Union Pacific Railroad and was destined, according to local speculators, to become the "city of the future." [1]

Founding Corinne

Knowing that this town, embraced by a sweeping curve of the Bear River, would be not only a railroad division town but also the junction between the Union Pacific from the East and the Central Pacific from the West, speculators had arrived long before official selection of the site was announced. As early as October 20, 1868, the *Salt Lake Reporter* had stated "everybody and his wife . . . is bound for Bear River. The railroad company will make that place the end of a division." [2] As soon as this fact became generally known, those who proposed to make real estate investments began to weigh the advantages of the various possibilities for the location of a junction city between the mouth of the Weber River and the northwest point of Great Salt Lake. Their primary concern was to determine which of the possible locations would be the most convenient point of departure for the stage

---

[1] USLC, John H. Beadle, "Scrapbook," Oct. 20, 1868.
[2] Ibid.

and freight lines that would be running from the railroad to Idaho and Montana.

Contenders for designation as the junction were Ogden, an already established city; Bonneville, five miles west of Brigham City; and the hopeful little village of Connor City, known to most simply as "Bear River." It soon became apparent that the fertile land at the tip of Bear River Bay in the Great Salt Lake promised the greatest number of advantages: it offered the shortest, fastest, easiest route to the flourishing Montana markets; it lay on the west side of Bear River within a very few miles of the established wagon road laid out by Captain Stansbury; the river afforded a source of water for irrigation of the hundreds of acres of arable lands on both sides of the river—"the only pure water in any abundance between the Wasatch and Humboldt Mountains"; and, to some, the Bear River showed possibilities for river navigation for bringing the ores from the south end of the lake to the railroad.[3]

While some speculators were betting on points nearer the mountains, others were busily preparing for the rush of business they expected to come to the banks of the Bear. By the end of January 1869, there was a saloon selling "sage brush whiskey" and a few staple provisions, one family had claimed all the land in the bend of the river, several merchants had established themselves there, and a "hotel" had been finished.[4] When John Hanson Beadle visited there on February 18, he found fifteen houses and 150 inhabitants. He reported that "there is no newsstand, postoffice or barber shop. The citizens wash in the river and comb their hair by crawling through the sage brush. A private stage is running from this place [Brigham City] to Promontory, passing through Connor. The proprietor calls it a *Try*-weekly, that is it goes out one week and *tries* to get back the next." [5]

The railroads and the government, so slow in coming to a decision about the location of the junction city, kept speculators waiting edgily, although some located claims as near to the river crossing as they could get them on the even sections of land.

[3] Ibid., Feb. 21, 1869; *Montana Post*, Apr. 2, 1869.
[4] *Corinne Journal*, May 25, 1871; Beadle, "Scrapbook," Feb. 21, 1869.
[5] Beadle, "Scrapbook," Feb. 18, 1869.

Bypassing a final decision, the Union Pacific engineers surveyed both Bonneville and Connor City, but on March 27, 1869, it was announced that Connor had been selected as the junction city. Just two weeks before, General J. A. Williamson, as the town's principal founder, had changed the name to Corinne.[6]

As soon as the survey had been completed, it was recorded in Douglas County, Nebraska, on March 24, 1869, and the lots were placed on sale the next day. The city plat was drawn on a grand scale (three square miles), providing for the great metropolis predicted by the more visionary of its founding citizens. The narrow business frontages on Montana Street and South Front Street drew most of the very active bidding, with some lots changing hands more than once during the day. The prices paid were estimated as ranging from $5 to $1,000, and the *Salt Lake Telegraph* reported on March 27, 1869, that "the choice locations... were considered bargains at that." The sale of more than 300 lots on the first day amounted to $30,000, and by summer sales reached $70,000. Estimates of the amount of the railroad's interest in Corinne were as high as $100,000. Many of the 300 to 400 people at Corinne had come from the railroad camps at Echo and Wahsatch, and were old hands at being first at a new boom town in order to get a good location. Others were Salt Lake merchants who had found competition too difficult in the Mormon city.[7]

Less than two weeks after the sale of lots, when the Union Pacific pulled its first engine across the new bridge over the river into Corinne on April 7, the *Salt Lake Telegraph* said, "the utmost excitement prevails upon the subject of Corinne, and hundreds are still flocking there. From two hundred and fifty to three hundred tents, shanties and buildings have been erected, and each day sees their number increased."

Living in the Burg on the Bear

For a time Corinne appeared to be merely one of a string of rowdy, uproarious construction camps preceding her and stretch-

---

[6] Ibid., Mar. 15, 27, 1869; *Corinne Mail*, Dec. 22, 1874.

[7] Territory of Utah, Box Elder County, County Recorder, Map of Corinne, March 24, 1869; *Utah Reporter*, Apr. 7, June 4, 1870; *Corinne Mail*, Dec. 22, 1874; *Montana Post*, Apr. 2, 1869; *Corinne Journal*, May 25, 1871.

ing beyond her to the west. The town was "fast becoming civilized, several men having been killed there already, the last one was found in the river with four bullet holes through him and his head badly mangled." [8] Some businessmen established themselves there, only to pack up after a few days and move on to some more likely place, agreeing with the *Salt Lake Telegraph* of April 26, 1869, that "a thriving town, with whatever natural advantages, cannot be resolved from the foetid elements rankling at Corinne.... I opine that the amount of Montana trade drawn to this direction will afford here but a flickering vitality in a season when they cannot be shipped via the Missouri River ... in justice to the public the facts should be known."

The actual state of affairs remains vague. John Hanson Beadle said that when he moved to Corinne in early April there were nineteen saloons and two dance houses, and the "supply of 'sports' " easily met the requirements of a railroad town. Workers drifted to Corinne for rest and recreation, and on Sunday, the "men went hunting and fishing, and the 'girls' had a dance or got drunk." [9] The *Salt Lake Telegraph* reported on April 13, 1869, "one house, or tent, of feminine fraility, one bar room and chop house, one grocery, one saloon with 'convenient appartments,' ... one punk roost, one keg saloon, two mercantile adventures, ... one town liquor store, one billiard hall, one washing, ironing and plain sewing erection, several promiscuous ladies in eight-by-ten duck domiciles, ... [and] one or two wholesale and retail liquor establishments."

But many had confidence that Corinne would rapidly develop into one of the largest shipping centers on the Central Pacific and Union Pacific lines. The well-established freighting route to Montana was a principal factor in making Corinne the ideal freight transfer point rather than Ogden. As a freighter looked north from his wagon camp in the depot yard at Corinne, he could contemplate a dry, firm road straight up Malad Valley to his destination. Ogden, two days of heavy travel away, didn't have a chance with a teamster who measured his profits in days on the road. [10]

---

[8] *Deseret News*, Apr. 7, 1869.

[9] John H. Beadle, *The Undeveloped West, or Five Years in the Territories*, p. 120.

[10] *Utah Reporter*, Nov. 27, 1869; *Helena Herald*, May 28, 1870.

Corinne, Utah, in 1869. Photograph by William H. Jackson. *National Archives.*

However, the initial rush of business, triggered by the influx of people as the railroad construction camps closed, slowed during the summer of 1869 as the city waited for eagerly sought freight contracts. Some people moved away, while others elected to wait out the doldrums. Many had expected that all other routes to Montana, including freighting by steamboat up the Missouri, would now fall into disuse. But in 1869 the Missouri River route was heavily used because shippers and merchants, uncertain about the completion date of the transcontinental railroad and doubtful about the site of a freight transfer point, had elected to gamble on high water and the steamers for another season.[11]

While business in Corinne showed a slow start, the pattern began to change in the fall of 1869 as the flow of goods shifted to the new railroad. One commentator noted, "There is not a man doing business here today but what knows that there never was a time since Corinne was laid out that the mountain orders could be met and filled without considerable patch-work and delay.... We have known orders to go begging here for ten days at a time, nobody having the goods to fill them, and still merchants say it is dull.... All we ask of you now is to wake up to your own interests, canvass the ground, and act accordingly." Apparently the merchants did canvass the ground. By December 31, 1869, the Union Pacific had shipped a total of 1,125,960 pounds to Corinne. When active trade began a month earlier than expected that spring, many were ready to take advantage of it. In April 1870, sales of over $4,000,000 had taken place; one warehouse alone shipped 1,000 tons of freight to Montana in the first six months. Banking transactions exceeded $5,000,000; real estate formerly worth less than $100,000 was now valued at over $1,300,000; and Corinne claimed to have paid internal revenue equal to three-fifths of that collected from the six most populous counties in Utah.[12]

After the fall freighting ended, oxen, mules, and horses wintered along the bottomlands of nearby rivers while their masters enjoyed the metropolitan delights of the new town and prepared for the next hauling season. Teamsters were heartened by the

---

[11] *Helena Herald*, May 18, 1870.
[12] *Utah Reporter*, Dec. 14, 1869, Apr. 7, 1870; *Helena Herald*, May 18, 1870.

sign of Creighton and Munro, agents for the Far West Fast Freight Line, and E. G. Maclay Company, agents for the giant Diamond R firm, building warehouses to accommodate the expected flow of goods. By early March 1870, some of the freighters were already on their way to Montana with small trains and light loads to cope with the mud and late snowstorms at Pleasant Valley on the Continental Divide. Mid-April found the "plain north and west of town ... dotted with freighter's camps, and stock corrals, while large cattle herds are pasturing on the prairie between us and the lake." [13] On May 13, 1870, the *Helena Herald* reported that a Diamond R train of five wagons arrived, having made the trip from the railroad in twenty-two days. On May 24, the *Corinne Reporter* listed the departure of a Garrison and Wyatt train of ten teams with trail wagons—eight yoke of cattle to the team—each team loaded with 12,000 pounds for a total of 120,000 pounds. Shipments north built up rapidly; the month of May saw 2,176,820 pounds received and dispatched through Corinne for Montana. The year-end total for 1870 reached 6,898,732 pounds.[14]

There was also passenger service to Montana, and its cash contributed to the tills of Corinne's businessmen. Stage lines formerly operating their Montana routes from Salt Lake City now transferred their base of operations to Corinne. Moreover, during 1870, and for most of the next decade, as many as fifty people a day disembarked at Corinne to outfit themselves for the trip north. The sale of horses, rigs, and supplies constituted another sizable business during the travel season.[15]

Freighting from the Railroad

During 1870, the freighting pattern for Corinne was shaped and in turn determined the life and pursuits of the people. In early March, the local newspaper would record "lively" business as teams and freighters crowded in to get their share of

---

[13] *Utah Reporter*, Apr. 21, 1870.
[14] Ibid, June 5, 1870; U.S. Congress, "Report on Reconnaissance of Northwestern Wyoming, 1873," *House Exec. Doc. 285*, p. 57.
[15] *Utah Reporter*, Apr. 19, 1870.

goods. Late March or early April found the first trains on their way to the Malad Divide, with May and June bringing exciting hours of work and prosperity for town merchants. Then the summer dullness would set in during July, although occasionally the local newspaper could rejoice about 100,000 pounds of freight being shipped in one day—"it wasn't much of a day for freight either, in fact it is considered quite out of season. With this showing in the dullest month of the season, what may we expect when the fall business sets in, in August and September?" [16]

In late August and on into September and October, visitors to Corinne complained that no accommodations were available, and Corinne businessmen were encouraged to consider establishing more hotels and restaurants to take care of the rush. Everything was hurried to beat a possible early winter at Pleasant Valley and avoid getting "snowed in on the divide." The local editor of the *Utah Reporter* on August 16, 1870, could point with pride to the "three immense bull trains . . . loading at the freight palaces on the off side of the track," one of which consisted of 20 wagons and 160 oxen. Or he could challenge freighters on September 17, 1870, with the comment that "Mr. Wade . . . [made] the round trip to Helena and back in thirty-one days. Who can beat that in overland freighting?" [17]

November concluded the hectic freighting days. Corinne would settle down to a winter of ice-skating parties, occasional evening visits to the Opera House to discuss the "Mormon question," and just biding time until another season of freighting resumed.

Corinne rather gloried in its unique situation as the only Gentile city in Utah, and enjoyed somewhat its altercations with Mormon polygamists. When it was remarked in 1871 that a new Gentile city might be built five miles south of Salt Lake City, the *Corinne Journal* reacted in alarm on May 2, arguing that Corinne could handle all the trade of southern Utah by means of steamers across the Great Salt Lake.

Corinne was "Montana-minded," considering itself almost an appendage of the northern territory, and trade from the south

---

[16] *Helena Herald*, July 14, 1870.
[17] *Utah Reporter*, Aug. 16, Sept. 17, 1870.

was of minor interest. Realizing that the chief basis for its economic development was the transfer and forwarding business, Corinne quavered in terror before every plan that would replace the wagon traffic with a railroad into Montana.

The Utah Northern Railroad

The start of the narrow-gauge Utah Northern Railroad from Brigham City to Cache Valley in 1871 created the first panic. With the completion of the road to Franklin, Idaho, in 1874, Mormon writers and even some Corinne citizens predicted the doom of the town on the Bear. But the Panic of 1873 delayed financing to continue the rails north. The boggy road through Marsh Valley north of Franklin kept teamsters on the Malad route, and the necessity of transferring goods from broad-gauge railroad cars to narrow-gauge cars at Ogden added to handling charges. These factors kept Corinne alive for another few years.

Corinne had desperately agreed to a spur rail line from Brigham City to connect with the Utah Northern, and some optimists in the town hoped this action might save Corinne as a shipping point. But when the Union Pacific took over the Utah Northern in 1877 and advanced the rails twenty miles north of Franklin by January 1878, the *Salt Lake Tribune* foretold the end: "The shipping season in the town is closed, and perhaps forever." And yet 1877 had been one of the most successful years in Corinne's history—5,700 tons of freight to Montana and Idaho, and 1,128 tons of ore received from the two northern territories.[18]

A few teams and wagons pulled into the familiar stops near the freight yard during 1878, but most were bound only short distances—to Malad or other nearby towns. The Salt Lake *Independent* correctly assessed Corinne's demise as a freight transfer station: "Corinne is one of the things of the past. It will in another year be simply a way station on the Central Pacific Railroad." By December 10, 1878, the freighting business had ended at Corinne when the Utah and Northern Railroad opened its terminus at Blackfoot, Idaho. The town immediately began to

---

[18] *Salt Lake Tribune*, Dec. 2, 1877.

deteriorate, and Alexander Toponce, for a long time an interested citizen, chronicled its demise: "The buildings went without paint, stores and dwellings stood vacant. Many of them were torn down or moved out on farms. People lived in houses rent free. Corinne men were found all over the west. The few who remained lived on the hope of what would happen when the irrigation water was brought on the broad valley." [19]

Not only did Corinne lose its freighting business, it also lost its identity as the chief Gentile town in Utah. "In August of 1877 the Mormons came to claim the near dead body of their adversary. A ward was organized with H. J. Faust as Bishop." When Warren B. Johnson started a walk from the Pacific to the Atlantic in 1882, he arrived in Corinne about dark on the evening of September 23, 1882. He asked a local resident for permission to sleep in the barn and asked casually, "Are there many Mormons in Corinne?" The lady of the house answered, "We are all Mormons here." [20]

Corinne, as the "Gateway to Montana," played a unique part not only in the history of Utah but also in the history of Idaho and Montana. During the first eighteen months of its existence it was transformed from a construction camp of the Union Pacific into a bustling, lively freighting center. Its high hopes dwindled as soon as another railroad pushed up the Montana Trail across the Malad and Monida divides to a connection with the Northern Pacific Railroad. But to the citizens of "Corinne the Fair" or the "Burg on the Bear," the choice of names depending on your place of residence and your preference in religion, the months of 1869 and 1870 were full of excitement and buoyant optimism for the future of the "greatest city" between St. Louis and San Francisco.

---

[19] *Salt Lake Independent*, Jan. 6, 1878; *Salt Lake Telegraph*, Dec. 10, 1878; Alexander Toponce, *Reminiscences of Alexander Toponce*, p. 233.

[20] Odell Scott, "Corinne City, Utah," Ms in the possession of Betty and Brigham D. Madsen; Warren B. Johnson, *From the Pacific to the Atlantic*, p. 173.

9

Staging North from the Railroad

While the Union Pacific crept steadily westward to meet the
Central Pacific, Wells, Fargo & Co. frequently had to adapt its
routes, schedules, and fares to the changing locations of the track
terminus. As spring approached in 1869, the company announced
that it expected to reduce fares to "very low figures"—$60 from
Helena to Salt Lake City. In February, the route via Virginia
City to Helena was changed to run directly from Helena to Salt
Lake City, with a daily coach from Virginia City connecting with
both the "up and down coaches." The change saved a day, so that
the trip from Helena to the railroad could be made in 66 hours or
to Omaha in 140 hours. By April 1, the railroad had reached
Ogden, and the stage run was changed to meet the train there
instead of at Wahsatch, thus eliminating a rugged passage
through Parley's Canyon east of Salt Lake City. Within a week
the run was changed again—this time to Corinne, thus shortening the travel time by half a day. Fares did not change as drastically as had been hoped, however, nor did the schedule. At the
end of April, six days were still required for the journey from
Helena, and the fare had been reduced only to $100 instead of the
hoped for $60.[1]

Wells Fargo, which had bought out Ben Holladay's interests
in the Overland Stage in 1866, received frequent praise for the
quality of its equipment and service on the Montana route. One
passenger wrote the *Helena Herald* on July 8, 1869, describing
the stage line as "the best stocked line in the West. The stations
and stables along the entire route are in first class order, the
coaches are in good condition, and the horses, as a rule, are

---

[1] *Montana Democrat*, Feb. 31, 1869; *Salt Lake Telegraph*, Feb. 25, Mar.
31, 1869; *Montana Post*, Apr. 2, 23, 1869.

among the best for speedy travel that could well be selected."
Competition from local stage companies did not seem to interfere
with the brisk business enjoyed by the Wells Fargo line. A passenger who tried to reserve a seat on Colwell and Carver's Salt
Lake–Ogden line complained that the entire coach had been chartered already and that it was too late to get a seat on the Wells
Fargo coach. Such a situation was so familiar to Ben Hampton of
Bear River Crossing that when he arrived in Salt Lake City en
route home from a trip, he bought a buggy for the final leg of the
journey because "the coach is always so crowded there is no
chance of getting in." [2]

More new coaches were shipped in for the line during the
middle of July, and the fare was reduced to $75 soon after. It soon
became apparent, however, that the officers of Wells, Fargo &
Co. had been sadly mistaken in assuming that the transcontinental railroad would require several more years for completion. On
August 20, 1869, the *Salt Lake Telegraph* carried the announcement that "Wells Fargo & Co. have come to the sensible conclusion to abandon entirely the Stage business and to confine
themselves to the Banking and Express businesses." [3]

Gilmer & Salisbury on the Montana Road

On August 26, the *Helena Herald* announced that Wells,
Fargo & Co. had sold the Overland Stage and Express Line to
J. T. Gilmer and Munro Salisbury of Salt Lake City. These two
energetic young men had been running stage lines in Utah and
were eager to expand their territory. Gilmer had begun as a
stage driver in 1859 for Russell, Majors, and Waddell between
Denver and Salt Lake City and had ten years of firsthand experience. Gilmer & Salisbury were able to buy "sixty or seventy
thousand dollars worth of new coaches that were never used
... for about a quarter of what they cost" from Wells Fargo. [4]

---

[2] *Deseret News*, June 16, 1869; USHS, "Hampton–Godbe Correspondence,"
Letter from Rosina Godbe to William S. Godbe, Great Salt Lake City, June 2,
1869.
[3] *Helena Herald*, July 8, Aug. 5, 1869.
[4] *Salt Lake Telegraph*, Aug. 20, 1869; *Helena Herald*, Aug. 26, 1869;
USLC, "John T. Gilmer."

Gilmer & Salisbury immediately began to modify and improve the service between Utah and Montana, including reducing the rates. One change effected by the end of November 1869 was a daily mail service between Helena and Corinne at Gilmer & Salisbury's expense—an action commended highly by Salt Lake and Montana papers. Their generosity was not quite as expansive as it appeared, however—there was already a daily stage between Virginia City and Salt Lake City and one going every other day to Helena, Diamond City, and Deer Lodge. This meant that a relatively short connection within Montana could provide daily mail service to Utah. The people of the territory were so pleased with the company's efforts that when an earthquake occurred in Montana in December, the *Utah Reporter* remarked that the quake took "twenty-four hours longer coming ...than Gilmer & Salisbury coaches." [5]

Mail Service to Montana

Frequent route and schedule changes, together with the vagaries of the weather, often affected mail delivery and not infrequently prompted complaints or suggestions for improvements. In April 1869, for example, mail for Utah and Montana was taken from the train in Ogden and sent to Salt Lake City to be forwarded to Montana by coach. Meanwhile, passengers from the same train were able to begin their northward stage journey directly from Ogden, thus reaching Montana at least a day ahead of the mail. Weather east of Salt Lake City often meant blocked trains and delayed mail delivery, even though stages were getting through to Montana. People who once were content to wait months for news from the East now fretted about anything that interfered with regular mail delivery—even a twenty-four hour delivery schedule was enough to cause discontent.[6]

In Montana, dissatisfaction with local mail service seemed chronic. The first week in July 1869, C. C. Huntley invested in some new Abbot & Downing Concord hacks to bolster his line

---

[5] *New Northwest*, Sept. 17, 1869; *Utah Reporter*, Nov. 13, 27, 30, Dec. 16, 1869; *Helena Herald*, Nov. 25, 1869.

[6] *Montana Post*, Feb. 26, Apr. 9, 1869; *Helena Herald*, June 3, 1870.

between Deer Lodge and Helena. Supplied with new Concord harnesses, the hacks were touted as "the lightest, best, most comfortable and handsome vehicle in the coach line" promising a "safe, speedy, and pleasant trip over the continental backbone." Not two weeks later the *New Northwest* at Deer Lodge was complaining about the poor mail service and grumbling that "anything like celerity in the transmission of mails, justly anticipated from tri-weekly or half daily service, is something extra-ordinary. With the net work of tri-weekly service routes existing ... we have a right to expect and demand a more efficient means of communication." [7]

On December 3, 1869, when Huntley's trips to Deer Lodge from Helena had been reduced from twice a day to triweekly, the editor of the *New Northwest* again turned his editorial wrath on the mail service. This time he objected to the government plans outlined in the notices for mail route applications: (1) half-day and triweekly service was reduced to weekly service "nearly all over Montana"; (2) government expense was increased without increasing service; (3) routes were established "between places in Montana that no *Montanian* ever heard of"; (4) "towns with 200-300 newspaper subscribers [were left] with no service at all"; and (5) [the result would be] "a system of ignorance, extravagance, and uselessness that the Grant administration ought to be ashamed of."

In the spring of 1870, a delegation to Washington, D. C., was able to secure a daily mail service from Corinne to Helena. The contract was let to Gilmer & Salisbury for $14,250 for triweekly service, although the company was carrying mail daily on their stage to Corinne. Other contracts with Gilmer & Salisbury included the run from Virginia City to Bannack ($950), Beaverhead to Deer Lodge ($2,520), and a "suspended" contract from Virginia City to Deer Lodge ($550). An open letter from William H. Taylor to the people of Montana a year later complained that a $12,000 contract with Gilmer & Salisbury between Ryans (near present Dillon, Montana) and Deer Lodge had not resulted in better service and that anyway the company was already being paid for the same route under other contracts. Supporters of

---

[7] *New Northwest*, July 9, 23, 1869.

Gilmer & Salisbury claimed that the contract was for triweekly service and that daily service had been provided by the firm "in pure charity." [8]

In the summer of 1871, the editor of the *Corinne Reporter* made an effort to explain the merits of shipping gold by mail rather than by express. Under a law that permitted any kind of goods weighing under four pounds to be shipped by mail, $1,000 in gold (which weighed less than four pounds) could be mailed for $3.75, while the same amount cost $12.50 by express. The editor also pointed out that insurance and security were the same either way, and the government made about $50,000 a year on the four-pound packages. It appeared that more gold was being shipped by mail than by freight or express! [9]

Missed schedules and poor routing were the main complaints concerning mail service. Accusations were made, too, of chicanery in the manipulation of contracts. One man was said to be getting $72,000 annually for a route that could be handled for $27 "by one man and a plug horse." [10]

Despite the public outcry about inefficient mail service during the decade of the 1870's, Gilmer & Salisbury made profits on their contracts and enjoyed a lucrative passenger business. The firm had succeeded in getting all the mail contracts for Montana at a good price, and by the middle of March 1870 daily coaches to Virginia City were leaving Corinne filled with passengers who had engaged their "sitting room" well in advance. Indeed, business was so brisk that the company soon was preparing to make the Helena run daily also. By July 1, the *Utah Reporter* estimated that at least 2,000 people had gone north on the Gilmer & Salisbury stages during the season. [11]

In addition to carrying passengers and mail, Gilmer & Salisbury also served as official carriers of the Montana fast freight that was handled by the Wells Fargo Express Company, which had no transportation facilities of its own after Wells, Fargo &

---

[8] Ibid., Dec. 3, 1869, Mar. 10, 1871; *Helena Herald*, Mar. 31, 1870, July 3, 1871.

[9] *Corinne Reporter*, July 22, 1871.

[10] A. C. Bolino, "An Economic History of Idaho Territory, 1863–1890," Ph.D. diss., St. Louis University, 1957, p. 162.

[11] *Utah Reporter*, Mar. 15, June 11, 1870; *New Northwest*, July 1, 1870.

The old Billings-Lewistown Stage going up the Rimrocks near Billings. *Courtesy of Kenneth F. Roahen.*

Co. sold all its staging property, including coaches, stock, and stations. Agents for the express company were set up in key terminals in Utah and Montana. The stage company was well paid for these services. For example, even though bankers were given a $400 discount when the largest gold shipment in a single day went out ($80,000 in bullion), one firm paid a shipping bill of $2,250.[12]

Competing on the Road

Such lucrative business naturally attracted competition. One owner of a small stage line announced unscheduled runs from Corinne to Helena that would start "whenever the load gets ready." He traveled only by day and expected passengers to fend for themselves in the matters of food and sleeping arrangements. With a fare of only $25, he rarely had to wait more than a day or two to fill his coach with riders. More serious competition came from C. C. Huntley, who operated a network of stage lines in Montana. On the sixty-mile run over the Continental Divide between Helena and Deer Lodge, C. C. Huntley and Gilmer & Salisbury both cut their fares to $5 and vied in making the best time while interested onlookers placed bets on their favorites. On September 9, the "two coaches were speeding it all the way over," until finally the Gilmer & Salisbury driver, W. H. Taylor, "dashed into Helena on the keen run," just five hours and three minutes after leaving Deer Lodge. Losing the race must have been quite a blow to Huntley, who the same day had received two new eleven-passenger coaches made by Coan and Ten Broeck of Chicago that were supposed to be an improvement over the Concords and better suited to mountain travel. In the long run, C. C. Huntley lost even more to the Gilmer & Salisbury interests—in October 1870 he sold them his express outfit.[13]

The fall season of 1870 was quite routine in the regularity of the service provided by the stage company. In October a new fare from Missoula to Corinne was announced as $92.50, and in November the *Helena Herald* observed "an unusual amount of

---

[12] *Helena Herald*, Aug. 23, Sept. 6, 1870.
[13] *Utah Reporter*, Aug. 30, 1870; *Helena Herald*, Sept. 9, Oct. 20, 1870.

Wells, Fargo & Co. station in Virginia City about 1865. *Montana Historical Society, Helena.*

express matter" from Corinne to Helena. During the winter a few routes were altered or extended, and fares were adjusted accordingly. In December, the Postmaster General ordered tri-weekly service between Deer Lodge and Ryans, thus eliminating the necessity of going from Deer Lodge to Helena in order to go south to Corinne. Now passengers from Deer Lodge Valley could meet the Helena coach at Ryans and save from 60 to 100 miles on a trip south. Though the distance was shorter, the time was longer; and the saving in fare was pretty well used up paying for a night's lodging at Ryans while waiting for the Helena coach. The fare from Deer Lodge to Corinne via Helena was $82.50, while the fare via Ryans was $75.00. Hugh Kirkendall felt that his Fast Freight and Express line could easily compete with this and advertised that his company would carry passengers to Corinne from Deer Lodge in eight days for $25. As might be expected, new scheduling by Gilmer & Salisbury eliminated the overnight stop, thus saving almost two days in travel time. Among other accomplishments that winter was an extension of the stage line to Fort Benton, advertised "with good stock, new coaches, and quick time." In addition, by negotiating with the Union Pacific, Gilmer & Salisbury were able to offer through tickets to Omaha at a reduction of $27.50 each way.[14]

Summer saw even more changes. The four-horse stages that had brought so much passenger appreciation when Gilmer & Salisbury first took over from Wells Fargo had been replaced in some sections with two-horse jerkeys; now, four-horse coaches again were put in service the length of the line from Corinne to Helena, and a daily through coach was scheduled. The fare was reduced from $50 to $45, prompting the *Montanian* to ask, "Who can't go to America now?" [15]

Stagecoaching in 1872

The winter of 1871–72 began with deceptive mildness, but February 1872 was a different story. Passengers were still get-

---

[14] *Helena Herald*, Oct. 14, Nov. 18, 1870; *New Northwest*, Dec. 9, 16, 1870, Feb. 3, June 3, 1871; *Corinne Journal*, May 2, 1871.

[15] *Helena Herald*, July 28, 1871; *Montanian*, Aug. 17, 1871.

ting through to Helena from Corinne regularly, chiefly because, according to X. Beidler, "there are three hundred miles of good sleighing." Business on the line dropped drastically, however, because the Union Pacific trains were blocked east of Utah. Train passengers were subsisting on crackers and cheese, and the *Helena Herald* appealed for relief "of snow-bound or frost-constipated railway trains." Jack Gilmer made an agreement with the Union Pacific to run stages around the blockade for $1,000 a day to get the mail through, but passengers had to wait and hope for other transportation. Roads in Montana were barely passable. The editor of the *Montanian* had to walk and guide his horse on a private sleighride from Virginia City to Sterling because "the beaten path will bear up a horse, but one step to the right or left and in he goes over head and ears." [16]

Preparations for the usual spring increase in passenger travel began in March when a carload of fine eastern horses was shipped into Corinne for the stage company. At this time "the Union Pacific announced new rates for combined rail and stage fares to Montana cities: First class, $111.75, second class, $91.75, and third class, $61.75." Responding to the challenge of Montana businessmen that "the terrible stage ride of three hundred and fifty miles ... frightens capitalists and prevents them from coming to see us, they imagine that we are entirely out of the world," the stage company repainted and reupholstered their coaches and cut their time to Helena. Nevertheless, some capitalists scorned the stage line and chartered a coach and relay teams "all the way to Helena." [17]

A major event of the summer of 1872 was the journey of General James J. Garfield on Gilmer & Salisbury stages as he made a personal visit to the Flathead Indians for treaty negotiations. His diary indicated his enjoyment of the experience. "[Aug.] 13, Tuesday. Took the stage holding nine passengers inside and two outside with the Driver. Moved up the Bear River Valley at a spanking trot.... The scenery has been one of grandeur constantly varying.... I have greatly enjoyed my study of the drivers.... They are a rough warm-hearted peculiar people and

---

[16] *Helena Herald*, Feb. 8, 14, 1872; *Montanian*, Feb. 22, 1872.
[17] *Corinne Reporter*, Apr. 5, June 27, 1872; *Montanian*, Oct. 26, 1871; *Helena Herald*, May 2, 1872.

have a distinct place among American characters.... 18, Sunday. A glorious days ride, among the mountains." On the other hand, the Earl of Dunraven acquired a very different point of view two years later when he traveled in a rented coach, "a strange vehicle, mostly composed of leather." He found that upset schedules resulted in "having dinner at 7 a.m., supping at noon, and breakfasting somewhere about sundown." He was disappointed because there were "no precipices, no torrents ... nothing grand, terrible, or dangerous. The idea that you are crossing the backbone of the continent, and scaling a vast mountain range, appears preposterous." He complained further that during their four days and nights on the stage, the passengers were "shot about like shuttles" over the baggage stacked inside the coach.[18]

The Epizootic of 1872-74

In December of 1872, the press began to report early rumblings of incipient disaster; the epizootic was rampant in California and along the Pacific Coast. This highly contagious disease of horses spread rapidly throughout the intermountain region. An infected horse would "cough for days and will then run at the nose, ... eyes will be watery, ... [and] secondary symptoms are those of dropsy." Stock owners were advised that "more horses have been killed in the east by medicine than by the disease." The best care seemed to be complete rest, adequate time for recuperation, a diet of moist, warm bran mash, and moderate medication. Two medicines were recommended. One was a solution of one or two grains of sulphate of copper in four ounces of distilled water, to be injected into the nostrils two or three times a day; the other was an inhalation of carbolic acid to relieve the bronchial tubes and lungs. No wonder many horses did not survive the first attack! A relapse seemed to be "inevitably fatal." [19]

Between the epizootic and the severity of the weather in February 1873, the stage company had a rather difficult time.

---

[18] Oliver W. Holmes, ed., *James A. Garfield's Diary of a Trip to Montana in 1872*, pp. 5-10; Earl of Dunraven, *Hunting in the Yellowstone*, pp. 53-62.

[19] *Helena Herald*, Feb. 6, 1873; *Montanian*, Feb. 6, 1873; *Corinne Reporter*, Feb 8, 1873.

Jack Gilmer tried to reassure the public by announcing that while his horses did have the epizootic it was not severe enough to "render them unfit for work." In the same paper, however, another news item stated that all the horses in Corinne were afflicted and that "most important is the Montana Stage line [Gilmer & Salisbury], the animals of which are affected in large numbers." [20]

Storms and extreme cold continued into March and complicated the strain on the beleaguered Gilmer & Salisbury lines. But as the roads improved and better weather reduced the equine infection, the stages were able to get back to making the run in three days, and it was again necessary to book passage three days ahead to get to Helena. Most of the passenger traffic seemed to be directed northward. Many of the early spring travelers were Montana residents returning after a winter in warmer regions, although many were " 'tender feet,' who are going north to seek fortunes among the placers." [21]

The winter of 1873–74 was the worst since 1866, with snow lying two to three feet deep in the Snake River Valley and with drifts up to thirty feet deep at the Monida and Malad divides. To make matters worse, the stage horses were again afflicted with the epizootic and "coughed almost incessantly" as they were driven through the snow.[22]

During the summer of 1874, an average of eight to ten passengers embarked daily for Montana towns, but by October, the usual fall reversal in the direction of travel became apparent, with the stages from the north being "loaded every night with merchants, tourists, cattle men, and adventurers." News reports during the winter of 1874–75 were filled with stage stories such as the night ride from Helena to Deer Lodge, when the thermometer registered 45⁰ below zero. The driver, Johnny Davis, walked through the snow to guide the stage, while E. M. "Gov" Pollinger, superintendent on the road, drove the team. The passengers spent most of their time "shoveling snow and getting the team on their feet." The bad weather continued into the spring,

---

[20] *Corinne Reporter,* Feb. 3, 1873.
[21] Ibid., Apr. 10, 1873.
[22] *Helena Herald,* Mar. 19, 27, 1874.

and as late as April 1875, John Kibbler chose to walk from Corinne to Virginia City, made the journey in ten days, and at Pleasant Valley overtook the Gilmer & Salisbury stage that had started from Corinne the same day he did.[23]

Stations on the Route

The only respite from the mind-shattering, bone-rattling ride in a stagecoach was an overnight stop at one of the various home stations that had been established every fifty miles along the route, or a brief pause at one of the thirty or forty swing stations where teams were changed and cramped limbs could be stretched. Locations of these stations rarely varied from those established by Wells Fargo before completion of the transcontinental railroad, though changes in personnel or in ownership of a ranch where a station might be located could sometimes change the name of an old and well-known station. The gradual improvement in service which Gilmer & Salisbury made along their trunk line included upgrading their home stations and swing stations, and personnel was shifted from one place to another as business demanded it.

The various station agents came to be well known to regular travelers along the Montana Trail, even though an agent might be shifted occasionally from one station to another. Some agents developed their own ranches in the vicinity of stations and remained settled there, perhaps for a lifetime, going from one nearby station to another to work for successive stage companies. Two such ranchers were the Adams brothers, John Newton and William Joseph, who "ran cattle and horses" for the stage company, furnished hay and wood to the stage lines, and from time to time served as station agents or drivers at such points as Eagle Rock and Market Lake.[24]

Another example is the Corbett family. Emma Ott Corbett weighed 441 pounds when she arrived at Eagle Rock, and she

[23] *Corinne Daily Mail*, Sept. 14, 1874; *New Northwest*, Jan. 15, 1875; *Montanian*, April 22, 1875.

[24] Edith H. Lovell, *Captain Bonneville's County*, p. 148; William S. Pettite, *Memories of Market Lake*, pp. 27, 65; *Idaho State Journal*, July 27, 1962; *Idaho Falls Post-Register*, Sept. 19, 1966.

refused to be weighed again. She had a quick temper, was a sure shot, and was known to wave a gun about while inviting passengers to come in and refresh themselves at her station. Mail sacks were left by her bed at night because she was a light sleeper, and because of her "courage and ability to handle difficult situations" she was moved "from one troubled spot to another." But Mrs. Corbett had a husband who was also a good shot, courageous, and hot tempered. For over thirty years there were clashes, until it appeared that Emma was winning "over her much thinner and older husband." After a divorce in 1883, she remarried and continued to tend Camas station.[25]

Over the years some of the stations became notorious for their bad meals or for their poor hospitality. Letter writers and newsmen tended to emphasize the inconveniences, so home stations rarely rated such praise as the *Helena Herald* heaped on the Lewis house at Franklin, Idaho: "[it] supplies a bounteous table, and clean, cozy lodgings to travelers, all of whom . . . tarry there over the night, taking supper and breakfast." Episcopal bishop Daniel S. Tuttle always enjoyed getting away from the "beans and bacon of Market Lake and Sand Hole to the green oasis of Pleasant Valley with the good chicken and splendid cooking of Mrs. Hall." But most stations sooner or later acquired such opprobrious nicknames as "Root-Hog Station" at Blackfoot, or "Dirty Woman's Station." [26]

Travelers soon learned what to expect at a stage stop. Regular passengers had learned to fend for themselves, but newcomers sometimes found their fare to be sardines and crackers if they did not join the intitial rush to the table. Agents usually had a wash basin and towel waiting outside the door, where people could remove a layer or two of alkali dust. Then a meal was served—usually abundant, but also monotonously similar to other meals served on the route. Stage-cramped passengers were often delighted when circumstances forced a driver to "lay over" for the night, even when it meant sleeping on the floor of the station. Martha Edgerton Plassman told of one winter evening she spent

[25] *Idaho State Journal*, July 27, 1962; Pettite, *Memories of Market Lake*, p. 99; Merril D. Beal "Personal Papers," Pocatello, Idaho.

[26] *Helena Herald*, July 27, 1876; WCML, Daniel S. Tuttle, "Montana Reminiscences," p. 22.

The old Whitehall Station in 1868. "Gov." Pollinger is leaning against the post in front. *Wells Fargo Bank, History Room, San Francisco.*

Pollinger Station, established in 1869—later Gaffney Station. *Montana Historical Society, Helena.*

Red Rock Stage Station, Montana, in 1895. *Montana Historical Society, Helena.*

in a station as the only woman with a coach load of men. A light was brought in and revealed two beds in the room, one of which was assigned to Martha. When she asked where the others would sleep, the reply was, "in here." After asking for and being promised a curtain, Martha went to bed and was then told she would have no curtain. When she protested to her traveling companion and asked what to do, he told her, "When in Rome, do as the Romans do." So she did. Later she could hear the men coming in and spreading their blankets on the floor, but when she awoke the next morning, the room was empty.[27]

After any stop, as soon as the meal was over, there was a rush for the coach and the coveted seat beside the driver. The loser tried next for the seats at the front or back of the coach, never for those in the middle. The middle was usually only a bench with no backrest; back support was provided by a wide leather strap which had to be removed every time someone entered or left the back seat. The rush for seats after each stop was an especially harrowing experience for "Mr. B.," who in the winter of 1877–78 had come down from Helena with his wife, four children, and another couple. At Red Rock, Mr. B. ran in the station to get some warm milk for the baby and came back to the coach to find "a stout, coarse-looking woman in his seat, a strapping boy of twelve at her side, a canary bird in her lap, a pillow, a buffalo robe, two pairs of blankets, two shawls and a valise in her immediate neighborhood, and three of his children shoved down into the center of the coach." Failing at vigorous oral protest, Mr. B. picked the lady up bodily and put her in the middle seat; then, at every station, she jumped out to proclaim that he had beaten her and mistreated her. He offered to pay her fare to Franklin if she would wait for the next coach, but she refused the offer, so the two wrangled all the way to Franklin.[28]

Traveling Companions

The only relief from the tedium of the ride was to strike up a conversation with one's companions in misery. If one were fortu-

---

[27] Alexander Toponce, *Reminiscences of Alexander Toponce*, p. 242; MSHS, "Those Early Days were Tough for Greenhorns," Clip file; MSHS, Martha E. Plassman, "Incidents of Stage Travel . . . ," Clip file.

[28] *Helena Herald*, Feb. 21, 1878.

nate, the group in the coach could be good company for the entire trip. Or a lively driver would often entertain with staging stories. Almost any kind of diversion was welcome. When Colonel W. F. Sanders was "imprisoned" in a coach with several American passengers and one Chinese, the Americans passed the time by singing. They sang until they were hoarse, then asked the Chinese passenger to sing. He broke into a wail that appeared to have no end, so they interrupted him to ask what the song meant. It turned out to be a song of love and longing for home. Frequently a passenger or two had been thoughtful enough to provide himself with some "liquid encased in glass," which might be shared with others for "protection against the cold." [29]

One man even appreciated being asked to walk and hang first "upon one side of the stage and then upon the other . . . to keep the vehicle 'right side up with care.'" Walking was no pleasure, however, for Brevet Brigadier-General Rusling on a tour as Inspector for the Quartermaster Department in 1873:

> We had matrasses along, which we carried on top by day, and at night arranged into a passable bed. So, too, we had india-rubber pillows, and robes and blankets in abundance. . . . We left Bear River about 10 P.M. in an ugly storm of rain and sleet, well tucked in for a night's ride; but in an hour or so were roused up by the stage coming to a dead-halt, and the driver singing out—it sounded half-maliciously—'Good place to walk, gents! Bad place ahead!' Out we got for a dismal walk of a mile or more, through a soft and yielding bottom, where the horses could hardly pull the empty coach through, and then in again with muddy boots and disgusted feelings generally. . . . At night our mattrasses proved too narrow for three, after all, and Halsey's shoulders or knees were punching into either L. or me.[30]

Francis Roe, on the other hand, found her traveling companions somewhat less than congenial on one occasion after her stage had stopped for fresh horses. The fresh horses were wild mustangs that began to buck and jerk the stage about until "one by one those men got out, and just as the last one stepped down on one side, the heads of two cream-colored horses appeared at the

---

[29] MSHS, "Those Early Days were Tough for Greenhorns," Clip file.

[30] W. L. Humason, *From the Atlantic Surf to the Golden Gate*, p. 25; James F. Rusling, *Across America*, p. 219.

open door on the other side, their big troubled eyes looking straight at me. During my life on the frontier I have seen enough of native horses to know that when a pair of excited mustang leaders try to get inside a stage, it is time for one to get out, so I got out!" [31]

Each man in turn, including the driver, ordered her back in. Indignant at being ordered because "it was bad enough to have to obey just one man, when at home, and then have four strange men—three of them idiots, too"—order her about, Mrs. Roe refused to get in, but stood very close to the stage in case the horses should decide to start out on a dead run. As she heard the brake being released, she jumped on the step,

> and catching a firm hold each side of the door, was about to step in when one of those men passengers grabbed my arm and tried to jerk me back, so he could get in ahead of me! . . . If my hands and arms had not been unusually strong . . . I would have undoubtedly been thrown underneath . . . for the four horses were going at a terrific gait, and the jerky was swaying like a live thing. . . . I scrambled inside. . . . But that man! He pushed in back of me and, not knowing the nice little ways of jerkies, was pitched foward to the floor with an awful thud but after a second or so he pulled himself up on his seat, and there we two sat in silence and in darkness.[32]

Even the best care of a skilled driver could not always prevent accidents. One accident in 1873 was related years later by Martha Edgerton Plassman. Having arrived in Montana with the earliest settlers, she well knew that "to pay for a stage passage did not insure the traveler a ride the whole distance in a coach; it simply meant that the stage company would undertake to convey the passenger someway, and at some time, to his destination." The ticket buyer might be asked to ride in a sleigh, a jerky, a boat, a lumber wagon, or even to walk. On this occasion a sleigh had been the mode of conveyance most of the way from Montana to Eagle Rock, Idaho. Martha said, "For three days and two nights we kept to the sled, except for the brief interval when it overturned as we attempted to go onto the bridge spanning

---

[31] Frances M. A. Roe, *Army Letters from an Officer's Wife, 1871–1888*, pp. 210–11.

[32] Ibid., pp. 211–12.

Snake River, and I slid halfway down to the treacherous stream below." [33]

Being Waylaid by Road Agents

Fear of accidents, however, did not instill the terror that could be inspired by the sudden appearance of road agents. One of the first stage robberies after Corinne was established as the southern terminus of the stage line occurred at Morier's station on July 13, 1869. A treasure box containing $7,000 was stolen while the drivers were changing horses. Within two weeks, the thief, a stock tender named James Jamison, had been caught and the money recovered.[34] Two more robberies, on August 31 and September 6, prompted several men to organize and pursue the robbers, no doubt spurred on by hopes of a generous reward. Both holdups occurred about ten miles north of Malad, in very nearly the same spot and in almost the same manner. The *Helena Herald* reported that all the treasure was insured and that Wells, Fargo & Co., "are the only losers," but Wells Fargo agents moved quickly. The General Superintendent of the company distributed posters reading: "Ten Thousand Dollars Reward.—Wells, Fargo & Co.'s Express was robbed near Malad City, Idaho, on the night of August 31st and September 6th of over Fifty Thousand Dollars. For the capture of the robbers and recovery of the money we will pay one fourth of the amount stolen or in proportion for any part thereof." [35]

One man who responded to the call was Albert H. Cook, a St. Louis police sergeant visiting in Salt Lake City. While Cook was engaged in "ferreting out" the robbers in the first crime, he received a telegram saying $27,000 had been lost in the second robbery, so he returned to Corinne and joined Dan Robbins, company division agent. The two drove seventy-five miles in six hours to the scene and were soon on the robbers' trail, accompanied by a small posse. "Within almost hearing distance" of the

[33] MSHS, Plassman, "Incidents of Stage Travel."

[34] *Helena Herald*, July 22, Sept. 9, 1869; *Deseret News*, Aug. 4, 1869.

[35] BL, "Bancroft Scraps, Utah Miscellany," vol. 109, p. 346; *Idaho Statesman*, Sept. 14, 1869; *New Northwest*, Sept. 17, 1869; *Salt Lake Telegraph*, Sept. 9, 1869; *Helena Herald*, Sept. 9, 1869.

robbery scene, the posse came upon the robbers' horses grazing in a canyon. As Mr. Cook related in a letter to his brother, "We followed and undertook to drive them out of the brush, which was so dense that we could not see ten feet ahead. We drove them up a ravine, where they turned and fired on us, hitting Dan Robbins three times. . . . We kept up the fire until we killed one of the robbers, and wounded the other five times. . . . We recovered every dollar of the money. We had to carry Dan Robbins six miles on a litter and fifteen miles in a wagon before we got him to a house." Mr. Robbins recovered, although for a time his friends feared that his life would be sacrificed "for a set of miserable thieves." Frank Long, the dead robber, had been a stage driver for Wells Fargo on the Boise road and had had a key made to fit the express box. He already had stolen $9,000 from an express box earlier.[36]

It was nearly a year before robbers hit again. This time there was no treasure box aboard, and the passengers' armed resistance forced the attackers to retreat. The attack occurred on July 28, 1870, near Pleasant Valley, and one week and a day later another attempt was made—this time successful. Without a shot fired, the bandits secured both the Helena and Virginia City treasure boxes and over $4,000 from the three Chinese passengers.[37]

Finally galvanized into more positive action, Wells Fargo stationed guards along Dry Creek, Portneuf Canyon, and other points. In addition, two mounted guards accompanied the stage at night. X. Beidler told of his experiences as a guard along this route. "It got so dangerous to ship treasure . . . that the Wells, Fargo & Co., concluded to raise the percentage for carrying the treasure and put on more messengers and guards. From Pleasant Valley to Sand Hole Station in the night two of us messengers had to ride horse back, riding in advance behind or on the sides of the coach." Beidler did not have a very high regard for his fellow guards and messengers, especially for one named Big Nick who had once "thrown up his hands and given up $6,000

---

[36] *Helena Herald*, Sept. 16, 23, 1869; BL, "Bancroft Scraps, Utah Miscellany," vol. 109, p. 346; *Salt Lake Telegraph*, Sept. 11, 12, 1869.

[37] *Helena Herald*, July 29, Aug. 6, 1870; *Utah Reporter*, Aug. 1, 2, 6, 1870; *Deseret News*, Aug. 10, 1870; BL, "Bancroft Scraps, Montana Miscellany," vol. 90, p. 91.

(and got his dividend)," and Frank Orr, "a brocky-faced thief." On one trip with these two men, Beidler observed Big Nick and Frank Orr whispering together, so he watched them more closely and altered his practice of riding with the driver when traveling on the stage to guard the treasure. He assigned Orr that seat and rode inside with Big Nick. Also, he told the driver, Tom Caldwell, that "something was up . . . and that if we were halted tonight not to put his foot on the break but to hit his horses on the back or he would be killed, and that our only show would be a running fight, and told him I will have my head and shoulders out of the coach window on your side. We had not gone over a mile before 'big Nick' asked me 'what will we do if we are halted.' I said, 'I am getting $250 per month to fight to save treasure and I will shoot at the first thing that crawls.'" Beidler guessed when the holdup was imminent and instructed the driver to go through on the run. As the stage raced past the holdup men, Beidler shot two of them. The stage "got to Hole in the Rock, 8 miles, in quicker time than the Utah Northern [Railroad] ever made it since." Nick later admitted to Beidler he had received a dividend from the previous $6,000 robbery and that he and Orr were to get a "whack" of the $120,000 this time.[38]

After the arrest of Orr and Big Nick, little was seen of stage robbers for nearly two years. Then, at the end of August 1872, the *Corinne Reporter* warned that "stage robbers now infest the roads in Idaho and Nevada, to the terror of travelers in those places." Not long afterward, on September 14, a coach was waylaid near Silver Star. As the stage passed through the shade of a bluff about midnight and a cry of "Halt!" was heard, John Featherstone, the express manager, replied, "Halt yourselves, ye sons of ——!" and discharged two barrels of buckshot in the direction of the voice. At breakneck speed, the stage raced ahead to Morier's station, where the frightened passengers, mostly women and children, refused to continue their journey in the same coach with a treasure box. They were not the first to object to riding in a coach that carried the express box; passengers had been complaining about it for years.[39]

---

[38] Helen F. Sanders, *A History of Montana*, pp. 286–87; *Helena Herald*, Aug. 18, Sept. 15, 1870.

[39] *Corinne Reporter*, Aug. 30, Sept. 19, 1872; *Helena Herald*, Sept. 19, 1872.

A second attempt in October was more successful, but when one passenger could produce only $8, he was warmly reprimanded by the robber with, "What the h——l have you been doing all summer?" [40] After this robbery, the road agents were interrupted by the winter weather and made no more holdup attempts until July 16, 1873. On that day, Charlie Phelps was driving the "up" stage, confidently assuming that because the "down" stage would have more gold, it would be more likely to be stopped. However, a mile and a half north of Robber's Roost, two shots rang out, and Charlie whipped his horses into a run. Half a mile later, he stopped the stage, saying he had been shot in the abdomen. He died next day, and was buried in the Malad cemetery, where a headstone was erected honoring his heroism. Again a reward was offered, and Gilmer & Salisbury agents joined the Wells Fargo agents in a seach for the felons, but were unsuccessful. [41]

One pursuit that did succeed that summer was the two-year search for the thieves who had broken into an express box in July 1871, and made off with the contents. George N. Rugg, a stock tender at Red Rock station, had persuaded the station keeper and his partner to assist him in robbing the stage, but the three were afraid of the "stern and fearless" express messengers. So while the drivers were at dinner, Rugg took the box from the coach, got the clasp open, removed the gold, and filled the chest with "boulders." The theft was not discovered until the stage reached Eagle Rock, where a new driver awaited the coach. There, according to custom, the treasure chest was opened in the presence of both the new crew and the old one. The enraged messengers, who had been guarding the rocks all the way from Red Rock, seized the driver and tried to force him to confess, but finally let him go.

In the meantime, the thieves were busy burying the gold near the Red Rock station, where it remained until Rugg's partners dug it up and took it to Canada. All Rugg ever got was $126. Poor Rugg, who seemed to be "nearer a d——d fool than

---

[40] *Helena Herald*, Oct. 24, 31, 1872; *Deseret News*, Oct. 23, 1872; *Corinne Reporter*, Oct. 19, 1872.

[41] *Montanian*, July 24, 1873; *Corinne Reporter*, July 17, 18, 1873; Arthur C. Saunders, *The History of Bannock County, Idaho*, p. 98.

Stage robber George N. Rugg. *Wells Fargo Bank, History Room, San Francisco.*

any scoundrel we have heard of lately," went to Utah and tried to blackmail his partners into giving him his share, but his letters were intercepted. He finally confided in a man who in turn reported the story to the authorities.

Rugg had been under suspicion from the start. Almost immediately after the theft, employees had threatened him with hanging. Al Graeter of Wells Fargo actually had dangled Rugg in the air three times while trying to frighten him into confessing. Investigators also threatened Rugg with X. Beidler, that intrepid representative of the vigilantes who was well known for his readiness to hang any culprits who might be caught.

When the truth finally came to light, the three perpetrators were jailed and tried. Having been persuaded to turn state's evidence, Rugg was released; the other two were sent to the Montana penitentiary where they served seven years and were pardoned in May 1880. The two later "became respected ranchers in another part of the state." Rugg, however, perhaps bearing out Montana's evaluation of his being more of a fool than a scoundrel, went to California and robbed another stage of its Wells Fargo express. He was sent to the California State Prison on November 8, 1877, and died there on July 27, 1880.[42]

On July 2, 1874, the southbound coach was stopped at Dry Creek and held until the northbound stage arrived, and both were plundered of about $1,360. The *Montanian* noted at the time that "these robbers are discreet, and never attack the 'treasure coach,' which is an arsenal on wheels." [43]

While many of these latter-day stage robberies could still provide thrills for tenderfeet and good copy for frontier newspapers, editors generally filled their columns with more prosaic accounts of freight wagons loading and teams departing. The business of moving goods north from the railroad was of prime bread-and-butter importance during the 1870's. Rumors began to circulate in the fall of 1874 in Corinne that Gilmer & Salisbury might move their station to Franklin, Idaho, now that the Utah

[42] *Montanian*, July 31, Oct. 30, 1873; *Helena Herald*, Oct. 30, 1873; MSHS, "Robbery of Gold–Laden Coach . . . ," in *Cut Bank Pioneer Press*, Mar. 16, 1931, Clip file; Wells, Fargo and Company Express, *Report of Jas. B. Hume and Jno. N. Thacker*, pp. 35, 50, 65.

[43] *Salt Lake Tribune*, Sept. 10, 1873, July 2, 1876; *Helena Herald*, Sept. 11, 1873, July 13, 1876; *Montanian*, July 9, 1873.

Northern Railroad had reached that point. As late as March 1875, however, the Corinne paper was still insisting that the stage terminus would not move to Franklin. Nevertheless, Gilmer & Salisbury moved to Franklin in May and began service from that point on June 3, 1875, marking the end of that era of staging along the Montana Trail.

10

The Diamond R Rolls Out

During its heyday as a railroad terminus town, staging north formed only one economic base for the city of Corinne. The establishment of a railroad freight depot at Corinne transformed the business of supplying goods, as well as people, to Montana. Staples from Omaha and fruit from California ordered via the Union Pacific or Central Pacific would be delivered on schedule in Helena after a three- or four-week wagon trip from Corinne. Clearly, forwarding merchants needed to find a more rapid means of getting the goods north. On September 16, 1869, the *Helena Herald* berated the freighting companies for not inaugurating a fast express. Stagecoaches were being taxed to their "utmost capacity" with freight goods, at a great cost in transportation charges to merchants. A fast freight was needed to bring goods north in six days from the railroad at a cost of $.20 per pound. Seeing an excellent opportunity, the large wholesale grocery firm of Creighton and Munro of Omaha bought out Megeath and Company of Corinne and became one of the biggest forwarding houses in town.[1]

Freighters from Corinne

On April 2, 1870, Hugh Kirkendall, who had been hauling freight from Fort Benton to Helena for many years, announced in the *Helena Herald* preparations to move goods both from "the Railroad and River ... WITH PROMPTNESS AND DISPATCH." And the Far West Fast Freight Line was ready to issue through bills of lading for freight from New York, Boston, Chicago, St. Louis, and Omaha to all points in Montana, with

---

[1] *Helena Herald*, Aug. 12, Sept. 16, 1869; *Utah Reporter*, Dec. 14, 1869.

Hugh Kirkendall (in doorway in shirtsleeves) established his Montana Fast Freight Line between Helena and Corinne in 1870. *Courtesy of William D. Livingstone.*

Creighton and Munro acting as company agents in Corinne. But the most important news came from the "giant establishment of the north," the E. G. Maclay & Co., owners of Diamond R, which built a warehouse in Corinne and named George B. Parker its agent. In March, the company dispatched a train of 100 wagons from Montana to pick up the first freight of the season from the railroad.[2]

As a citizen of Corinne pointed out, now a Helena business-man could telegraph New York City and start his teams for the railroad the same day. By the time the teams reached Corinne, the order would have been filled and carried west by the Union Pacific. Within five days, sixteen-mule trains or ox trains would be loaded with from 40,000 to 60,000 pounds and be on their way north. On April 21, 1870, the Diamond R shipped 20,000 pounds to Helena by one mule train. By the first week in May, a total of 250,000 pounds had been dispatched for Montana. Creighton and Munro sent out 214,414 pounds during the week ending May 14; and Garrison and Wyatt, ox team freighters for Kirkendall, moved out of Corinne with ten eight-yoke teams, each team pul-ling 12,000 pounds of freight—a total of 120,000 pounds. For the last week in May, E. G. Maclay shipped out 283,953 pounds of supplies while Creighton and Munro sent 278,596 pounds.[3]

The newspapers often described some of the trains carrying supplies to Helena in the summer of 1870. Two "immense" bull trains of the Diamond R were loading at "the freight palaces on the off side of the track. The crack of the bull whip swung by the accomplished 'skinners' resounds from every camp." The trip to Helena was expected to take thirty-two days. "The great train of Mr. Schodde" was also loading to take 110 tons, "the largest shipment ever made from here at one time." If tonnage were not enough to brag about, one could always cheer the speed of Mr. Wade's train, which made the round trip to Helena in thirty-one days. Much of the freight goods carried by these large outfits went to the northern army posts, with the government planning to send 3,000,000 pounds of military supplies via Corinne during

---

[2] *Helena Herald*, Jan. 18, Mar. 5, May 21, 28, 1870; *Utah Reporter*, Mar. 12, 1870.

[3] *Helena Herald*, Mar. 4, 1870; *Utah Reporter*, Apr. 26, May 5, 17, 24, June 3, 1870.

Owners of the Diamond R Freight Co. from left to right: C. A. Broadwater, Matt Carroll, E. G. Maclay, George Steele. *Courtesy of William D. Livingstone.*

that summer of 1870. An average of six carloads of freight a day were sidetracked at Corinne during the summer shipping months with western Montana as the destination. During May 1870, Corinne's warehouses received 2,172,820 pounds of goods from the Central Pacific.[4]

North from the Railroad in the 1870's

By late October the *Utah Reporter* was predicting that the freighting season for 1870 would end in about four weeks, when the winter storms on the Continental Divide would prohibit wagon travel. An unusually mild season, however, left the roads in excellent condition, which prompted some wagon masters to leave on the arduous month's trip as late as the middle of December, "notwithstanding the prospect of winter close at hand." This meant arriving in Helena in mid-January, an almost unheard of stroke of luck for both freighter and Montana merchant. The winter snowstorms did finally come. In April 1871 four trains of goods were stuck at Pleasant Valley until fifty men armed with shovels widened the sleigh track and opened the road to ground level.[5]

The most stupendous news of 1871 was the announcement by the Diamond R Overland Express and by Hugh Kirkendall's Montana Fast Freight and Express Line that the two fast freight companies would each start an unheard of eight-day service from the railroad to Helena or Deer Lodge with connections at Morier's Junction for Virginia City. The express would run with relays every few miles, just as the stage did; the wagons, each drawn by six mules, would travel day and night; express rates would not exceed $.10 per pound during April and May; and the trains would start north every other day. Kirkendall announced a purchase of twenty new wagons at $330 each for the service, which led the *Utah Reporter* to declare, "Hugh is about as much a benefit to Montana as a railroad would be." The Diamond R won

---

[4] *Helena Herald*, Sept. 1, 17, 1870; *Utah Reporter*, Apr. 2, June 5, 12, Aug. 16, 17, 27, Sept. 17, 1870.

[5] *Utah Reporter*, Oct. 17, 1870; *Helena Herald*, Dec. 15, 1870; *New North-*

the first express race to Helena, its wagons making the trip in the remarkable time of seven days.[6]

For about three months the two rival concerns vied for the profitable fast express business. In the week ending May 20, Kirkendall shipped 204,756 pounds of merchandise north and carried eighty-nine passengers, at $25 each, stowed in among the baggage. The excellent profits finally led the two concerns to reduce their cutthroat competition by consolidating on July 15 as the Diamond R Express Company, with E. G. Maclay as manager and Hugh Kirkendall as superintendent. Daily service was then inaugurated.[7]

The spring freighting for 1871 got under way by April 16, when the first Diamond R fast freight train left for Helena. The roads were still bad; two of Kirkendall's first freight wagons capsized on the Portneuf Canyon toll road. By mid-May, the Corinne newspaper was reporting 350 yoke of Diamond R oxen leaving for Montana in one day, Parkinson's train rolling out with 60,000 pounds, and the California and Montana Transportation Company of the firm of Creighton and Munro readying its wagon transports. Local newspapers began to publish fast times— a Diamond R mule train to the north in twenty-three days or an oxtrain of the same company in twenty-eight days. The Central Pacific Railroad reported a total tonnage of 3,065,486 pounds received at the station during April.[8]

The *Corinne Reporter* began to publish faithfully nearly all shipments north. A typical week's manifest for the Diamond R appeared on July 14, 1871 (see p. 205).

While the residents along the northern boundary of Utah shared in the profits of forwarding from Corinne, Ogden and Salt Lake City suffered a freighting depression. The *Salt Lake Tribune* complained that the railroads had ruined the profession of teamster. But visitors stopping over at Corinne found frequent opportunities to drive teams up north if they were "dead broke," as was Ebenezer Crouch when he landed there. He drove a four-

---

[6] *New Northwest*, Feb. 3, Apr. 7, 1871; *Helena Herald*, July 31, 1871; *Utah Reporter*, Mar. 10, Apr. 5, 22, 1871; *Corinne Reporter*, Apr. 29, 1870; *Montanian*, Apr. 20, May 4, Aug. 17, 1871.

[7] *Corinne Reporter*, May 6, 8, 20, July 15, 20, Dec. 6, 1871.

[8] Ibid., Apr. 8, 17, 22, 29, May 5, 6, 16, 1871; *Montanian*, June 1, 1871.

FREIGHT SHIPMENT.

Manifest of freight forwarded by the Diamond R Line during the week ending July 13, 1871:

	LBS.
By Hugh Kirkendall's mule train to Helena...........................	9,049
By Wells, Fargo & Co. to Norristown, Pennsylvania...................	60
S F Buford's train to Virginia City, M T............................	4,466
Wilson & Rich's train to Bozeman	19,061
W C Wright's train to Silver Bow	2,821
Diamon R Express to Helena........	9,297
Diamon R Express to Deer Lodge	14,084
Diamond R Express to Whitehall, Gaffney's, Watson's Station and Port Neuf Cañon.....................	1,372
Guinson & Wyatt's train No 1 to Helena............................	101,483
W Davidson's train to Deer Lodge	4,453
Hugh Kirkendall's train to Helena, Bezeman, etc......................	8,721
J H Neely's train to Va City........	8,000
Guinson & Wyatt's train No 2 to Helena............................	101,320
Diamond R Express to Helena......	6,769
J H Neely's train to Malad..........	979
do to Va City..........	1,940
R B Hill's train to Ross' Fork......	2,057
T Monroe's train to Deer Lodge.....	21,810
Diamond R Express to Missouli, Helena, Eagle Rock, etc............	8,968
C P R R for Far West Fast Feight Line	37,049

Grand total—364,274 pounds.

A listing of freight fowarded by the Diamond R that appeared in the *Corinne Reporter* on July 14, 1871. *Marriott Library, University of Utah.*

horse team and recorded that the road was lined with teams, "and some pretty rough outfits most of them were. Many of them negroes that had been freed from slavery and had come west and hired out to whack bulls.... When ... the team would get stuck in the mud there would surely be some cracking of whips and swearing." [9]

A severe snowstorm hit Helena on November 4, 1871. Only a few days before, Garrison & Wyatt had set out from Corinne with their last loads of the season to spend the winter at their homes in Helena. They were caught by the storm, along with many other trains. The Diamond R train No. 3 was abandoned at Pleasant Valley summit, the cattle being driven to Williams ranch twenty miles north. At Virginia City flour was $8 per hundred pounds and expected to rise soon to $10. By December 7, there were six ox trains snowbound between Malad and Pleasant Valley. The *Montanian* grumbled at "that rushing outfit," the Diamond R, "both slow and fast," which had not delivered printing paper to their newspaper office in Virginia City. In rebuttal, the *Utah Reporter*, smug in Utah where it was not 16° below zero, argued that the Diamond R and other big trains were doing their best to get through despite snowstorms "almost unparalleled in their severity," and asked for forbearance on the part of a not-too-often disappointed public. The fact that Maclay intended to continue his express service through the winter months at a sure loss was applauded by the editor because the service would provide an accommodation never before enjoyed during the winter season.[10]

The Union Pacific Railroad also came in for its share of criticism when avalanches and blockades halted service during the wintertime. When a huge amount of long-delayed freight arrived on May 2, the editor of the *Utah Reporter* could not refrain from commenting that "a road so miserably managed is liable to be out of running order any time." [11]

Soon, though, a reader of the *Corinne Reporter* could tell that spring was approaching by the number of advertisements

9 *Salt Lake Tribune*, June 28, 1871; BYUL, Ebenezer Crouch, "Autobiography of Ebenezer Crouch, Sept. 12, 1923," p. 53.
10 *Corinne Reporter*, Nov. 4, Dec. 2, 7, 13, 1871; *Montanian*, Nov. 23, 30, 1871.
11 *Corinne Reporter*, Jan. 4, May 3, 1872.

suddenly appearing announcing the readiness of the California and Montana Transportation Company and E. G. Maclay Company to forward any and all goods by the fastest ox teams to Montana points. The optimistic editorials also announced that freighting for 1872 would surely exceed the previous year's totals by at least a thousand tons.[12]

When Schodde's train with 200,000 pounds aboard pulled out on June 22, the *Corinne Reporter* thought that the amount of freight taken was hardly missed in the warehouse. A few weeks later, a Diamond R train with 60,000 pounds moved up the Malad Valley, the fifty-two mules in the team sparkling in their new harnesses.

After the second trip of the season, a wagon master might declare a two-week rest period for a "summer vacation." Sometimes a nearby town saloon beckoned, and after several drinks, a lack of restraint occasionally led to a gang fight. Before departing from Corinne, the summer freighters might be tempted to part with some of their profits for a new wagon from the "Central Market of the West." They could choose from among the finest makes: Shutler, Bain, Fish Brothers, or they could order a home-made wagon from Pat O'Neil, Osborn & Johnson, or G. A. Bruce.[13]

Mid-August saw the trains coming back from the north for their third trip of the season to Montana, and among them were the Helena to Fort Benton freighters now that the Missouri River steamboat traffic had ended for the year. The end of September saw a decrease in the arrival of Montana freight via the Union Pacific, and within two weeks the Mormon and other "irregular" freighters began to unload their last southbound cargoes in Corinne.[14]

The late fall of 1872 was as dry as the previous autumn had been blizzardy and cold. The Diamond R warehouse was closed for the season on December 10, although some wagon trains continued to leave for the north. But by December 19, the *Montanian* announced that no train of importance was en route for Virginia City. Mules and oxen were being turned out on the

[12] Ibid., Feb. 13, Mar. 14, 1872.
[13] Ibid., May 23, June 22, July 12, Aug. 22, 26, Sept. 2, 1872.
[14] Ibid., Aug. 19, 24, Sept. 27, 1872; *Helena Herald*, Oct. 31, 1872.

winter ranges, and the only cloud to darken the freighter's horizon was the rumor that the epizootic again was rampant on the Pacific Coast and was rapidly spreading inland.[15]

Winter was the season for negotiating contracts, and when Hugh Kirkendall won the contract in mid-February to furnish the Blackfoot Indian Agency with its annual supplies, as a "rustling Indian feeder," he prepared his teams and wagons to complete the agreement "before the 'epizoo' has time to reach as far north as Helena." The following month the news came that E. G. Maclay & Co. had been awarded the contract "for military transportation pertaining to the route to Montana," having bid $1.02 per 100 pounds per 100 miles, just one cent under Garrison & Wyatt's proposal. The high freight rates brought more demands for a railroad from Corinne to Helena, as the San Francisco *Alta Californian* joined the chorus with the information that the 1872 freight costs for the merchandise transported over the Montana wagon road had exceeded $2 million.[16]

During four years of experience in hauling supplies from the railroad to Montana, E. G. Maclay, under the insignia of the Diamond R, had organized the largest freighting outfit on the road by 1873, with over 600 head of mules and at least 100 wagons. In 1873, there were probably about 600 other freighters, large and small, engaged in trade to Montana. Many local Utah men hired out to the Diamond R at $1.00 to $1.50 a day to drive nine yoke of oxen or ten or more mules hitched to three wagons. The Diamond R kept field notes of its expenses, one account reporting such diverse charges as $32.50 at the Portneuf Canyon Toll Gate for 16 wagons and 33 span of mules, $.50 for repairing a wagon brake, and $1,107.48 for blacksmith work in Corinne.[17]

Hazards on the Trail

Problems on a freighting trip could slow a train down, as confirmed by William Woodward of Logan, Utah, who kept a

---

    [15] *Helena Herald*, Nov. 14, 1872; *Corinne Reporter*, Dec. 13, 1872.

    [16] *Helena Herald*, Feb. 13, Mar. 17, 1873; *Corinne Reporter*, Mar. 18, 1873; BL, "Bancroft Scraps, Montana Miscellany," vol. 90, p. 13.

    [17] Joel E. Ricks, ed., *The History of a Valley: Cache Valley, Utah–Idaho*, p. 184; USHS, J. W. Kennington, "Freighting in Cache Valley," p. 2; MSHS, "Diamond R Papers," pp. 9, 48, 61.

diary of his trip north. He left Corinne with five loaded wagons on October 1, 1873, traveling about 15 miles the first day. The next day he and his crew spent all morning looking for stray animals, but still made 14 miles. After a night of rain, they only made 9 miles over the heavy roads. On the tenth and eleventh, the animals strayed off again; then heavy snow fell on the thirteenth and fourteenth forcing the train to "lay over" for two days. Later, after heavy going through the sand past Sand Hole and Camas Creek, the five wagons started up Beaver Canyon and an axle broke. Woodward replaced it using tools borrowed from Mr. Harkness at the Toll Gate. After passing Pleasant Valley, Pine Buttes, Junction, and Sage Creek, the train came to a very steep hill that was so slick from new-fallen snow that the teamsters had to unload part of the goods and then go back downhill to retrieve them. They only made half a mile that day; and the next day they broke another axle, which Woodward replaced with one purchased from a neighboring Garrison & Wyatt train. Just beyond White Tail Deer Creek, one of Woodward's mules "got scared & run around an an axel-tree broke." This time he borrowed an axle from a young man at a ranch. On Monday, November 10, Woodward unloaded at Helena. The next day he was able to secure several passengers for Corinne and started south. Beyond Point of Rocks he camped at a place "some of the people called Land of promise. No wood nor feed." Two days later he discovered that one of the passengers had lost a prized whip, so he traveled back 3½ miles to retrieve it. Woodward arrived at Corinne on November 27, having made the trip north in 38 days and the trip south in 18 days.[18]

Goods Going West and Return Cargoes

Throughout the first five years after the driving of the Golden Spike at Promontory, Utah, Union Pacific shipments to Montana via Corinne remained fairly constant—between 6 and 7 million pounds of goods annually. In 1872, 7,501,280 pounds passed through the town destined north.[19]

---

[18] USHS. William Woodward, "Journals, Diaries, Notes, Account Books, Letters, Essays, Plats, 1851-1901."

[19] U.S. Congress, "Report on Reconnaisance of Northwestern Wyoming, 1873," *House Exec. Doc. 285,* p. 57.

Rates charged by freighters varied considerably depending on the season, the condition of the roads, and the availability of wagon trains. During the winter, freight charges usually stayed around $.10 per 100 pounds, although the winter of 1870 saw rates go up to $.19 a pound. By late spring and summer, charges might drop anywhere from $.03 to $.05. The average rate hovered near $.04½. Creighton and Munro charged the army $.07½ for goods to Fort Shaw and $.06½ to Helena in October 1869 and $.10½ per 100 miles in 1873. A Diamond R waybill for June 3, 1873, listed the following rates for bull train No. 2: to Blackfoot, Idaho, $2.00 per 100 pounds; to Bozeman, $5.00; to Missoula, $3.75; to Deer Lodge, $4.12; and to Fort Ellis, $4.50.[20]

A sample of the great variety of merchandise sent to Montana could be found in one *Corinne Reporter* article of April 27, 1871; "eighty horse power engine, the blacksmith's shop complete, vehicles of all descriptions, . . . great piles of clothing and dry goods; mowers, reapers, shovels, brooms, matting, carpets, hardware, spices, fruit, varnish, veneers, and every conceivable article of trade or manufacture."

Cargoes of Montana merchandise for the return trip to Corinne were not easy to obtain during the first two or three years after 1869. Occasionally a wagon train could pick up 30,000 pounds or so of wool to carry south, but hides and furs were more abundant. Of increasing importance was the rich ore that soon became a common return cargo. Twenty tons of valuable "silver rock" were shipped in December 1869 via Corinne to reduction works in Newark, New Jersey, and Swansea, Wales. It was estimated to be worth $10,000 per ton, which made it possible to pay the mining and shipping costs and still return a profit.[21]

---

[20] *Montana Post*, Jan. 1, 1869; *Helena Herald*, March 27, May 8, 1873; Daughters of Utah Pioneers, Box Elder County, *History of Box Elder County*, p. 34; BL, "Bancroft Scraps, Montana Miscellany," vol. 90; Charles Bovey Collection, Fairweather Hotel, Virginia City, Mont., California Fast Freight Line Way Bill, July 19, 1870; "Overland Diamond R Freight Line Papers," Way Bill, Nov. 8, 1872, in the possession of Lewis Brackman, Helena, Mont.; Henry P. Walker, *The Wagonmasters*, p. 220; U.S. Congress, "Report of Secretary of War for 1870," *House Exec. Doc. 1*, p. 260; MSHS, "Diamond R Papers," Way Bill From Corinne to Ellis and Deer Lodge.

[21] John F. Bishop, "Beginning of the Montana Sheep Industry," *The Montana Magazine of History*, vol. 1, (Apr. 1951), p. 8; *Corinne Reporter*, Dec. 16, 1869, Oct. 11, 1871.

Bill of lading for a shipment made by the Diamond R from Helena to Fort Shaw, Montana, in 1878. *Courtesy of Lewis O. Brackman.*

Even in later years, tens of thousands of tons of less rich ores remained in the mining districts because there were no reduction facilities. Corinne entrepreneurs attempted to meet this need by constructing the Alger Reduction Works, which was apparently never successful in attracting Montana ores. With the great copper discoveries at Butte, some of this mineral began to travel south by freight wagon for shipment east. In the decade of the 1870's, increasing amounts of Montana ores were carried to Corinne, making the round trip even more profitable.[22]

The mines of southeastern and central Idaho were not as many nor as wealthy as those of Montana, but periodic discoveries and rushes kept ox and mule trains going to the Salmon River and other new diggings. The big news in Idaho in this period, however, was the discovery of gold in the Caribou Mountains north of Soda Springs, near Gray's Lake. The rush started in the spring of 1871 and was in full swing by the next year. Of greater importance to the Central and Union Pacific railroads were Boise and its surrounding areas, which probably imported 8,000 to 12,000 tons of goods annually.[23]

With completion of the transcontinental railroad, it became only a matter of time before branch lines began to threaten the wagon freighters' monopoly of the Montana Trail. Winter storms, the hazards of trail freighting, increasing demand, and high freight rates were continuing issues demanding better means of transportation for goods. In the early 1870's Corinne's preeminence as a freight forwarding center was seldom actually threatened, although rumors of proposed branch railroads made entrepreneurs fearful for its continuing domination of the Montana trade. Mormon plans for a railway from Salt Lake City to the settlements in Cache Valley and Bear Lake Valley soon became a reality and ultimately heralded the end of Corinne as a major shipping point north.

---

[22] *Corinne Reporter*, Apr. 24, May 18, 1871; James M. Hamilton, *From Wilderness to Statehood*, p. 267.
[23] *Corinne Reporter*, July 22, 1871; *Idaho Statesman*, Dec. 19, 1871.

11

Threat of the Narrow Gauge

When the Union Pacific chose to route its line north of the Great Salt Lake, Salt Lake City was left in splendid isolation forty miles to the south. Brigham Young determined to correct the omission as soon as possible by building his own railroad to Ogden to connect with the transcontinental line. Only seven days after the Golden Spike was driven, another ceremony was held by the Mormon prophet and his aides—a groundbreaking ritual to inaugurate construction of the Utah Central Railroad. By November, the road reached from Ogden to Kaysville, with Mormon workers cheerfully contributing their teams and time without thought of pay. The *Salt Lake Telegraph* pointed out on November 14, 1869, one pleasant feature of this different type of railroad building: John W. Young, son of Brigham Young and superintendent of construction, told the men he wanted track laid into Salt Lake City "without the name of Deity being once taken in vain." [1]

The Utah Central Railroad was completed on January 10, 1870. The round-trip fare from Brigham City was only $3.50, and the Mormon people rejoiced, despite the sarcasm of the Corinne newspaper in always referring to the U.C.R.R. as the "Un Certain R.R." [2]

The Utah Northern Railroad

Now that the Mormons had built one railroad, why not build another to offer service to their brethren living in Cache Valley and Soda Springs? And what about the profits to be made from extending the road beyond Bear Lake into Montana? As early as

---

[1] *Deseret News*, May 19, 1869.
[2] *Deseret News*, Apr. 20, 1869, Jan. 26, 1870; *Utah Reporter*, Jan. 15, 1870.

August 23, 1871, rumors were circulating at Ogden that a roadbed was to be built to Soda Springs via Cache Valley, with the grading to be finished by winter as far as Franklin, Idaho. It was announced that John W. Young was to be president of the new company, which was to be known as the Utah Northern Railroad. Eastern capitalists had agreed to furnish rails and rolling stock for a narrow-gauge line if local residents would prepare the roadbed and furnish ties. The promoters explained that the chief advantages of a narrow-gauge over a standard-gauge track were a one-third saving in construction and operation costs and a greater adaptability to mountainous terrain. The minimum radius of curvature on a standard-gauge was 955 feet; on a narrow-gauge it was 220 feet. The farmers of Cache Valley and the residents of Ogden agreed to furnish labor to build their sections of the road in return for stock in the company. Tracks were to start from a connection with the Central Pacific Railroad at Willard, Utah, the people of Weber County agreeing to extend the narrow-gauge from Willard south to Ogden.[3]

In Boise, it was the general conviction that the Union Pacific Railroad was behind proposals for the new Utah Northern Railroad since the Central Pacific Railroad operated the depots at Corinne and at Kelton, Idaho. A branch road from Ogden would be able to control the Montana trade and bypass these two Central Pacific freight stations. The projected terminus at Soda Springs was considered to be merely a blind until the Union Pacific could gather the resources to leap the Snake River plains and reach the Beaverhead Valley.[4]

At Corinne, the editor of the local paper started what eventually became a continuous sarcastic campaign against this threat to the existence of the town. He pointed out the additional costs to shippers of transferring goods from standard-gauge to narrow-gauge cars at Willard. The Mormon people at Brigham City and Cache Valley paid little heed and pushed ahead with the grading until December 6, 1871, when a blizzard curtailed work until spring.[5]

---

[3] *Ogden Junction*, Aug. 23, Sept. 13, 20, 1871; *Salt Lake Tribune*, Sept. 2, 6, 1871; Merrill D. Beal, *Intermountain Railroads: Standard and Narrow Gauge*, pp. 4, 8; *Deseret News*, Sept. 27, 1871.

[4] *Idaho Statesman*, Sept. 23, 1871.

[5] *Corinne Reporter*, Sept. 6, Nov. 15, 1871; *Deseret News*, Dec. 6, 1871, Jan. 10, 1872.

Fighting the Narrow-Gauge Threat

To counter the threat of a narrow-gauge line through Cache Valley, a meeting was held on March 29, 1872, in Corinne to plan construction of a broad-gauge line north to Helena. Within ten minutes, $17,000 was pledged to establish the Utah, Idaho, and Montana Railroad. The seven-man board of directors included General Patrick Edward Connor, John Tiernan, Fox Diefendorf, James Campbell, Oscar D. Cass, John W. Graham, and O. J. Hollister—all of Corinne. Hollister was sent to Washington, D.C., to obtain a charter for a right-of-way across the public lands to Helena, which was granted on May 28. This magnificent turn of events seemed to indicate that Corinne would remain the distributing point to the north "for many generations to come." On June 17, a groundbreaking ceremony was held for the Utah, Idaho, and Montana Railroad. A survey party finally completed its work by August 31, but only a few miles of grading were ever finished. The *Corinne Reporter* failed to generate interest in the road even when it reminded readers on November 11, 1872, that the Utah, Idaho, and Montana Railroad was their only "anchor" because it looked as though the Utah Northern would soon reach Logan, resulting in an " 'untimely cutting off' of our trade, for the Young family are determined to leave us out in the cold." [6]

Branch Lines

By June 13, 1872, the *Deseret News* was advertising that two trains a day would run from the Central Pacific junction at Willard to Hampton's Bear River Crossing. The citizens of Ogden finally realized that all the transfer business to the Utah Northern was taking place at Willard. In late October 1872 a meeting was held and bids were let to construct the roadbed connecting Ogden and Willard. Beyond Hampton's Bear River Crossing, crews ran into a major obstacle at the eighty-two-foot-wide gap at Cottonwood Hollow, but the hollow was finally filled. Crossing the Mendon Divide toward Logan also meant much team and pick and shovel

---

[6] *Corinne Reporter*, Mar. 29, Apr. 17, May 28, 29, June 1, 1872; Clarence A. Reeder, Jr., "The History of Utah's Railroads, 1869–1883," Ph.D. diss., University of Utah, 1970, pp. 225–26.

labor. When Christmas came, Logan was still without a railroad connection. Despite the snow and cold, the Cache Valley farmers kept at their task, and the railroad was extended to Logan on February 3, 1873. Celebration of completion of the line was postponed, however, due to bad weather. By dint of much shovel work, Cache citizens managed to keep the road open for a few days between storms.[7]

To insure that Central Pacific freight would be shipped north from Corinne via the Utah Northern Railroad, leading citizens of Corinne and managers of the Utah Northern agreed to build a branch line from Brigham City by July 1, 1873. The Utah Northern agreed to run its trains to Corinne only until the road from Willard to Ogden was completed and only as long as it was profitable. It was further agreed that the junction with the Central Pacific at Corinne would not be moved anywhere except to Ogden. The last spike for the line was driven on June 11, after which the participants at the ceremony "then directed their attention and energies toward a half dozen kegs of beer which were thoughtfully prepared for the occasion." The Utah Northern purchased a large warehouse in Corinne for the Diamond R to provide storage for freight to Montana on the new line.[8]

At this time, Salt Lake train passengers to the north had to take the Utah Central to Ogden, the Central Pacific to Corinne, and, finally, the Utah Northern to Brigham City and Logan. Completion of the Utah Northern segment between Ogden and Brigham City would eliminate one change of cars and the trip to Corinne. On February 5, 1874, the last rail was laid and the Utah Northern was complete from Ogden to beyond Logan.[9]

Pushing the Railroad North

Progress in building a roadbed and laying track to Franklin, Idaho, did not meet expectations of Utah Northern promot-

---

[7] *Deseret News*, Apr. 3, May 29, June 13, 26, Sept. 26, Oct. 30, Dec. 4, 1872, Feb. 12, 1873; M. Beal, *Intermountain Railroads*, p. 13; Reeder, "History of Utah's Railroads," pp. 228–29.

[8] *Corinne Reporter*, Jan. 17, 23, Apr. 21, June 11, 1873.

[9] *Deseret News*, Oct. 1, 1873, Feb. 11, 1874; Reeder, "A History of Utah's Railroads," pp. 231–33.

ers in 1873. By November 17, the road had only reached Smith-field, Utah, before winter snows and zero weather stopped con-struction.

Completion of the Utah Northern as far north as Logan sig-naled the end of Corinne's domination of the Montana trade. Henceforth, Logan—and later Franklin—would offer competi-tion for the forwarding business to Helena and other Montana cities. Zion's Cooperative Mercantile Institution of Salt Lake City established a branch at Logan in May 1874, which led the anti-Mormon newspaper, the *Salt Lake Tribune*, to warn that the "brethren are plotting against the business prosperity of Co-rinne." And the Diamond R, largest shipper of goods north, had already moved its headquarters to Logan and directed several of its mule and bull trains there to pick up freight for Montana. Wells Fargo set up an express office in Logan announcing that freight would be forwarded to Salt Lake City at the rate of $2 per 100 pounds.[10]

Teamsters estimated that about eight days per round trip were saved by hauling to Montana from Logan, in addition to eliminating the necessity of crossing the Malad Divide. But A. B. Knight of Virginia City still thought "the Narrow *Gauge* a fraud." [11] When the first heavy snowstorm hit, the tiny train became embedded in snow at Cottonwood Hollow, and it looked to many as though the railroad would be worthless during the winter season.

As soon as possible in April, John W. Young and Moses Thatcher had teams and men at work grading through northern Cache Valley. Laying a mile of track a day, they reached Frank-lin on May 2, 1874; and two days later regular freight and pas-senger service began from Ogden to the Idaho border. Soon the Diamond R shifted its headquarters from Logan to Franklin, and firms from Corinne moved their warehouses to the new terminus. A postal car system was established to carry the Montana mail to Franklin for forwarding north.[12]

---

[10] *Salt Lake Tribune*, May 10, 1873; *Corinne Reporter*, May 12, July 7, 1873; *Deseret News*, June 25, 1873.

[11] Charles Bovey, Collection, Virginia City, Mont., letter from A. B. Knight, Corinne, July 3, 1873.

[12] *Deseret News*, Dec. 17, 1873, Mar. 4, 18, Apr. 22, 29, May 6, June 3, July 22, 1874; *Montanian*, July 23, 1874; Reeder, "History of Utah's Railroads," p. 235.

The people of Montana spent much of their winter speculating on railroad matters. The *Omaha Herald* persisted in believing that Montana would soon be "out of the wilderness" by "the aid of those dreadful Mormons" and their Utah Northern Railroad. Another flurry of speculation came from talk of a Corinne-to-Oregon railway. The Oregon legislature had considered a subsidy bill for a narrow-gauge Portland–Dalles–Salt Lake Railroad, to connect with the Utah Northern somewhere on the Snake River.[13]

Conjecture about new railroad lines left most people unmoved, but talk about pushing the Utah Northern farther toward Montana seemed quite believable in light of the Mormon success so far. When George S. Kennedy of the firm of Creighton and Company of Franklin wrote from New York that Joseph Richardson, general manager of the Utah Northern Railroad and a member of the Union Pacific board of directors, would be in Helena in June to discuss further construction prospects, Utahns and Montanans alike were ready to believe that the Union Pacific was preparing to invest a substantial sum in the narrow-gauge company. But by September, news came that Richardson would not consider extending the Utah Northern without financial aid from Montana Territory.[14]

Nearly every city of any size in Montana had held a railroad meeting or talked of holding one during the winter of 1874–75. Bozeman residents appointed a committee to pursue the subject; business leaders convened in Deer Lodge and proposed a narrow-gauge line connecting to Utah; and Jefferson County residents adopted a resolution for the forthcoming Territorial Convention asking for a north-south road. Utah Northern supporters kept urging aid for their line. The chief obstacle to support of the Utah Northern was that it was a local corporation whose "expenses consume all the receipts." [15]

Finally, in February of 1876, the Montana Legislature passed a bill subsidizing the Northern Pacific Railroad for $3,000,000 in bonds and the Utah Northern for $1,500,000 in bonds. Utah

---

[13] *Deseret News*, Mar. 11, June 24, Oct. 22, Dec. 9, 1874.
[14] *Montanian*, Sept. 3, 1874; *Deseret News*, Apr. 22, Sept. 23, 1874.
[15] *Deseret News*, Mar 17, 1875; *Corinne Daily Mail*, Apr. 1, 1875; *Montanian*, June 3, 1875.

Northern officials refused the proffered grant chiefly because they had to complete 200 miles of track to reach the Montana border before any money would be paid.[16]

In February of 1877, the Montana Territorial Legislature made another attempt to interest the Utah Northern when Governor Potts approved a bill offering the railroad $1,700,000 in bonds at a rate of 7 3/10 percent interest, payable annually. The road was to be built from Franklin to the Big Hole River, a distance of 300 miles, and for every 20 miles completed a pro rata portion of the bonds was to be delivered at $5,000 per mile. Utah Northern owners again rejected the offer because a stipulation in the bill required payment to Montana of a small percentage of the profits of the railroad.[17]

The Union Pacific Takes Over

After the death of Brigham Young, the Union Pacific promoters were able to purchase Mormon church stock in the narrow-gauge company. Jay Gould and Sidney Dillon quietly bought up $80,000 worth of Utah Northern shares from Utah stockholders at $.10 on the dollar and bonds and stock from Joseph Richardson worth $400,000. Through some complex transactions, eventually Sidney Dillon, who was also president of the Union Pacific, and Benjamin Richardson gained control of the Utah Northern stock. With Dillon's purchase, there was no longer any doubt that the new Utah Northern was a wholly-owned subsidiary of the Union Pacific. By means of a complicated set of legal and financial maneuvers, the old Utah Northern was sold on April 3, 1878, to the Union Pacific for $100,000, which created a new railroad corporation without bonded debt.[18]

While the New York financiers planned behind closed doors, residents of Utah and Montana looked in vain for some sign of construction activity on the narrow-gauge line. Interest was

---

[16] *Deseret News*, Feb. 23, Apr. 12, 1876.

[17] Ibid., Feb. 14, 28, March 7, 1877; Reeder, "History of Utah's Railroads," pp. 242-43.

[18] Reeder, "History of Utah's Railroads," pp. 243-46; Robert G. Athearn, "Utah and Northern Railroad," *Montana Western History*, vol. 23 (Oct., 1968), pp. 2-23.

Utah and Northern Railroad in Beaver Canyon, Idaho, 1884. *Utah State Historical Society, Salt Lake City.*

aroused in June of 1877 when word came that two surveying parties were being sent out to determine which of two routes— from Corinne or from Evanston, Wyoming—was the better way to Montana. In early October, Utah and Montana were electrified by the appearance in Salt Lake City of the entire Union Pacific board of directors, who took a tour of the line, towed by the "vigorous little engine [which] like a bantam rooster crowed merrily to the morn, and ran along the three-foot track." The directors decided to reroute the road through Bear River Canyon, eliminating the hazards of the Cache Valley Divide, and with that exception, gave their approval to the line as far as it had been constructed. Work on the long-awaited extension from Franklin north began in October 1877. By November 28, it was completed 20 miles beyond Franklin.[19]

The Corinne and Franklin Rivalry

With removal of the Diamond R headquarters, first to Logan and then Franklin, and relocation of J. A. Creighton & Company to Franklin at the new track terminus, Fred J. Kiesel and Company became the chief forwarding agents in Corinne. Demonstrating his faith in the future of Corinne, Kiesel built a large new warehouse. Kiesel had had a bitter experience with Mormon competition previously in the Bear Lake area, being driven out by "the intolerance of the Mormons." Kiesel claimed his clerk had been killed by Mormons, and the Mormons in turn attributed the clerk's death to Indians. "I would have trusted myself with the Indians in those days quicker than with the Mormons," said Kiesel.[20]

In 1874, with Franklin threatening as a rival, Corinne still surged with business. The *Salt Lake Tribune* of July 28, 1874, gave credit for this to the J. A. Creighton & Company agent in Franklin, George Kennedy, who was interested in selling Studebaker wagons to Franklin freighters at $300 a piece and was refusing to load any wagons at all until one of his models had

---

[19] *Deseret News*, July 25, Oct. 10, Nov. 28, 1877; Reeder, "History of Utah's Railroads," p. 247; *Helena Herald*, June 14, 1877.

[20] *Helena Herald*, Mar. 19, June 5, 1874; MLUU, "The Bancroft Collection of Mormon Papers," Fred Kiesel, reel 20, p. 54.

Bill of lading for the Diamond R. *Courtesy of Lewis O. Brackman.*

Note the charge for advancing goods from the railroad on the bill of lading from Fred J. Kiesel & Co. *Courtesy of Lewis O. Brackman.*

been purchased. He paid his teamsters such low wages in Franklin that they left in great numbers for Corinne, where they could obtain better profits.[21]

Kennedy was finally driven to solicit Malad teamsters "with large inducements," to leave their old route and move to Franklin. The *Corinne Mail* of October 20, 1874, noted that "some merchants declare they lost thousands of dollars on a single shipment by the change from Corinne to Franklin, . . . and every freighter who pulled out of Franklin has been disgusted and condemns the road. All would freight from Corinne at less rates, and as a natural consequence Corinne is itself again." With an average of about three-fourths of the freight loading for Montana still originating at Corinne, by year's end "the Franklin route [was]... scarcely thought of." [22]

However, on October 1, 1874, the *Montanian* complained that many of the middlemen in Corinne raised freight rates above the contract price when goods reached their depots. Montana merchants could not afford to wait and debate the legalities of these increases. If a Montana businessman complained, he was informed he could sue someone in Omaha or Pittsburg to obtain redress. But the need for goods was so great, few murmurs were heard.

Early in the fall of 1874, there were about 500 tons of goods stored in Corinne warehouses awaiting shipment north, and about 20 tons in railroad cars. During September, Corinne received 1,454,275 pounds of freight; in October 1,953,034 pounds. It was estimated that Kiesel and Company shipped 2,500 tons of goods to Idaho and Montana during the last five months of the year.[23]

Staples continued to make up the bulk of goods, but there were some changes in commodities—from canned goods and whiskey in the early years to a more varied assortment of articles including sewing machines and threshing machines. Salt from the Oneida Salt Works in Idaho became increasingly

---

[21] *Salt Lake Tribune*, July 28, Sept. 12, 1874.
[22] Ibid., Oct. 3, 1874; *Corinne Daily Mail*, Oct. 6, 20, Nov. 15, 18, Dec. 21, 1874.
[23] *Corinne Daily Mail*, Sept. 12, Oct. 22, Nov. 9, Dec. 17, 1874; *Montanian*, Dec. 17, 1874.

important for smelters and refineries reducing ores. And Utah fruits and vegetables continued to provide a welcome change in the Montana diet, with such delicacies as apples and onions selling "like hot cakes on a frosty morning." Return cargoes from Montana consisted mostly of rich ores destined for eastern smelters.[24]

In the spring of 1875, Kiesel and Company added an extension to its warehouse, and the forwarding firm of McCormick and Hardenbrook was completing a huge new warehouse. The first train of the season left Corinne on April 29. Blockades on the Union Pacific caused delays for about 1,000 cars of freight destined for Corinne, and a number of large freighting outfits were forced to camp at Corinne until mid-May, when railroad service was restored.[25]

George Kennedy was still trying to attract teamsters to his depot at Franklin, but without much success. One reason may have been the location—the depot lay in an alkali flat. When it rained, it took Alva Noyes and his crews nine days to get their three wagons one-half mile from the station to firm ground. Some freighters did travel to Franklin to determine if there were goods waiting to go north, but were disappointed. Levan and Brown reported only about twenty tons waiting, and Dan Hill and Alex Harris waited almost four weeks for freight before giving up in disgust and heading for Corinne—where they loaded immediately.[26]

In 1875, the amount of freight being transferred from railroad cars to freighters' wagons in Corinne was greater than ever before, and again Franklin presented no competition. While statistics in the *Montanian* demonstrated that freighters from Franklin could make the trip to Virginia City in less time, Corinne was still the preferred freight depot for most teamsters. By late August, 100,000 pounds a day were being delivered by

[24] ISUA, Leonidas A. Meacham, "Interviewed by John F. Ryan, 1936"; Barzilla W. Clark, *Bonneville County in the Making*, pp. 53–54; *Montanian*, Oct. 1, 1874; *Helena Herald*, Sept. 10, 1874.

[25] *Corinne Daily Mail*, Feb. 5, Mar. 15, 26, Apr. 20, May 1, 10, 1875; *Helena Herald*, May 20, 1875.

[26] Alva J. Noyes, *The Story of Ajax: Life in the Bighole Basin*, pp. 19–20; *Corinne Daily Mail*, June 12, July 29, Sept. 2, 3, 7, 1875.

the railroad to Corinne, and the week ending August 25 saw 370,000 pounds of goods leaving for Montana. By September, Corinne was shipping nearly 500,000 pounds a week.[27]

In 1876, wagon transport from Corinne exceeded all previous years. At year's end, Kiesel and Company had shipped 10 million pounds of goods north and McCormick and Hardenbrook had shipped 4 million pounds—a total of 7,000 tons. During 1876, Butte sent 1,000 tons of ore south valued at $150,000 at a cost of $35,000 in freight charges.[28]

About 150 wagons were camping near Corinne in April of 1877, waiting to be joined by other large trains on their way from winter stations in Montana. Tons of coarse salt from plants on the Great Salt Lake were hauled north to various smelters in Montana for use in ore refining, emphasizing the rapid development of mining processes. This soon resulted in shipments of stamp mills to the various mining towns of Montana and Idaho. The freighting firm of Thomas & Caldwell moved one mill weighing 104,254 pounds to Gerson Canyon, Idaho. Walker Brothers of Salt Lake City hired Nels Bennett to move their mill from East Canyon in Utah to Walkerville, near Butte. By late November, Joseph W. Walker wrote to his wife that "the mill is a great success, fourteen bars already shipped amounting to $40,000.00 & two more ready to ship." Mining magnates who did not own stamp mills still had to rely on wagons to get their ores to refineries. In one week, ending August 5, 1877, for example, 112,000 pounds of ore reached Corinne from Butte.[29]

The Indian War of 1877

In August of 1877 wagon traffic was halted by an Indian war for the first time since the discovery of gold in 1862. As the Nez Percé, under Chief Joseph, fled eastward before General O.

---

[27] *Montanian*, June 10, 24, Aug. 26, Sept. 16, 1875; *New Northwest*, Sept. 3, 1875; *Corinne Daily Mail*, Aug. 25, Sept. 22, 1875.

[28] *Ogden Freeman*, Nov. 28, 1876; *Helena Herald*, Dec. 7, 1876.

[29] *Salt Lake Tribune*, Apr. 13, 1877; *Ogden Freeman*, Apr. 17, June 19, 1877; MLUU "Walker Family Correspondence," letter to his wife, Salt Lake City, Utah, from Alice Gold and Silver Mining Company, Walkerville, Mont., Nov. 27, 1877; *Helena Herald*, Aug. 5, 1877.

O. Howard's pursuing troops, their flight took them across the Montana Trail, where they encountered a wagon train carrying, among other things, ten barrels of whiskey. They opened the whiskey and then "things got out of hand." The rampaging warriors burned the wagons and killed three drivers and two passengers.[30]

The attack immediately reduced freight traffic north of Eagle Rock. An *Idaho Statesman* correspondent said on September 1, 1877, that he "found the freighters and ranchmen along the Montana stage road in a very demoralized condition." They left their wagons and valuable freight and took their stock to places of safety. The Indian troubles interrupted freighting for a few weeks at the height of the season, and many deliveries were delayed until hostilities quieted in December.

During the year Corinne paid little attention to the threat of the Utah Northern Railroad building beyond their weak rival, Franklin. But when news arrived in October that the Union Pacific had purchased the Utah Northern and was building road beyond Franklin, the *Salt Lake Tribune* said of Corinne on January 1, 1878, that "the shipping season . . . is closed, and perhaps forever." [31]

Improved national economic conditions and the rapid growth of a market for consumer goods in western Montana led officers of the Union Pacific to consider extending the narrow-gauge through the wastelands of Idaho to the golden profits of Montana. At the end of 1877, eastern corporate action was making a dramatic change in travel on the Montana Trail.

---

[30] U.S. Congress, "Report on Agreement with Indians in Idaho, Feb. 3, 1874," *House Exec. Doc. 129*, p. 3; Mark H. Brown, *Flight of the Nez Percé*, pp. 25, 282, 284–85; *Idaho Statesman*, Aug. 18, 23, Sept. 1, 1877; *Helena Herald*, Aug. 19, 23, 30, 1877; *Salt Lake Tribune*, Aug. 21, 24, 1877; *Deseret News*, Aug. 29, 1877.

[31] *Ogden Freeman*, Oct. 26, 1877; *Helena Herald*, June 28, 1877; Jesse H. Jameson, "Corinne: A Study of a Freight Transfer Point in the Montana Trade, 1869–1878," M.A. thesis, University of Utah, 1951, pp. 108–89.

12

Hanging Up the Reins

Many people were still skeptical after reorganization of the Utah and Northern Railway by the Union Pacific directors in the autumn of 1877. For four years they had listened to optimistic reports of the road's being pushed to Marsh Valley, to the Snake River, or even to Monida Pass, with little result. Railway equipment during these years was of "the most primitive character . . . and the laughing stock" of the patrons. Oxteams traveling parallel with the road to Corinne competed with the railroad "both in price and time." When construction began anew in late 1877, few took the word seriously, and the "bull teams continued to wend their way towards Corinne as of old." [1]

The Utah and Northern Reaches Blackfoot

But the spring of 1878 brought much railroad activity. Under the supervision of Washington Dunn, a veteran Union Pacific engineer, Mormon graders quickly extended the line across the Bear River to Dunnville in Round Valley (present Banida), twenty miles beyond Franklin. The Union Pacific officials were determined to improve their recently acquired road, and a broader grade was built, longer ties laid, and heavier track iron installed. Cache Valley farmers flocked to the construction area, where a man and a team could earn between $1.75 and $2.50 a day—and not in scrip either, but in hard U. P. cash. Dunnville, reached in April, became the first construction terminus on the extension to Montana and set the tone for all the other camps.

---

[1] MSHS, "Historical Resume," in *Holiday Supplement to Dillon Tribune, 1883-1884.* Clip file, pp. 2-4; Merrill D. Beal, *Intermountain Railroads: Standard and Narrow Gauge*, p. 50.

Dunn had several "mail order" houses built in the East, and his crews bolted the sections together. They were flimsy affairs made of thin lumber with cloth partitions. Like other railroad construction towns, there were "many saloons, dance halls, gambling hells, and wild women" at Dunnville, but the God-fearing Mormons, who composed the majority of the work crews, created a different kind of atmosphere than the other "hell-on-wheels" camps of the Union Pacific.[2]

The Corinne forwarding house of Kiesel and Company, several wagon firms, and other businesses moved to Dunnville. W. C. Lewis moved his hotel from Franklin; Wells, Fargo & Co. established an express office; and Gilmer & Salisbury set up their stage office. Everyone recognized the temporary nature of the town, since construction crews were rapidly laying half a mile of track a day down Marsh Valley.[3]

On June 28, Watson's stage station was reached and a town called Oneida immediately sprang into being. It was located about a mile south of the stage station, just west of present Arimo, Idaho. A visitor described the camp in the *Ogden Freeman* of June 28, 1878, as "already better than Dunnville was at any time." By July 2 there were about forty families living in Oneida and six stores, three hotels, five saloons, and two billiard halls.[4] By September the population had jumped to 250. A correspondent to the *Salt Lake Tribune* described Oneida as a town on wheels made up of sign boards from Corinne and even portions of that town itself. There were no churches, although most residents attended "to their duties as Christians, and every morning a string of devotees might be seen to go beyond the sage brush, east of town, to watch the sun rise, and, ask the Almighty where the next terminus is to be." In addition to Kiesel and Company, there were stores operated by Hodson, Schlisinger, Eliel, Sebree, and Ferris & Holt. Other establishments included Dyer's Restaurant, the O. K. Bakery, three blacksmith shops, four wagon agencies, and a few saloons—the Gem, Occidental, Nevada, Bank Exchange, Fancher's, Cayuse, and Chamberlain's Iron Clad.[5]

---

[2] Beal, *Intermountain Railroads*, pp. 51–54; *Deseret News*, Jan. 23, Mar. 13, Apr. 10, May 1, 1878; *New Northwest*, Jan. 11, 1878.

[3] Beal, *Intermountain Railroads*, p. 55; *Deseret News*, May 15, 1878.

[4] *Salt Lake Tribune*, July 2, 1878; *Ogden Freeman*, June 28, 1878.

[5] *Salt Lake Tribune*, Sept. 1, 1878.

When late September came, the end of the track was about three miles below Black Rock stage station in Portneuf Canyon and twenty-two miles beyond Oneida. The railroad had been built down Marsh Creek rather than the Portneuf River because Marsh Creek was smaller and straighter, required fewer bridges, and was not in the grasp of the H. O. Harkness toll road franchise, as was the Portneuf route. Black Rock, about two miles below present Inkom, Idaho, was on the Fort Hall Indian Reservation, and the agent immediately sent word to the Oneida businessmen that no trading establishments or stores would be allowed without permission from the Commissioner of Indian Affairs, who in turn refused authorization until the Bannock and Shoshoni Indians officially agreed. With track laying rapidly proceeding toward the Snake River, the Utah and Northern decided only to pause at Black Rock, hoping to reach Blackfoot on the other side of the reservation, where a more permanent town could be located. As soon as Oneida "was numbered with the slain," Blackfoot sprang into existence and became immediately important as the railroad freight shipping point to the Salmon River mines.[6]

Shipping from the Terminus

As the railroad advanced, wagon freighters had to sharpen their bargaining powers to receive proper rates. In 1877, Fred J. Kiesel and Company and McCormick and Hardenbrook shipped 5,700 tons of freight to Montana from Dunnville, and, with the Maclay Company, very much dominated the freight shipping business from the railhead. There were still wagon shipments coming from Corinne, but as soon as the terminus moved to Oneida, the road from the Central Pacific to the north via Malad Divide was intersected by the Utah and Northern Railroad and effectively removed Corinne from any competition as a freight-forwarding center.[7]

The Union Pacific officials, determined to capture as much

[6] Ibid., Sept. 24, 1878; *Helena Herald*, Oct. 10, 1878; MSUL, Mrs. Margaret E. Ferris, "Letters, 1874–1884," Oct. 28, 1878.

[7] *Salt Lake Tribune*, Jan. 1, Apr. 3, 1878; *Deseret News*, May 8, 1878; *Idaho Statesman*, Jan. 17, 1878.

"Jerkline twelve" on the old freight road in 1883. *Montana Historical Society, Helena.*

of the Montana freight as possible, entered into a contract with E. G. Maclay's Diamond R in March to receive the Utah and Northern freight at the railroad terminus. A warehouse was set up at Dunnville by Fred J. Kiesel and Company, which had sub-contracted from the Diamond R firm. Maclay also entered into agreements with other subcontractors to haul goods.

This entry by the Union Pacific into the forwarding business, and the approach of the narrow-gauge, led many Montana businessmen to transfer their orders from Missouri River steamboats to the railroad. As the *Deseret News* put it on May 8, 1878, the Montana freight business was increasing "most astonishingly, even surpassing the anticipations of the recent purchasers." At Ogden a dozen men were now employed in changing merchandise from the broad-guage to narrow-gauge cars; formerly three or four men had handled the task. From ten to twenty carloads of freight passed over the Utah and Northern line daily.[8]

At the other end of the road, the Diamond R faced some difficulty in getting enough wagons to carry the goods north. In addition to using their own teams, the company did not offer sufficiently high freight rates to encourage independent freighters to attempt the long and arduous trip. As the *Ogden Freeman* said on May 21, 1878, "they [freighters] are offered the paltry sum of two cents per pound for making a round trip of 600 to 800 miles." Mormon teamsters, formerly making up a greater part of the independent freighting outfits, were now busily engaged making money in hauling and grading the railbed. By June, teamsters were asking $.04 per 100 pounds at both Corinne and the terminus as transportation became scarce.[9]

Increasing wagon freight to Montana brought much newspaper comment beginning with the first train of the season, which rolled into Helena on May 31, 1878, thirty days from the terminus. By August 1, the *Herald* grumbled that "Main street has been completely blockaded with wagons unloading during the entire day." With the expiration of the Union Pacific-

[8] *Ogden Freeman,* Mar. 5, 1878; *New Northwest,* Mar. 15, 22, 1878; *Deseret News,* May 8, 1878; MSHS, "Agreement between E. G. Maclay & Co., & H. C. Niebbold, April 14, 1878."

[9] *New Northwest,* May 17, June 21, 1878.

Diamond R contract in September, Oneida and Black Rock residents expected business to pick up as higher rates attracted more teamsters. About 800 tons of goods were stored at the end of the track. Some of the goods had lain there for several weeks because "freighters are loth to haul while rates are low." [10]

Freight rates did rise; and by November, R. C. Knox noted 150 wagons loading at Oneida when he left. He passed 265 journeying to Montana on his way north and 447 going south. The *Helena Herald* reported on January 16, 1878, that E. G. Maclay and Company had forwarded 6,500 tons of goods from the terminus to Montana during 1878, while shipments by way of the Missouri River amounted to 9,680 tons. Freight shipped by other terminus firms probably added enough to the Maclay total to equal the volume of goods from the Missouri.

Surprisingly, prices in Montana did not reflect a decline as a result of the approach of the narrow gauge. As Carrie Strahorn remarked, "The scarcity of fruit seemed like a famine of luxuries." Oranges were $1.00 each, pears were $.25 apiece, and apples were $.75 a pound. Salt from Idaho's Oneida Salt Works brought $80 to $90 a ton. [11]

Changing from Stagecoach to Railroad

With the advance of the railroad terminus to the north, stagecoach passengers to Montana began to face the possibility of a ride on the "wheel-barrow line," or narrow-gauge railroad, as part of the journey from the States. During early 1878, travelers on the stage rejoiced over the unusually mild winter. The roads were dusty but mosquito free until late in March and early April, when a continuing blizzard tied up wagon traffic on Pleasant Valley Divide for about four weeks. Gilmer & Salisbury's "Gov" Pollinger battled the snow drifts regularly and in most instances got the stages through on time. The advance of the Utah and Northern to Dunnville and later to Oneida shortened the arduous coach trip from Montana, and passengers looked expectantly to

[10] *Helena Independent*, May 31, 1878; *Ogden Freeman*, Sept. 3, 1878.

[11] Carrie A. Strahorn, *Fifteen Thousand Miles by Stage*, p. 88; *New Northwest*, Mar. 1, 1878; *Idaho Statesman*, Nov. 7, 1878.

Passengers walking beside a stagecoach on the Montana Trail. *Courtesy of William D. Livingstone.*

Helena–Fort Benton stage at Saw River Crossing, 1885. *Montana Historical Society, Helena.*

the day when the narrow-gauge would reach the Montana line and be "across the Rubicon" of the Continental Divide.[12]

The stage stations of 1878 had not changed very much from those established in the 1860's. The development of copper deposits at Butte increased travel to that place until about half the stage passengers were giving the copper capital as their destination. Gilmer & Salisbury, in September, started a daily line of stages from Helena via Deer Lodge to Butte.[13]

A through fare from Omaha to Helena was advertised as $100 for first-class accommodations, which included 100 pounds of baggage free by rail and 40 pounds by stage. Extra weight on the coach cost $.15 to $.20 a pound. From Franklin, the 425-mile stage ride to Helena cost $62.50.[14]

Passenger complaints about the discomforts of travel were not as numerous by 1878, although the Gilmer & Salisbury agents were still masters at putting "a prairie schooner load of freight on to a coach, after it is apparently full of passengers and mail." Either service had improved, or weary Montanans had decided to resign themselves to the sleepless, jarring ride to the Utah and Northern. One passenger remarked on the "dirty disagreeable holes" that he found the stations to be. Another remarked that whereas any tramp could get a meal in Montana hotels for $.50, stage passengers were expected to pay $1.00 for the same food.[15]

Perhaps the classic description of western staging during the period was that penned by Carrie A. Strahorn in her book, *Fifteen Thousand Miles by Stage*. On her first trip, she departed from Oneida, and somewhere in the desert wastes of Idaho she and her fellow passengers arrived at a cabin that contained four stalls for the horses and a ten-by-ten-foot combination parlor, kitchen, and bedroom. Over the outside door was a sign reading, "Hotel de Starvation, 1,000 miles from hay and grain, seventy miles from wood, fifteen miles from water, and only twelve inches from h-ll."[16]

---

[12] *Helena Herald*, Jan. 31, Feb. 21, Mar. 7, Apr. 4, 1878.

[13] Ibid., Sept. 12, 1878.

[14] Ibid., Apr. 18, 1878; Robert E. Strahorn, *To the Rockies and Beyond*, p. 122.

[15] *Ogden Freeman*, Nov. 1, 1878; *New Northwest*, Jan. 11, 1878.

[16] C. Strahorn, *Fifteen Thousand Miles*, p. 79.

Pioneering to Montana

In 1878, the Union Pacific used its advertising budget to good advantage to entice settlers from the East to go to Montana. Would-be pioneers were advised that if they could not afford to travel first or second class, emigrant rates were available for $45 for the trip from Omaha to Lovell's, just north of Beaverhead. At the terminus of the Utah and Northern, freight wagons would be available to carry them north, with meals being furnished at $.50 per day. Complaints were made, however, on May 21, 1878, in the *Ogden Freeman* that through tickets purchased in the East were not honored at the end of the railroad, the teamsters there merely pointing to wagons that were crowded "so full of goods up to the very bows, that there is no room." The forlorn pilgrims then had to search for any means available to complete their journey. Some outfitted themselves at Dunnville or Oneida and traveled in their own wagons to Montana; others packed up their blankets and walked north.[17]

Well-organized trains of emigrants eschewed the railroads and followed the well-worn Oregon Trail and the Montana Trail. By April, these western routes would be lined with Easteners on their way to make their homes in the Beaverhead country. But in the summer and fall of 1878, emigrants, stage passengers, and freighters spent a season of uncertainty as the Bannock War created almost a repeat performance of the Nez Percé troubles of the prior year. Fearful of an attack by the Indian raiders, the passengers on one stage designated one of their number to ride outside on the box with the driver because they feared the Jehu would "cut and run," that is, cut the traces, mount one of the horses, and take off. The Indian incidents were isolated and did not seriously hamper travel, with the exception of trips to the Salmon River area.[18]

The worst incident involved a freighter named Jesse Mc-Caleb, who was leading five huge oxteams loaded with 50,000 pounds of goods along Lost River when a party of Bannock Indi-

---

[17] WCML, Union Pacific Railroad, "Ho for Montana"; Robert E. Strahorn, *The Resources of Montana Territory and Attractions of Yellowstone National Park*, p. 67; *Ogden Freeman*, Jan. 1, 1878; *New Northwest*, Mar. 29, 1878.

[18] C. Strahorn, *Fifteen Thousand Miles*, p. 84; *Helena Herald*, Apr. 25, 1878.

ans attacked the train. McCaleb was killed, and his men then fought off the Indians for two days but lost five oxen and three horses in the battle. The Birch Creek Stage Station on the Salmon River road was also besieged, the stock tender and driver being wounded and the stagecoach burned. Finally, at Pleasant Valley, a group of Indians burned some haystacks, treed one of the stage employees for two days, and ran off forty-four head of stock from freighters camped nearby.[19]

The Railroad Comes to Montana

By late April 1879, a two-section steel bridge was completed across the Snake River at Eagle Rock about 100 feet downstream from the Anderson Brothers Toll Bridge. The Andersons donated 104 acres of land to the railroad as a site for shops, with the Utah and Northern promising in return to hold the terminus on the south side of the river from April to July. Merchants from Oneida and Blackfoot began to move to the new town of Eagle Rock, which was soon "overflowing with speculators. The rush is so great that sleeping accommodations are out of the question."[20]

Construction trains began to cross the new bridge by the middle of May, and everyone was looking forward to the next move to Camas Creek, forty miles away. At this time, the Utah and Northern Railway was charging $18 for the 250-mile trip, leaving Salt Lake at 7:00 A.M. and arriving at the terminus fifteen and a half hours later. The "itinerant" town of Eagle Rock was soon almost deserted as the crews moved first to Market Lake, then on to Camas, which became the new railhead on July 21. The *Helena Herald* on June 19, 1879, exulted over the new town: "Farewell to that miserable stage ride across the sandy desert .... Never again shall we have the privilege of working three or four hours in righting up a Concord on the barren plains of Idaho."[21]

---

[19] *Idaho Statesman*, Sept. 2, 1878; *Helena Herald*, Aug. 29, Sept. 12, 19, 1878; *Salt Lake Tribune*, Sept. 11, 1878.

[20] *Salt Lake Tribune*, Apr. 20, May 11, 1879; *Helena Herald*, May 15, 1879; *Idaho Statesman*, May 8, 1879; Beal, *Intermountain Railroads*, p. 65; *Ogden Junction*, Apr. 30, 1879.

[21] *Salt Lake Tribune*, May 25, July 29, 1879.

Utah and Northern Railroad crossing the trestle at Eagle Rock. Roundhouse and shops are in the background. *Utah State Historical Society, Salt Lake City.*

As soon as the weather permitted in 1880, track-laying crews started out for the Montana line, which was reached by March 9. On that day, a special ceremony was held. Telegraph wires were attached to two silver spikes so that all Montana could hear the blows of the sledgehammers. Captain E. T. Hulaniski, general agent, and L. J. Fisk, assistant superintendent of construction, gave speeches; cheers rent the air; and the spikes were driven. Montanans everywhere gave thanks for the longest three-foot gauge railroad in the world—290 miles from Ogden to Monida Pass.[22]

Freighting and Passenger Service in 1879

As the railroad had moved north toward the Continental Divide during 1879, the amount of freight dispatched via the Utah Northern had increased. At Eagle Rock, in early May, there were hundreds of teams and teamsters waiting for freight moved via the Utah and Northern, but most of the Mormon freighters had withdrawn from the Montana trade by this time. The railroad terminus was just too far from home. The rates were lower than ever before—$2.55 per 100 pounds from San Francisco to Eagle Rock, and $1.50 per 100 pounds from the end of the track to Helena. Yet, the *New Northwest* of May 23, 1879, noticed that California oranges were $3 a box in Salt Lake, at 200 to 300 a box, while Montanans at Deer Lodge were paying $.25 apiece for the fruit. The *Idaho Enterprise* reported on July 31, 1880, that 10,000 tons of merchandise were expected to be shipped from the railroad terminus to points in Montana and Idaho during 1880, which would comprise about half the total tonnage going into those two territories. As one awestruck citizen from Soda Springs wrote, "The great amount of freight shipped into the Territory of Montana from this point [the terminus] cannot be comprehended by parties not accustomed to transportation by rail." [23]

---

[22] *New Northwest*, Mar. 12, 1880; *Helena Herald*, Mar. 11, 1880; *Idaho Enterprise*, Mar. 11, 1880; *Deseret News*, Mar. 17, 1880.

[23] *New Northwest*, Mar. 28, 1879; *Idaho Enterprise*, July 31, 1879; Charles Bovey, Collection, Virginia City, Mont., letter from H. C. Kennedy to Ike, Terminus of UNRR, Mar. 14, 1879, Virginia City, Mont.; *Idaho Statesman*, Sept. 27, 1879.

Also during 1879 stagecoach travel mounted as the railroad advanced toward the north, and crossing Monida Pass by stage still gave a reminder of the hazards presented by the Continental Divide. Stage stations from the 1879 winter terminus at Beaver Canyon to Helena had not changed very much over the years. The 275-mile stage ride from Beaver Canyon to Helena took about thirty-six hours and cost $100 first class. The *Helena Herald* on June 5, 1879, looked forward to the time when the railroad would be completed to Helena and passengers would be able to ride in comfort to Ogden for a mere $30.

The transfer of business from stagecoach to railroad was not as smooth as expected. The Union Pacific had easily taken over the express company operations from Wells Fargo in 1878, changing several of the office agents in the process, but mail service had suffered interruptions. The Utah and Northern contracted to carry the mail to Oneida, while Gilmer & Salisbury agreed to pick up the mail at the end of the track. Therefore, when the rails reached Camas, there was a distance between that place and Oneida for which there was no contract. The railroad courteously agreed to forward the mail anyway.[24]

To prove that the Old West was not yet dead, someone attempted to hold up the stagecoach near Hole-in-the-Rock Station in June of 1879. About 9 P.M., one of four men concealed behind some rocks shouted, "Stop the coach!" and fired a single shot over the top of the vehicle. Three armed messengers, sent along because of the large amount of currency aboard, answered by unloading their shotguns and sidearms at the robbers. At the same time the driver "pushed the team along with whip and ribbons." Miraculously, no one was hit. The editor of the *Helena Herald* said on June 12, 1879, that it was the first attempt in years to rob a stage, and hoped it would be the last.

Lengthening the Line

After a "wretched" winter at Beaver Canyon, Montana, construction crews of the Utah and Northern pushed the road to a camp called Allerdice, which constituted a temporary way sta-

---

[24] *Helena Herald*, June 3, 1880; Robert E. Strahorn, *The Great West: Its Attractions and Resources*, pp. 219–20; *Salt Lake Tribune*, July 29, 1879.

tion until May 10, 1880, when Red Rock, a place with three hotels and "ten times as many saloons," became the terminus town of the narrow-gauge. Later the name was changed first to Spring Hill, then to Lima. The new terminus lay only 160 miles south of Helena, 155 miles from Deer Lodge, 120 miles from Butte, 108 miles from Virginia City, and only 80 miles from Salisbury.[25]

In late September 1880, the Utah and Northern officials announced that the winter terminus of the railroad would be located in the Beaverhead Valley about forty-eight miles north of Red Rock. Terminus businessmen quickly bought a portion of Richard Deakin's ranch for $10,500, established a townsite, and sold $14,000 worth of lots in the first twenty-four hours. When Sidney Dillon of the Union Pacific donated $500 toward construction of a church at the new settlement, the town was named Dillon. By October 10, Dillon had a population of 300.[26]

Until the tracks reached Dillon, teamsters continued to have difficulties traversing the Pleasant Valley Divide and were unable to move freight beyond Beaver Canyon. The few goods that did get through cost from $.05 to $.07 per pound. As late as April 1880, most goods still lay at the end of the tracks, but eventually Walsh's mule train reached Helena on April 24.[27]

By the time the rails reached Red Rock, the *Deseret News* was able to report 350 carloads of freight delivered to that point by June 2, 1880. The *Helena Herald* on June 3, 1880, disclosed that the warehouses at Red Rock were bursting with freight, "with such a rush and jam ... here now that it is hard to keep anything straight," according to one forwarding agent. And while many ox and mule teams were on the way to Helena, unless many more freight teams showed up, goods would not reach Helena for several weeks. As news spread of the high rates for transporting goods from the railroad, however, freighters converged on the terminus.[28]

By the end of 1880, 16,150 tons of goods had been shipped to

[25] Beal, *Intermountain Railroads*, p. 70; MSHS, "Historical Resume," pp. 2-4.

[26] *Helena Herald*, Sept. 9, 1880; *New Northwest*, Sept. 24, 1880; MSUL, Mrs. Margaret E. Ferris, "Letters," Sept. 10, 1880; Beal, *Intermountain Railroads*, p. 83; *Salt Lake Tribune*, Oct. 3, 1880.

[27] *New Northwest*, Mar. 26, 1880; *Helena Herald*, Jan. 15, Apr. 24, 1880.

[28] *Helena Herald*, July 19, 1880.

Montana by the Utah and Northern and freight wagons, and it was estimated that 18,000 tons would be forwarded by January 1, 1881—13,000 tons in merchandise and 5,000 tons in machinery for the mines.[29]

This increase in tonnage was equaled by a corresponding rise in the number of passengers carried by the Utah and Northern and the Gilmer & Salisbury stage lines. Anticipating a boost in the number of passengers, Gilmer & Salisbury ordered a number of new stages that would carry 30 riders each, which led the *Helena Herald* on February 12, 1880, to outline a thirty-six-hour timetable from the winter terminus at Beaver Canyon, an announcement that a few years before would have sent Montana into a "delirium of joy." [30]

During March, arrangements were made to take express and passengers by rail to Pine Buttes, a station sixteen miles north of Beaver Canyon, thus saving four hours and the "hard and disagreeable drive over the Pleasant Valley Divide." By this time the stage company was transporting a ton of mail a day to the news-hungry residents of Montana. To take care of the increased loads, the company put on a "Double Daily" from the terminus and watched the daily passenger roster rise from 35 on March 21 to 85 on April 1. By summer, Gilmer & Salisbury were operating some 5,000 miles of staging and inaugurated a route from the end of the railroad to Yellowstone Park. On October 8, passengers began to detrain at Dillon, making it possible to journey the 125 miles to Helena in only twenty-four hours.[31]

The elimination of the hard and dangerous stage ride across Pleasant Valley Divide certainly encouraged more travel, but the Union Pacific's continuing aggressive advertising campaign also persuaded many to undertake the journey to Montana. From Omaha, the schedule called for four and three-quarters days to Helena, with first-class paying $100, second-class $75, and emigrant-class $45. Soon travelers were being booked days in advance, and by late April four and five passenger cars were leaving daily from Ogden to go north.[32]

---

[29] Ibid., Dec. 2, 1880.
[30] Ibid., Jan. 1, 1880.
[31] Ibid., Mar. 25, July 19, 30, Oct. 8, 1880.
[32] Ibid., Apr. 15, 22, 1880; WCML, Union Pacific Railroad, "Ho for Montana."

Newspaper editors were indeed becoming hard-pressed to maintain an aura of the wild, wild West as they reported few accidents and holdups. But a railroad at Dillon and a well-organized stage company on the road to Butte and Helena did not mean an immediate end to weary rides to other western Montana towns. In addition to Gilmer & Salisbury branch lines, there were still free-wheeling independent operators who set up service at a moment's notice. One such driver was John Kelsey, an ex-Mormon. He recorded that his first fares were a fat comedian, the comedian's wife, and a banjo player. When the comedian failed to pay the transportation charge, Kelsey fought him for it and was arrested and fined $10. On another occasion, a correspondent gave the *Helena Herald* a vivid description on March 18, 1880, of an independent driver who fought snowdrifts for twenty-four hours, fourteen of which he spent shoveling a path on the road between Deer Lodge and New Chicago. At the end of the day he was still determined to "get through or bust." [33]

Pushing on to Butte

The railroad's goal in 1881 was to reach Butte, and by July the terminus was at Melrose, 35 miles away. With the help in September of a "fresh batch of Mormon graders from Cache Valley, Utah," the tracks reached Silver Bow junction on October 26. Butte was then only six miles away, and on December 21, the first passenger train pulled into that city. It was 11:10 P.M., snow was falling, and a chilling wind swept around the tracks, but several hundred citizens braved the elements to applaud the arrival of civilization.[34]

Freighting from the various railheads in 1881 tended to follow the previous year's pattern. Until early summer there were not enough wagons to forward goods from the railroad, but gradually enough arrived to accommodate shippers. The new firm of Sebree, Ferris and Holt became the principal forwarding agent at Dillon, and this company, along with others, kept their main

---

[33] *The Mountaineer* (Big Sandy, Montana), Mar. 16, 1942.
[34] MSHS, "Historical Resume," pp. 2-4; *Helena Herald*, Sept. 15, 1881; Beal, *Intermountain Railroads*, pp. 85-87.

houses at Dillon and merely established branches at Melrose and
Silver Bow when the railroad reached those points. The terminus
at Melrose, about thirty miles beyond Dillon, took away all the
freighting business on the west side of the Continental Divide and
left Dillon to supply Helena and the areas east of the mountains.[35]

The shortening of the line from the Utah and Northern to
Helena, Deer Lodge, Missoula, and other Montana cities did not
mean the end of wagon freighting on the Montana Trail. In addition to fast freight lines springing up at each terminal to forward
goods, the railroad also gave business to freighters when it
refused to haul dynamite over its rough roadbed. On one occasion
James P. Anderson and twelve other teamsters from Utah took a
contract to move a large quantity of dynamite from Utah to the
Montana mines. One driver recorded, "We were all somewhat
worried with all the loads of powder." Another train ahead of
them had suffered tragedy when some of the wagons "blew up and
outfits and men were blown to atoms." [36]

Gilmer & Salisbury in Montana

W. S. Howell, superintendent for Gilmer & Salisbury at
Helena, had his share of troubles as the railroad moves dictated
abrupt changes in stagecoach routes. Gilmer & Salisbury complained to the superintendent of the Utah and Northern that
their stagecoach arrived at Dillon on the morning of November
16 to find the train standing at the depot. The railroad agent and
conductor observed the big load aboard the stage, reasoned that
getting the eleven passengers settled on the train might delay
them as much as half an hour, and deliberately started for
Ogden, leaving the stage passengers to wait twenty-four hours
for the next train.[37]

The stage company, however, could not complain about any
lack of business. On March 31, there were twenty-one passengers

---

[35] MSUL, Mrs. Margaret E. Ferris, "Letters," Jan. 16, 1881; MSHS, "Historical Resume," pp. 2-4.
[36] USHS, Adolph M. Reeder, "Honor to Moroni Mortensen," p. 3.
[37] MLUU, Gilmer & Salisbury, "Letter Book," pp. 8, 27-28, 232.

on the Concord coach as it left Dillon "for upper Montana," and this number—or just under—seemed to be the usual load. Fares varied as the routes changed, but during most of the summer of 1881, the standard rates were: Deer Lodge to Butte—$5; Deer Lodge to Silver Bow—$4; Helena to Dillon—$16; Silver Bow to Missoula—$15; and Silver Bow to Helena—$10. In addition to passenger revenue, Gilmer & Salisbury reported in December to Wells Fargo in San Francisco that their main Montana line had shipped during the year by express $1,136,290.74 in gold, $2,305,702.00 in silver, and $689,800.00 in silver by freight lines.[38]

Occasionally, when independent operators threatened to take some of the stage passenger business, Gilmer & Salisbury had to deal rather summarily with the interlopers. A serious threat came from an opposition line owned by a Mr. Roberts at Melrose. Superintendent Howell told agent Riddle in Melrose to furnish a wagon and stock to a driver who was to "get below Roberts all the time." When another opponent named Brown started in business at Melrose, Riddle was told to make arrangements with Brown to supply coaches and teams for Brown's extra passengers at half the fare, "this will give him [Brown] a show to put his own fare down and Knock Roberts.... You must use your own judgment as to what is best, only do something and clean Roberts up." [39]

Road conditions continued to plague the efforts of the Jehus employed by Gilmer & Salisbury to get the stages through on time. As passenger traffic increased, the number of accidents rose correspondingly, and on some routes the company just closed down for the winter because "it would cost more than it would come to to do it."

Besides having to pay the cost of damages to passengers injured in accidents, operating and overhead costs for the stage company were quite high. In one letter to Omaha, Howell detailed the estimated costs of operating Route #42127, Dillon to Helena, for one month:[40]

---

[38] Ibid., pp. 116-18, 201-2, 248.

[39] Ibid., pp. 112, 156.

[40] Ibid., pp. 35, 88, 166, 366, 376-78, 450.

Hay & Grain	$ 1,689.36
Wood	50.00
5 Drivers @ 75	375.00
11 Stocktenders @ 50	550.00
2 ” @ 60	120.00
1 Division Supt.	150.00
1 General Supt. (Proportion of Salary)	75.00
6 Agents	345.00
1 Blacksmith	150.00
Horse shoes, Nails, Calks, Coal, etc.	200.00
Repairs on Coaches	300.00
” ” Harnesses	50.00
Incidental Expenses	50.00
Depreciation in value of property	1,000.00
Interest on investment $36,987 @ 1% per month	369.00
Total cost per month	$ 5,473.36

One of the large Gilmer & Salisbury operations in Idaho was the Blackfoot, Bonanza, and Wood River route running 156 horses, 4 mules with 4 coaches, 5 eleven-passenger wagons, 4 eight-passenger wagons, 8 jerkeys, 1 buckboard, 4 dead-axe wagons, 1 water wagon, 1 blacksmith wagon, and 9 sleighs. As veteran stage riders would immediately recognize, the equipment was not the best; no wonder R. C. Watson, Blackfoot agent, finally resigned his position, rebelling when his four-horse coaches were replaced by jerkeys. Howell explained to Watson: "Of course you can't put a four Horse load on a Jerkey, but if the Jerkeys are light and you get up light sleighs for the snow, I don't see why you can't run all right." Writing to O. J. Salisbury about the matter, Howell said, "The only trouble so far [as] I could gather from [Watson's] letter was that he had been asked to cut the road down to Jerkeys. I don't see . . . why he should cry about that." [41]

Early in 1882, the Helena headquarters was ordered to consolidate some of the staging divisions. The coaches formerly used on the road between Silver Bow and Butte were to be transferred to the route from Bozeman to Miles City. These four wagons were lighter than those used on the main line, but carried almost as

---

[41] Ibid., pp. 144–49, 198, 209, 217.

many passengers. Gilmer & Salisbury announced an eighteen-hour schedule from Dillon to Deer Lodge, but warned that their transportation capacity to Helena was only "two Horse" and that anyone going to Missoula would have to wait his turn after through passengers from the East had been taken. It was possible to leave the railroad at Silver Bow and travel to Deer Lodge, but again passengers would have to wait until the Easterners had been sent on. By March, Superintendent Howell was announcing plans to move more horses and equipment to the Missoula run. At the same time, the company began to sell through tickets from the railroad to some points on the Bozeman–Miles City route.[42]

In late February of 1882, Superintendent Howell was still hoping that the passenger and express traffic to Helena would come from Dillon, but the Union Pacific officials began to press to change the transfer point to Butte. An alternate route by way of Deer Lodge seemed preferable to Howell, although his company would then receive only a fare of $10 per person instead of $16 for the route from Dillon to Helena. To accelerate the change to Butte, the railroad made the rate from Ogden to Butte exactly the same as to Dillon. It was an uneven battle! Although Howell raised the freight prices between Helena and Butte to $.04, Helena merchants could still receive goods via Butte at $.02 per pound less than by way of Dillon. Gilmer & Salisbury capitulated, and the staff was faced with the task of furnishing enough horses and stages to keep both lines running until the change could be effected on April 1. Business on the main stage line to Helena was booming. Howell doubled his teams and wagons three or four times in one week, and even when the trains were blocked by snowdrifts for two days, he still didn't get the road "cleaned up." [43]

The End of the Road

For the next two years Gilmer & Salisbury continued to serve northwestern Montana from its terminus at Butte, until the

---

[42] Ibid., pp. 345, 355, 391, 401, 414, 416, 418, 432.
[43] Ibid., pp. 368, 373, 376, 386, 416, 422, 439.

Northern Pacific and Utah and Northern rail lines agreed to a connection at Garrison, which the Utah and Northern branch of Union Pacific reached in the fall of 1884.

For the freighters who for many years had followed the Montana Road from Salt Lake City and Corinne north, their long-haul business was now ended. Many teamsters continued to load up at the way stations of the Utah and Northern for short side trips to smaller towns, but the way stations were "dreary looking places." The editor of the *New Northwest* wrote the best epitaph for stagecoach travel when he described his day-and-a-half train journey from Deer Lodge to Ogden. It was, he said,

> a happy contrast to the five days' time that was formerly occupied in the winter trip, with a chance to "hoof it" through mud or snow, and emerge from the coach in Utah with all the aches that name has been given to. Now, you go flying, warm, cozy, and comfortable, except in the event of being "snow-bound" or "ditched," in which case you starve respectably or are neatly and thoroughly killed.
>
> After all, are we not likely to sigh for the good old times of stages again on part of the route this winter? The U & N Co. does not seem to have shedded or fenced Pleasant Valley and other snow divides. It would not suprise me greatly if weeks should intervene during the winter without communication with the South. One of the old six-horse teams, with a veteran on the box, will wallow through snow that will stop a locomotive.[44]

A few Montanans may have shared this nostalgic look at the past with the editor, but most of their neighbors could only rejoice that after many years of frustration and waiting, the wagon ride to the Great Salt Lake was over.

Conclusion

From the time when Captain Stansbury pronounced it "the best natural road I ever saw," the Montana Trail had become the main thoroughfare between the City of the Saints and southern Idaho and western Montana. The pioneering efforts of a few freighters moving goods north by wagon to the Bitterroot Valley during the

---

[44] Beal, *Intermountain Railroads*, p. 92; BL, "Bancroft Scraps, Idaho Miscellany," vol 111; Merrill Beal, Personal Notes; *New Northwest*, Nov. 4, 1881.

1850's became a flood by 1862-63 when gold was discovered at Bannack City. Mormon settlers, discouraged in their farming efforts by grasshopper invasions, began to take farm-wagon loads of produce and supplies to the mining camps as a means of acquiring a little cash. Within a short time, however, the major effort of moving goods from the Mormon metropolis was taken over by better-organized and well-financed freighting concerns like the Diamond R Company, and the route to the north annually became a heavily traveled road during the snow-free months from April to November.

Similarly, the transportation of passengers to the golden gulches of Montana evolved from primitive outfits, such as that started by Jack Oliver, to the more sophisticated concerns of Ben Holladay and Wells Fargo. The Abbot, Downing Company of Concord, New Hampshire, even designed a special stagecoach for the rough mountain roads of this western area. Nevertheless, many travelers chose to pay the cut-rate fares charged for passage aboard the express wagons and ox-drawn trains that moved slowly along the dusty trail.

Stagecoach operators and teamsters alike muttered inprecations at the toll keepers of the ferries, bridges, and roads along the way. Impoverished legislatures in Utah, Idaho, and Montana had hoped that by granting toll charters they were providing the means for making travel along the trail safer and more comfortable. Such aspirations usually were swept away by spring floods or undermined by the refusal or inability of the operators to maintain their bridges and roads. All travelers were happy when the charters were finally revoked in the late 1870's.

There was another route into Montana, up the Missouri River by steamboat; but it also suffered a drawback—seasons of low water, when the boats would be stranded far below their destination at Fort Benton. Even so, river steamers remained the principal means of moving bulk goods to Montana during the spring and summer months of the 1860's and 1870's when such transportation was possible. At other times of the year, and for quick and reliable deliveries of rush orders or perishable goods, the Montana Trail was the premier road.

The completion of the transcontinental railroad in 1869 shortened the wagon journey from Utah by about 70 miles and from Omaha by several hundred miles. This easy access to the West brought increasing numbers of adventurers and pilgrims seeking their fortunes in western Montana and made the new town of Corinne on the Central Pacific Railroad the freight transfer point for goods being shipped north.

More and more, the large freighting concerns now came to dominate the transportation market to Montana, although Mormon farmers continued intermittently to haul produce, tools, and other high-value commodities to the north.

During the 1870's, the Montana Trail achieved particular importance as a busy western thoroughfare. As already noted, in November of 1878, the statistically-minded traveler R. C. Knox counted 862 wagons loading at Oneida or traveling between there and the north, with probably another 150 or so picking up cargoes at the various towns in Montana. Thus an estimated 1,000 wagons were engaged in freighting along the road during just the month of November, and most freighters would have already made at least two or three trips that year. This meant that perhaps as many as 4,000 wagon loads of goods moved north along the trail in 1878.[45]

Stagecoach travel also became particularly heavy, especially as the decade of the 1870's advanced. The recent studies by W. Turrentine Jackson of Wells Fargo operations between Utah and Montana from 1866 to 1869 emphasize the importance of the years before the completion of the railroad; and the driving of the Golden Spike encouraged many more travelers to take a ride in a Concord stage, courtesy of the new firm of Gilmer & Salisbury.[46]

Of all the areas of the West, Montana had suffered the unique experience of being one of the most isolated. Surrounded on the west by the mountain fortress of central and northern

---

[45] *Idaho Statesman*, Nov. 7, 1878. A comparison between Knox's estimation of the number of wagons moving north and traffic on the Santa Fe Trail points up the significance of the Montana Trail. According to Josiah Gregg's account, between 1822 and 1843 there were never more than 100 to 250 wagons per year on the road from Independence to New Mexico, except for 1843 when 450 wagons were counted. Josiah Gregg, *Commerce of the Prairies*, pp. 331–32.

[46] W. Turrentine Jackson, "Wells Fargo Stagecoaching in Montana: Into a New Territory," *Montana: The Magazine of Western History*, vol. 29, no. 1 (Jan. 1979), pp. 40–53; idem, "Trials and Triumphs," vol. 29, no. 2 (Spring 1971), pp. 38–53; idem, "The Overland Mail Contract for 1868," vol. 29, no. 3 (Sept. 1979), pp. 56–68; idem, "Final Months," vol. 29, no. 4 (Oct. 1979), pp. 52–66.

Idaho, on the east by hostile and unrelenting Indians, and on the south by the Continental Divide, the people of the region learned early to stock up on supplies during the grasshopper days of summer in order to survive the four months of winter when they would be snowed in. The States were far away and hard to reach. The people of Montana were forced to endure their mountain-fastness seclusion for almost twenty years before the joining of the Utah and Northern Railroad with the Northern Pacific in 1884 brought to an end the long wagon and stagecoach journey from Utah. During that time, the Montana Trail had been the one sure lifeline for supplies and travel. Now nearly everyone rejoiced that the steam whistle was at last replacing the neighing of stage horses and the lowing of oxen. There was little regret that wagon trains and stagecoaches would no longer be seen on the Montana Trail.

Appendix A

Rules for the Road

Responsibilities were carefully spelled out for the wagon masters of Garrison & Wyatt Freight Lines and/or their supervisor of wagon masters, Colonel S. C. Ashby. The first set of rules concerned Ashby's responsibilities and the "in town" activities of the wagon masters; the second set was "rules for the road":

RULES AND REGULATIONS FOR FREIGHTING

1st In case a train arrives early in the morning if by hurry & one or two extra man being hired to unload — they may be hired & to start back same day. But if I find that the Train can't be unloaded & started out before next day there is no necessity of any extra help.

2nd In case any of the Teamsters get Drunk the Wagon Master is to send said Drunken man or men to Camp & hire other men in their place & whatever is paid these Laborers — the same is to be charged to said Drunken man.

3rd In the event that any package of freight is stolen or lost on the trip it is to be distinctly understood that the Teamsters driving said wagon in which this freight is short is to be held personally responsible for same & charged to his a/c In case that a change is made on the road of Drivers — the man bringing said wagon into town may be innocent of any theft & if it is doubtful as to who is the guilty man — the man driving may go clear The Wagon Master is to [be?] notified immediately that certain pkgs or shortages are short in such a mans wagon & rather insinuate to the Wagon Master tho he must investigate the matter & let Ashby know who is the guilty man The Wagon Master in making Beef Bills & Repair Bills & Stable Bills if any necessary is to certify to same being correct before Ashby pays any such bills. Any Wagon Master coming into town on business belonging to this Train can feed his horse if necessary & same to be chrgd to said Train & if said Wagon Master stays upon his account or for his own pleasure — the said Wagon Master is to be charged with feeding said horse himself. In giving orders to any Butcher Blacksmith or Stable Man Ashby must notify said party to have the Wagon Master certify to such bill before he leaves town.

When a train comes in and the Drivers want money they must be putt off until they are done unloading as if they are paid as soon as they come in they are very apt to go off and get Drunk

Any man who the Wagon Master knows is going to quit — pay this man no money until you settle with him & pay him in full When the train gets close to Town the Wagon Master wants to find out how many Men are going to quit — the Wagon Master is to come to Ashby & tell him how many Men he will want to start back — Ashby can the next morning stick up a Notice if he wants to hire so many men — or he may wait until the Train come in and as soon as they commence unloading — idle hands will be apt to come around & want a job — then is the time to hire them & put them to work at the usual wages per month, in this way money is saved instead of hiring Laborers by the hour When Wagon Master comes in ask him how much Grub he has & hand a list of what he has & also then & there make out a list for him to return with & hand it in to Col Vawter to be put up so that it will be ready when the Train is Unloaded & not keep the Train waiting for their Grub. No Grain will be furnished Train Horses.

In shoeing Kijus only shoe when absolutely necessary & then only in front

In shoeing Mules if they need it badly they can be shod all around — if not needed only in front

Corinne Trips Make a list of Rations Given each train going there in the Wagon Masters Train Book —

In making notices for Bull Whackers never specify how many are wanted simply *"Bull Whackers Wanted"*

Avoid Irishmen — unless for Burnett — let him have what he wants

Never tell a Bull Whacker when wants to hire how many men I want — but put him off & tell him to come around in an hour or two & in this time — it gives an opportunity to choose better men

RULES AND REGULATIONS FOR WAGON MASTERS

Wagon Masters are positively forbidden to camp together when out upon the road when traveling in the same direction or in opposite directions — Unless they are compelled to use water both from the same place and even their corralls must be not less than 300 Yds. apart.

Wagon Masters are instructed to inform each Teamster when they load up & start out that they will be held personally responsible and any man coming in and upon the delivery of the frgt find that there is anything short upon his wagon — he will be charged with same — & wagon masters must tell their men plainly these facts in the start Each Driver will be made to pay for any Sheets damaged by his carlessness also with any Sheet Ropes lost and Bows Broken in his wagon by his Neglet or any Frgt damaged by his Neglet or carelessness or his Team or any wagon or wagons that are upset & Damaged by carelessness or neglect

In case of Hard storms at night the Night Hearder shall report to the Wagon Master that he is unable to keep the cattle The Wagon Master will then go or send a man to assist to Keep the Cattle In approaching or leaving Town where Grass is always scarce (Wagon Masters) will particularly caution Herders against Loosing any cattle near Town. The above Rules and Regulations as to the running of our Trains — Wagon Masters will do well to see fully enforced — and any failure upon their part to carry out these orders — They will then be held personally responsible*

---

*MSHS, Colonel Shirley C. Ashby, "Diary and Notebook."

Appendix B

Road Etiquette for Teamsters

The editor of the *Helena Herald*, in his issue of May 30, 1872, discoursed at length on "Road Etiquette" for the edification of those freighters who could and would read it. After commenting on good manners at the table and in the bed when two men shared, he reflected:

> Now, there are certain rules of good breeding that apply to the road as well as the table or the fireside. . . . When two teams meet, good breeding requires that each give half the road. Yet we often meet teamsters who refuse to obey this simple rule. . . . A man with a heavy lumber wagon has no more right to crowd a light carriage into the ruts or bushes than a burly lubber would have to force his weaker bed-fellow to sleep on the rail. . . .

> When one teamster wishes to pass another on a dusty road, he should ask the privilege of doing so, especially if there is a lady in the forward wagon. When the forward team finds that his own team travels slower than the other, he should hold his horses to their slowest pace till the other passes. . . .

> We think a little attention on the part of teamsters to the simple rules of good breeding, will do as much to prevent accidents and secure comfort and good feeling on the road as any set of laws that could be enacted.

Appendix C

Song of the Overland Stage Driver

A well-known "Song of the Overland Stage Driver," penned by Nat Stein, agent for Ben Holladay in Virginia City, Montana, was published in the *Montana Post*, April 8, 1865. Although not memorable for poetic style, its rough-hewn passages offer a paean of acclaim not only to the stage driver, but also to his less exalted compatriots.

I sing to everybody, in the country and the town,
A song, upon a subject that's worthy of renown;
I han't [sic] got a story of Fairy-land to broach,
But plead the cause of sticking to the box-seat of a coach.
    Statesmen and warriors, traders and the rest,
    May boast of their profession, and think it is the best;
    Their state I'll never envy; I'll have you understand,
    Long as I can be a driver on the jolly Overland.

There's beauty never-ending, for me, upon the plains,
That's worth a man's beholding, at any cost of pains;
And in the Indian country it offers me a fund
Of glee, to see the antelope and prairie-dogs abscond.
    Statesmen and warriors, &c.

The mountains and the canons, in turn afford delight,
As often as I pass them, by day or in the night;
That man must be a ninny, who'd bury up alive,
When all it costs to revel through creation, is to drive.
    Statesmen and warriors, &c.

Alike are all the seasons and weathers, to my mind,
Nor heat nor cold can daunt me, or make me lag behind.
In daylight and in darkness, through rain and shine and snow,
It's my confirmed ambition, to be up and on the go.
    Statesmen and warriors, &c.

You ask me for our leader, I'll soon inform you then,
It's Holladay, they call him, and often only Ben;
If you can read the papers, it's easy work to scan
He beats the world on staging now, 'or any other man.'
    Statesmen and warriors, &c.

And so, you must allow me, the Agent at his books
And selling passage-tickets, how woe-begone he looks!
'Twould cause his eyes to twinkle, his drooping heart revive,
Could he but hold the ribbons, and obtain a chance to drive.
  Statesmen and warriors, &c.

The Sup'rintendent even, though big a chief he be,
Would find it quite a poser to swap off berths with me;
And if Division Agents, though clever cloves and fine,
Should make me such an offer, you can gamble I'd decline.
  Statesmen and warriors, &c.

The Station Keepers nimble, and Messengers so gay,
Have duties of importance, and please me every way;
But never let them fancy, for anything alive,
I'd take their situations, and give up to them my drive.
  Statesmen and warriors, &c.

And then the trusty fellows who tend upon the stock
And do the horses justice, as reg'lar as a clock,
I love them late and early, and wish them well to thrive,
But their's is not my mission, for I'm bound you see, to drive.
  Statesmen and warriors, &c.

A truce to these distinctions, since all the hands incline,
To stick up for their business, as I stick up for mine;
And, like a band of brothers, our efforts we unite,
To please the travelling public, and the mails to expedite.
  Statesmen and warriors, &c.

It's thus, you're safely carried throughout the mighty West,
Where chances to make fortunes are even found the best;
And thus, the precious pouches of mail are brought to hand,
Through the ready hearts that centre on the jolly Overland.
  Statesmen and warriors, &c.

Appendix D

"A Freighting Trip to Montana"

Very few freighters were literate enough or had enough interest to record the incidents of travel on the trail to Montana. Therefore, William Woodward, a Mormon freighter from Cache Valley, Utah, has some significance for his diary record of several trips to Montana. The following is the most descriptive.

Wednesday 24 [September 1873] Went to Corrinne by train to see about freight to Montana. Arrived back at Logan about 10.30 PM Staid at Mrs. Olsen's

Thursday 25 Rode home with Bro Doney to Franklin & tied the colt behind his wagon.

Friday 26 Argo & St Leon went hunting the horses. I was mending harness

Saturday 27 George went to hunt the Kit mare & did not find her. Argo went in the afternoon and found the mare. I hired C. W. Fox's mules for $25.00 for the trip to Montana.

Sunday 28 I hired Bro Bunkleys pony for $10.00 for the trip to Montana — drove through Richmond & Smithfield to Bear River & camped. T. Morrison went with us.

Monday 29 We could not find the old horses & Fox's mule. George & T. Morrison started for home to look for them.

Teusday 30 Argo found the horses & George found the mule — We then drove on to Cottonwood Creek about 13 miles & camped

1873 October

Wednesday 1. Rolled on to Corinne obtained frieght at once for Helena at 4¢ per lb & loaded 3 wagons that afternoon.

Thursday 2 loaded two more wagons & were near ready to roll. I sent Argo home by train to Logan

Friday 3. Rolled out about 15 miles & camped near a spring.

Saturday 4 We did not find all the animals till about noon; rolled on about 14 miles.

Sunday 5 Rolled on to Willow Creek about 15 miles

Monday 6 Sent a letter from Malad home. Crossed the Mald range of mountains & camped; made about 17 miles.

Tuesday 7 Morning Rainy — roads very muddy — laid over.

Wednesday 8. Rolled on past Carpenter's, & camped — roads heavy made about 14 miles

Thursday 9 It rained through the night — roads muddy. Rolled on in the afternoon down Port Neuf Canon about 9 miles.

Friday 10 Some of the animals strayed off. Rolled on to Black Rock station in the afternoon.

Saturday 11. Very late in getting the animals some were off in the hills Rolled into Snake River Vally & camped on a small creek

Sunday 12. Rolled on passed Ross Fork & through the sand to Black-foot River

Teusday 14 Snowed through the night & day — laid over.

Wednesday 15. Snowing today — laid over.

Thursday 16 Snowing today — laid over.

Friday 17. Rolled on to Cedar Point about 6 miles I was quite chilly to day

Saturday 18 Travelled up Snake River. Crossed Eagle Rock Bridge & camped about 5 miles from the Bridge up the River — went about 18 miles.

Sunday 19 Two of our animals went back over the Bridge. Went a few miles up Snake River—

Monday 20. We were late getting the animals — drove to Market Lake — Roads muddy. Sent two letters home.

Teusday 21 Pulled through some heavy sand and arrived at Sand Hole or Desert Wells.

Wednesday 22. Drove away up Kamas Creek to a Rocky Hill — Snowed through the night

Thursday 23 Drove through some heavy sand & camped on Dry Creek. Heavy North Wind — very cold

Friday 24 Drove to Beaver Canon about 15 miles.

Saturday 25 George & I started up the Canon with our teams when we looked back & T. Morrison had got an axeltree broke. We had to stop. I prepared to make an axel tree obtained the loan of a few tools from Mr. Harkness at Beaver Canon toll gate

Sunday 26 Fixed the axel tree & loaded up Rolled about 3 miles. I. H. Packer came up with us & camped.

Monday 27 Drove over the Pleasant Vally Range & camped near Pine Buttes Roads very heavy.

Teusday 28 Rolled on to the Junction & then to Sage Creek — very late when we arrived at camp.

Wednesday 29 Rolled on to a steep hill & camped — we tried to get up this hill to night but so much snow on it we could not

Thursday 30. This hill was very bad to pull up; we had to unload part of the wagons; only went about 1-1/2 miles.

Friday 31 Started over a little creek. T. Morrison Broke an axel in the Creek. We got one of Mr. Garrison — put it in & went down Price's Canon a few miles

1873 November

Saturday 1 Rolled down the canon and down a valley & camped on Blacktail Deer Creek. dark when we arrived at camp. went about 23 miles.

Sunday 2 Drove to Point of Rocks, about 20 miles

Monday 3 Crossed Beaver Head Bridge — we were delayed by some teams being in the road. I. H. Packer left us to day near twin Bridges — we camped near the main road.

Teusday 4 Crossed the Jefferson River near Fish Creek & camped near the Jefferson River.

Wednesday 5. Drove over Pipe Stone Creek, & White tail Deer Creek & camped on the banks of White tail Deer creek.

Thursday 6. Just as we were ready to start, one of my mules got scared & run around an an axel-tree broke. After considerable trouble I borrowed an axel of a young man at a Ranche, and we travelled a few miles

Friday 7 Crossed the Boulder Mountain & camped in the Boulder Valley — made a good drive.

Saturday 8. Crossed the Prickly Bear Mountain & camped below Jefferson.

Sunday 9 Rolled to Helena The road was hilly & many Ravines made it bad for teams & teamsters.

Monday 10 Onloaded.

Teusday 11 Rolled out to Montana; got several passengers for Corinne.

Wednesday 12 Rolled on to Boulder Valley.

Thursday 13 Crossed the Boulder Mountains and camped in Jefferson Valley on White tail deer creek.

Friday 14 Rolled on to Twin Bridges. Passed two teams from Franklin in the night.

Saturday 15. Rolled past Point of Rocks & camped at a place some of the people called Land of promise. No wood nor feed

Sunday 16. Rolled up Black tail deer creek, & camped near a small creek made a good drive to day.

Monday 17. One of the passengers lost my whip last night — I went back this morning & found it about 3-1/2 miles from camp. It commenced to rain & then to snow, & we were in Price's Canon & the snow came down fast — staid about 3 hours & then rolled on again to sage creek. Over the ridge from Sage Creek the roads were dusty.

Teusday 18 Drove over the divide of the mountains & camped on divide Creek.

Wednesday 19 Drove past Pleasant Valley to Little dry Creek.

Thursday 20 Drove to Kamas Creek Ford.

Friday 21 Late starting, snowing & raining, about night — we camped at a slough on Snake River got to camp at about 8 PM

Saturday 22 Crossed Snake River Bridge & camped about 6 miles down stream from the Bridge.

Sunday 23 Drove to Blackfoot River

Monday 24. Drove to the springs near Port Neuf Canon.

Teusday 25. Drove through the Port Neuf Canon and camped at a spring about 2 miles south of the toll gate.

Wednesday 26 I left the teams and passengers to go to Corrinne & I took one team for Franklin — staid over night at Bro. Howell's near Clifton

Thursday 27 Drove to Franklin about 17 miles to day.

Friday 28 This morning snow was on the ground*

---

*MLUU, "The Bancroft Collection of Mormon Papers," William Woodward, A Freighting Trip to Montana, Cache Valley Archives, microfilm roll no. 4.

Appendix E

Estimated Number of Tons of Freight Shipped from Corinne North to Montana
During the Years 1872-80*

Year	Tons
1872	5,000
1873	5,500
1874	6,000
1875	7,000
1876	7,500
1877	8,000
1878	9,000
1879	12,000
1880	18,000

*Prior to 1872, apparently no figures are available, even estimates, of the amount of freight shipped north to Montana from Salt Lake City and later from Corinne. By 1872, the Corinne newspapers and a few of the Utah and Montana journals began to mention, only incidentally, the tonnage of goods being sent north from the railroad. This table contains estimates for the years 1872-80 based on very scattered bits of information:

1. 1872—7,501,280 lbs. of goods were shipped via the Union Pacific, and if an estimated smaller amount of 4,000,000 lbs. is attributed to the Central Pacific Railroad, an estimate of 5,000 tons seems reasonable.
2. 1874—Kiesel & Co. shipped 2,500 tons of goods during the last five months of the year, and in the one month of September, Corinne dispatched 1,953,054 lbs. of merchandise to Montana.
3. 1875—2,100 tons of goods were sent north by June 1 and by late August, 100,000 lbs. a day were being received at Corinne for transhipment.
4. 1876—By September 100,000 lbs. of freight arrived each day at Corinne; by December 31, 1876, Kiesel & Co. had sent 5,000 tons to the north and McCormick & Hardenbrook had sent 2,000 tons.
5. 1878—The Diamond R reported having shipped 6,500 tons to Montana for 1878 and having brought back 3,000 tons of goods.
6. 1880—With the Utah and Northern Railroad in Montana, the one firm

of B. F. White Co. reported having forwarded 7,393,353 lbs. by July 10, and there were at least six other large firms engaged in the business. By December 1, 16,150 tons of goods had been sent north with an estimate that 18,000 tons would have gone by the end of the year.

7. A government report listed the following shipments of goods to Montana via the Union Pacific:

Year	Pounds
1870	6,898,732
1871	7,501,280
1872	6,129,644
1873	6,000,000 (est.)

8. For 1880, the *New Northwest* reported that the UNRR carried 17,000 passengers an average distance of 91 miles and transported 35,000 tons of freight. Of course, not all passengers or freight went to Montana.

Bibliography

Primary Sources

BL *Bancroft Library, University of California, Berkeley*

"Bancroft Scraps, Idaho Miscellany," vol. 111.

"Bancroft Scraps, Montana Miscellany," vol. 90.

"Bancroft Scraps, Utah Miscellany," vol. 109.

"Biographical Sketch of the Walker Brothers."

Broadwater, Colonel C. A. "Dictation."

Clayton, William. "Letter Books." Vol. 1.

Dunlap, Katherine. "Overland Journey, May 15–August 16, 1864."

English, William James. "Dictation."

Franks, George. "Dictation."

"History of Brigham Young."

"Holladay Overland Mail and Express Company Papers."

Miller, James Knox Polk. "James Knox Polk Miller Diaries."

Sanders, Wilbur Fisk. "Notes, Helena, Montana, Feb. 6, 1885."

"Utah Early Records." Ms 328.

BYUL *Brigham Young University Library, Provo, Utah*

Crouch, Ebenezer. "Autobiography of Ebenezer Crouch, September 12, 1923." With addenda by his daughter. Ms 614.

McBride, Heber R. "Autobiography." Ms 501.

Walker, Joseph R., and Brothers. "Account Books, 1860–1862." 7 vols. Ms 228.

HL *Huntington Library, Pasadena, California*

Cummings, B.F. "Journal—Salmon River Mission."

"Overland Mail Collection Scrapbook."

ISUA *Idaho State University Archives, Pocatello, Idaho*

Albertson, Pete S. "Reminiscences." Wadsworth, Washoe County, Nev., Nov. 11, 1886.

"Creighton & Co., Forwarding and Commission Merchants." Ms 41 (11).

Davis, Ray J. "Toll Fares." Ms 50.

Hawkes, Joshua. "Autobiography." Franklin, Idaho, Ellen Wright Camp, Daughters of the Utah Pioneers. Typescript.

Howard, Minnie F. Papers.

Idaho Historical Records Survey. "Interviews." Ms 83. Typescript.

Kiesel, Fred J. "Letters, Corinne, Utah, to George L. Shoup at Salmon City, Idaho, Aug. 29, Sept. 11, 1877." Ms 579.

"McNutt & Phillips Pioneer Store Financial Papers." Ms 41, vol. 2, pp. 1, 2.

McPherson, Murdock M. "Murdock M. McPherson's Recollections." Ms 15. Typescript.

Meacham, Leonidas A. "Interviewed by John F. Ryan, 1936." Idaho Historical Records Survey Interviews. Ms 83.

Morse, L. C. "Letter, Eagle Rock Bridge, to George L. Shoup, Salmon City, Idaho, Aug. 27, 1877." Ms 576.

Owens, Art T. "Interviewed by John F. Ryan, 1936, at the age of 82." Idaho Historical Records Survey Interviews. Ms 83.

Pettengill, Mrs. George. "Reminiscences." Daughters of the American Revolution Papers.

"Stage Fare & Stage Stations in Utah, Idaho and Montana." Ms 684.

LDSHD The Church of Jesus Christ of Latter-day Saints Historical Department, Salt Lake City, Utah

"Box Elder Stake Manuscript History, 1849."

"Cache Stake Manuscript History, Logan, August 9, 1866."

Young, Brigham. "Journal History."

MLUU Marriott Library, University of Utah, Salt Lake City, Utah

"The Bancroft Collection of Mormon Papers." U. S. Library of Congress, Manuscript Division, Microfilm, 30 rolls.

Bodily, Robert. "Journal." Mormon Diaries, Journals and Life Sketches. File 49.

Gilmer & Salisbury. "Letter Book." Ms 14.

Peterson, William Baltazar. "Historical Scrapbook of Preston & Vicinity." An Inventory of Historical Research Materials for Cache Valley. Reel 6.

"Walker Family Correspondence." Ms 80.

MSHS Montana State Historical Society, Helena, Montana

"Agreement between E. G. Maclay & Co., and H. C. Niebbold, April 14, 1878."

Ashby, Colonel Shirley C. "Diary and Notebook."

Barness, John, and Dickinson, William. Untitled article. Freighting clip file.

Carroll, Matthew (Matt). "The Diamond R Transfere Co." Diamond R file.

Conway, Dan R. "Story of the Old Concord Stage Coach. . . ." In *The Ismay Journal*, Oct. 8, 1925. Clip file.

Darling, Lucia (Mrs. Lucia D. Park). "Journal of a Trip Across the Plains in the Summer of 1863." Typescript.

"Diamond R Papers." Diamond R file.

"Experienced Bullwhacker," told by Ann Hawkins.

Foster, Marie. "Early Days of Freighting." Freighting clip file.

Freighting clip file.

"Freighting in the Early Days . . ." (story told by an old-time freighter). Clip file.

Higginbotham, Charles. "Life Lines of a Stage Driver." Typescript.

"Historical Resume." In *Holiday Supplement to Dillon Tribune* (bound with *West Shore*, 1883-84). Clip file.

Hosford, Thomas J., C. O. Trask, and George D. French. Affadavits on Work by Wm. Sturgis on Red Rock and Beaverhead Canon Road, March 12, 1866. "The Great Beaverhead Wagon Road." Typescript.

Kertula, T. J. "Early Montana Days Marked by Freighters' Rate Wars." Clip file.

Meredith, Mrs. Emily R. "Experiences and Impressions of a Woman in Montana, 1862-1863." Typescript.

Millard, J. H. "Letter, Omaha, to James U. Sanders, Helena, Dec. 18, 1918."

Morley, James Henry. "Diary, 1862-1865." Typescript.

"Old Way Book of Oliver Stage Line Tells of Travel between Helena, Virginia City." May 7, 1947. Clip file.

"Oregon Pioneer Crossed Plains with Kirkendall." Stagecoach and Covered Wagon clip file.

Plassman, Martha Edgerton. "Incidents of Stage Travel. . . ." In *The Openheim Observer*, Feb. 8, 1923. Clip file.

―――. "Ox Team." In *Jordan Times*, July 16, 1928. Clip file.

―――. "The Silver Mounted Carriage. . . ." Clip file.

Pollinger, E.M. "Early Day Stage Lines and U. S. Mail." Typescript.

―――. "Letter, Alaska Bench, Montana, Twin Bridges, May 28, 1904, to Col. J. E. Callaway."

"Portneuf Canyon . . . Danger for Stage. . . ." In *Stagecoach and Covered Wagon*, Sept. 11, 1941. Clip file.

Reichelt, Clyde. "Joe Hartmann." Freighting clip file.

"R. L. 'Dick' Potter, as told to Rozetta Bailey Sylten." In *The Saco Independent*, Aug. 1, 1936. Clip file.

"Robbery of Gold-Laden Coach. . . ." In *Cut Bank Pioneer Press*, Mar. 16, 1931. Clip file.

Sanders, Harriet F. "Diary of Harriet F. Sanders of a Journey from Omaha to East Bannack City, Idaho Territory, Summer of 1863, via Kearney, Laramie, South Pass, and Lower Snake Ferry." Typescript.

————. "Diary, Virginia City to St. Louis, February 21–March 17, 1866." Typescript.

Sanders, Wilbur Fisk. "Diary." Typescript.

"Stage War of '66." Clip file.

"Those Early Days were Tough for Greenhorns." Oct. 1, 1942. Clip file.

"A Thousand Miles of Road." In *West Shore*, n.d. Clip file.

Walker, Joseph T. "Diary."

————. "A Trip Across the Plains, 1863, 1865."

"Way Bill from Corinne to Ellis & Deer Lodge."

MSUL Montana State University Library, Bozeman, Montana

Bailey, David J. "Diary and Reminiscences: His Journey from Indiana to Montana, 1865."

Cavanaugh, Miles J., Sr. "Autobiography, 1863." Ms file 339.

Comfort, John M. Article in *Madison County Mentor*, Mar. 2, 1900. Ms file 369.

Ennis, Fannie Davis. "Early Days in Virginia City, etc." Ms file 76.

Ferris, Mrs. Margaret Eastman. "Letters, 1874–1884." Ms file 403.

Goshill, S. I. "A Wagon Train Diary, 1878." Ms file 104.

Kirkaldie, Franklin Luther. "Letters, May 1864–March 30, 1869." Ms file 43.

Maynard, Ethel Augustus. "Reminiscences, 1933." Ms file 107.

Norman, Theo. "Diary 1869–1879." Ms file 375.

Patten, F. E. W. "Journal of Travels . . . 1863." Ms file 396.

NA National Archives, Washington, D.C.

"Complaint by the District Attorney, Henry N. Blake, plaintiff vs. The Virginia City and Summit City Wagon Road Company, defendant." Filed Nov. 1871. District Court of First Judicial District, Montana Territory, in and for Madison County. Territory of Montana.

"Fort Hall Endorsement Books, 1876–79." Military Records Division. RG 98.

"General Records of the Department of State, October 14, 1864–July 16, 1872." Military Records Division. RG 59.

"Letters Received by the Topographical Bureau." Military Records Division. M506, roll 32.

"Mail Contracts, Utah, 1858–1862." Library of Post Office Department.

"Mail Routes, Montana, 1866-1870." Library of Post Office Department.

"Mail Routes, Utah, 1862-1866." Library of Post Office Department.

"Office of the Quartermaster General, Consolidated Correspondence File, 1794-1915." Military Records Division, Boxes 309-10, 363, 1174.

"Records of the Office of the Chief of Engineers." Military Records Division. RG 77. Bulky Package File no. 306.

"Records of the Office of the Quartermaster General." Military Records Division. RG 92.

"Records of the Office of the Interior Relating to Wagon Roads, 1857-1881." U. S. Department of the Interior. File microcopies no. 191.

"Records of United States Army Commands, 1784-1821." Military Records Division. RG 98.

"Territorial Papers, Idaho, July 11, 1863-Dec. 1, 1872." U. S. Department of State.

"Territorial Papers, Idaho, 1864-1890." U. S. Department of Interior. File microcopies no. 191. Roll 3. Letters Received June 21, 1864-Nov. 20, 1890.

"Territorial Papers, Montana. Acts and Resolutions—2nd Session of Montana Legislative Assembly, 1866." U. S. Department of State. Vol. 2.

"Territory of Utah, Utah Administrative Records, 1851-1869." Records of States of United States.

USHS Utah State Historical Society, Salt Lake City, Utah

Ellsworth, S. George. "An Inventory of Historical Resource Materials for Cache Valley, Utah-Idaho." Utah State Historical Society, Cache Valley Chapter, and Utah State Agricultural College, Logan, 1957.

"Hampton-Godbe Correspondence."

Kennington, J. W. "Freighting in Cache Valley." Dec. 22, 1938. Logan, Utah, WPA file.

Reeder, Adolph M. "Honor to Moroni Mortensen." Typescript. File 1447.

Ricks, Joel E. Collection.

U. S. Works Progress Administration (WPA). "Inventory of County Archives of Utah, Box Elder County, No. 2." Historical Records Survey. Dec. 1938. Ogden, Utah.

Woodward, William. "Journals, Diaries, Notes, Account Books, Letters, Essays, Plats, 1851-1904." Cache Valley Microfilm, reel 4, item 2, reel 5, item 1.

USLC U. S. Library of Congress, Washington, D.C.

Beadle, John Hanson. "Scrapbook." Editorials and dispatches from the *Salt Lake Daily and Weekly Reporter* (and other papers), Oct. 1868-Aug. 1869.

Belnap, Gilbert. "Autobiography."

Daems, Henry B. "The Voice of a Pioneer." 1951. Typescript.

"John T. Gilmer." 1884.

WCML William Andrews Clark Memorial Library, Los Angeles, California

"James and Granville Stuart Account Book in 1862-63 at Bannack City, Montana (then in Dakota)." Item #506—Calendar of Montana Collection.

Kessler, C. H., comp. "Typewritten Ms from scrapbook of newspaper clippings furnished Kessler by Mrs. A. J. Fisk." (Concerned with Capt. A. J. Fisk's Fourth Expedition to Montana Territory.)

"Overland Stage Co., Passenger Register, Wells, Fargo & Co., Mails, 1868." Ms 95.

"Remarks of Hon. William H. Clagett, of Montana, in the House of Representatives, April 18, 1972." Ms.

Tuttle, Daniel S. "Montana Reminiscences."

Union Pacific Railroad. "Ho for Montana." 1 p. March 1, 1880.

Wallace, B. C. "A Few Memories of a Long Life."

Private Collections

Beal, Merrill D. "Personal papers in the possession of Merrill D. Beal." Pocatello, Idaho.

Bovey, Charles. Collection. In the possession of Charles Bovey, Fairweather Hotel, Virginia City, Montana.

Carpenter, John Stilley. Papers. In the possession of Ella Carpenter Jensen, Salt Lake City, Utah.

"Overland Diamond R Freight Line Papers." In the possession of Lewis O. Brackman, Helena, Montana.

Price, Anella J., and Thelma Simpson. "History of Malad City, Idaho." 1963. In the possession of the *Idaho Enterprise*, Malad, Idaho.

Scott, Odell. "Corinne City, Utah." 1948. Ms in the possession of Betty M. and Brigham D. Madsen.

Government Documents

United States Congress

"Affairs in Utah and the Territories," by James Fowler Rusling. *House Miscellaneous Document 153*, 40th Cong., 2d sess., serial no. 1350, 1867.

"Annual Report of Surveyor General of Utah," by David H. Burr. *House Executive Document 1*, 34th Cong., 3d sess., serial no. 893, 1857.

"Expedition of Captain James L. Fisk to the Rocky Mountains," *House Executive Document 45*, 38th Cong., 1st sess., serial no. 1189, 1864.

"Inspection by General Rusling and Hazen." *House Executive Document 45*, 39th Cong., 2d sess., serial no. 1289, 1867.

"Memorial of the Legislative Assembly of Montana, April 13, 1866." *Senate Miscellaneous Document 111*, 39th Cong., 1st sess., serial no. 1239, 1866.

"Memorial from Trustees of Montana Central Railroad." *House Miscellaneous Document 73*, 41st Cong., 3d sess., serial no. 1463, 1871.

"Military Road in Montana, Memorial from Montana Legislature, Feb. 4, 1869." *House Miscellaneous Document 38*, 40th Cong., 3d sess., serial no. 1385, 1869.

"Northern Pacific Railroad Exploration Survey, Letter from Isaac I. Stevens to Lieutenant Mullan, Fort Owen, St. Mary's Valley, October 3, 1853." *Senate Executive Document 78*, 33d Cong., 2d sess., serial no. 758.

"Protection Across the Continent, 1866," by D. B. Sackett. *House Exec. Doc. 23*, 39th Cong., 2d sess., serial no. 1288, 1867.

"Reconnaissance of the Yellowstone River in 1871," by Captain J. W. Barlow. *Senate Executive Document 66*, 42d Cong., 2d sess., serial no. 1479, 1872.

"Report of Commissioner of Indian Affairs, Upson to Dole, Sept. 1, 1864." *House Executive Document 1*, 38th Cong., 2d sess., serial no. 1220, 1865.

"Report of Exploration of a Route for the Pacific Railroad from St. Paul to Puget Sound," by Isaac I. Stevens. *House Executive Document 129*, 33d Cong., 1st sess., serial no. 736.

"Report of Secretary of War for 1870." *House Executive Document 1*, pt. 2, 41st Cong., 3d sess., serial no. 1446, 1870.

"Report of the Secretary of War." *House Executive Document 2*, vol. 2, 35th Cong., 2d sess., serial no. 998, 1859.

"Report on Agreement with Indians in Idaho, Feb. 3, 1874, Salt Lake City, Utah Terr., Nov. 17, 1873," by John P. C. Shanks, T. W. Bennett, Henry W. Reed. *House Executive Document 129*, 43d Cong., 1st sess., serial no. 1608, 1874.

"Report on the Internal Commerce of the U. S. for the Fiscal Year 1889." *House Executive Document 6*, pt. 2, 51st Cong., 2d sess., serial no. 2738, 1890.

"Report on Reconnaissance of Northwestern Wyoming, 1873." *House Executive Document 285*, 43d Cong., 1st sess., serial no. 1615, 1874.

"Report on Yellowstone National Park by N. P. Langford." *Senate Executive Document 34*, vol. 1, 42d Cong., 3d sess., serial no. 1545, 1872.

"Report Upon the Pacific Wagon Roads, Feb. 19, 1859," by F. W. Lander. *House Executive Document 108*, 35th Cong., 2d sess., serial no. 1008, 1859.

"Utah Expedition Contracts, Feb. 10, 1858, Mar. 2, 1858." *House Executive Document 99*, 35th Cong., 1st sess., serial no. 958, 1858.

"Wagon Road from Niobrara to Virginia City, Jan. 19, 1866," by George N. Propper. *House Executive Document 58*, 39th Cong., 1st sess., serial no. 1256, 1866.

"West of the Rocky Mountains, Resources of the States and Territories," by R. W. Raymond. *House Executive Document 54*, 40th Cong., 3d sess., serial no. 1374, 1869.

Territory of Idaho

"General Laws of the Territory of Idaho, First Session through Sixth Session, 1864–1871." Idaho Legislature, Boise, Idaho.

"Justice Court Records, 1869-1873." Oneida County, Malad, Idaho.

"Miscellaneous Records." Oneida County, Malad, Idaho.

"Proceedings of County Commissioners, Soda Springs, Idaho Territory, 'Book A,' County Records." Oneida County, Malad, Idaho.

Territory of Montana

Council Journal of First Legislative Assembly of Montana Territory, Bannack City, Dec. 12, 1864. Virginia City, Mont.: D. W. Tilton & Co., 1866.

Council Journal of Second Legislative Session of Territory of Montana, March 5, 1866, to April 14, 1866, at Virginia City. Helena: Wilkinson & Ronan, 1870.

General Laws of Montana Territory, Fourth Session of Legislative Assembly, November 4 to December 13, 1867. N.p.: N.d.

House Journal of Third Session of Legislative Assembly of Territory of Montana, Nov. 5–Dec. 15, 1866. Helena: Wilkinson & Ronan, 1870.

House Journal, Fifth Session, Legislative Assembly of Territory of Montana, Virginia City–Dec. 7, 1868, to Jan. 15, 1869. Helena: Montana Post Pub. Co., 1869.

Laws, Memorials, and Resolutions of the Territory of Montana Passed at the Fifth Session of the Legislative Assembly, Virginia City, December 7, 1868, to January 15, 1869. Helena: Montana Post Publishing Company, 1869.

Laws, Memorials, and Resolutions of the Territory of Montana Passed at the Sixth Session of the Legislative Assembly, Virginia City, December 6, 1869, to January 6, 1870. Helena: Robert E. Fisk, Public Printer, 1870.

Laws, Memorials, and Resolutions of the Territory of Montana Passed at the Seventh Session of the Legislative Assembly, Virginia City, December 4, 1871, to January 12, 1872. Deer Lodge, Mont.: James H. Miller, Public Printer, 1872.

Laws, Memorials, and Resolutions of the Territory of Montana, Passed at the Ninth Regular Session of the Legislative Assembly, Jan. 3, 1876, to Feb. 11, 1876. Helena: Robert E. Fisk, 1876.

Territory of Utah

Acts, Resolutions, and Memorials Passed by First Annual and Special Sessions of Legislative Assembly of Territory of Utah, Sept. 22, 1851. Great Salt Lake City: Brigham H. Young, Printer, 1852.

Acts and Resolutions Passed at the Second Annual Session of the Legislative Assembly of the Territory of Utah, Second Monday of December, 1852. Great Salt Lake City: George Hales, Printer, 1853.

Acts and Resolutions Passed at the Adjourned Session of the Legislative Assembly of the Territory of Utah, June, 1853. N.p., n.d.

Acts and Resolutions Passsed at the Third Annual Session of the Legislative Assembly of the Territory of Utah, Second Monday of December, 1853. [Great Salt Lake City]: Arieh C. Brower, Printer, 1854.

Resolutions, Acts, and Memorials Passed at the Fifth Annual Session of the Leg-

islative Assembly of the Territory of Utah, Fillmore City, Dec. 11, 1855.
Great Salt Lake City: George Hales, Public Printer, 1855.

*Acts and Resolutions—Legislative Assembly of the Territory of Utah, Eighth
Annual Session—for the Years 1858-1859.* Great Salt Lake City: J. Mc-
Night, 1859.

*Acts, Resolutions and Memorials Passed by the Legislative Assembly of the Ter-
ritory of Utah During Ninth Annual Session for Years 1859-60.* Great
Salt Lake City: John S. Davis, 1860.

*Acts, Resolutions and Memorials Passed by the Legislative Assembly of the Ter-
ritory of Utah During the Eleventh Annual Session for the Years 1861-62.*
Great Salt Lake City: Elias Smith, 1862.

*Acts, Resolutions and Memorials Passed by the Legislative Assembly of the Ter-
ritory of Utah, 13th Annual Session, 1863-64.* Great Salt Lake City: Henry
McEwan, 1864.

*Acts, Resolutions and Memorials Passed by the Legislative Assembly of the Ter-
ritory of Utah, Fourteenth Annual Session, 1864-65.* Great Salt Lake City:
Henry McEwan, 1865.

*Acts, Resolutions and Memorials Passed at the Several Annual Sessions of the
Legislative Assembly of the Territory of Utah, Jan. 19, 1866.* Great Salt
Lake City: Henry McEwan, 1866.

*Acts, Resolutions and Memorials Passed and Adopted During the Sixteenth
Annual Session of the Legislative Assembly of the Territory of Utah, Jan.
18, 1867.* Great Salt Lake City: James A. Thompson, 1867.

*Acts, Resolutions and Memorials Passed and Adopted by the Legislative Assem-
bly of the Territory of Utah, Eighteenth Annual Session, 1869.* Salt Lake
City: Geo. Q. Cannon, 1869.

*Acts, Resolutions, and Memorials Passed and Adopted During the Nineteenth
Annual Session of the Legislative Assembly of the Territory of Utah, 1870.*
Salt Lake City: Joseph Bull, 1870.

Utah Administrative Records 1851-1895, Auditors Report. William Clayton,
Auditor, Nov. 3, 1860, Nov. 10, 1866.

Box Elder County. County Recorder. Abstract Book A.

———. Map of Corinne, March 24, 1869.

Theses and Dissertations

Barber, James V. "The History of Highways in Utah from 1847 to 1869." M.A.
thesis, University of Utah, 1949.

Bolino, A. C. "An Economic History of Idaho Territory, 1863-1890." Ph.D. diss.,
St. Louis University, 1957.

Edrington, L. Kay. "A Study of Early Utah-Montana Trade, Transportation
and Communications, 1847-1881." M.A. thesis, Brigham Young University, 1953.

Hansen, Alma W. "A Historical Study of the Influence of the Railroad Upon Ogden, Utah, 1868-1875." M.A. thesis, Brigham Young University, 1953.

Howell, Glade F. "Early History of Malad Valley." M.A. thesis, Brigham Young University, 1960.

Jameson, Jesse H. "Corinne: A Study of a Freight Transfer Point in the Montana Trade, 1869-1878." M.A. thesis, University of Utah, 1951.

McBride, Ralph L. "Utah Mail Service Before the Coming of the Railroad, 1869." M.A. thesis, Brigham Young University, 1957.

McLatchy, Michael Gene, ed. "From Wisconsin to Montana 1863-1889: The Reminiscences of Robert Kirkpatrick." M.A. thesis, Montana State University, 1961.

Reeder, Clarence A., Jr. "The History of Utah's Railroads, 1869-1883." Ph.D. diss., University of Utah, 1970.

Young, James Ira. "The History and Development of Franklin, Idaho, During the Period 1860-1900." M.A. thesis, Brigham Young University, 1949.

Books and Pamphlets

The Abridged Mormon Guide! Showing the Distances and Best Camping Places Over the North Platte Route from Omaha to Salt Lake City, U., Thence to the Salmon River, Bannock and Virginia Gold Fields. [Salt Lake City]: "Farmer's Oracle," Printers, 1864.

Allen, William R. *The Chequemegon.* New York: William-Frederick Press, 1949.

Bancroft, Hubert Howe. *History of Utah, 1540-1886.* San Francisco: The History Co., 1890.

————. *History of Washington, Idaho, and Montana (1845-1889).* San Francisco: The History Co., 1890.

The Banditti of the Rocky Mountains and Vigilance Committee in Idaho: An Authentic Record of Startling Adventures in the Gold Mines of Idaho. New York: Wilson & Co., 1865.

Banning, Captain William, and George Hugh Banning. *Six Horses.* New York: The Century Co., 1930.

Barsness, Larry. *Gold Camp: Alder Gulch and Virginia City, Montana.* New York: Hastings House, 1962.

Beadle, John H. *Life in Utah; or the Mysteries and Crimes of Mormonism.* Philadelphia: National Publishing Co., [1870].

————. *The Undeveloped West, or Five Years in the Territories....* Chicago: National Publishing Company, [1873].

Beal, Merrill D. *A History of Southeastern Idaho....* Caldwell, Idaho: Caxton Printers, 1942.

————. *Intermountain Railroads; Standard and Narrow Gauge.* Caldwell, Idaho: Caxton Printers, 1962.

————, and Merle W. Wells. *History of Idaho.* 3 vols. New York: Lewis Historical Publishing Company, 1959.

Beal, Mrs. J. W. "Montana's Early History: A Pioneer Woman's Recollections of People and Events Connected with Montana's Early History." In *Contributions to the Historical Society of Montana,* vol. 8, pp. 295-304. Helena: Montana State Historical Society, 1917.

Bidwell, John. *A Journey to California, 1841.* Introduction by Francis P. Farquhar. Berkeley: Friends of the Bancroft Library, 1964.

Birney, Hoffman. *Vigilantes.* Philadelphia: Penn Publishing Co., 1929.

Boller, Henry A. *Among the Indians: Eight Years in the Far West: 1858-1866.* Philadelphia: T. Ellwood Zell, 1868.

Brimlow, George F., ed. *Good Old Days in Montana Territory: Reminiscences of the Harrington and Butcher Families.* Butte: McKee Publishing Co., 1957.

Brosnan, Cornelius J. *History of the State of Idaho.* New York: Charles Scribner's Sons, 1918.

Brossard, Edgar B. "Father Alphonse Brossard's Freighting Experience." *In Trails and Pioneer Freighters Who Followed Them, Including Toll Gates, Bridges and Ferries of the West,* p. 89. Compiled by Kate B. Carter. [Salt Lake City]: Daughters of Utah Pioneers, Central Company, 1948.

Brown, Jennie Broughton. *Fort Hall on the Oregon Trail: A Historical Study.* Caldwell, Idaho: Caxton Printers, 1932.

Brown, Mark H. *The Flight of the Nez Perce.* New York: G. P. Putnams Sons, 1967.

Bruffey, George A. *Eighty-One Years in the West.* Butte: Butte Miner Co., 1925.

Burlingame, Merril G., and K. Ross Toole. *A History of Montana.* 2 vols. New York: Lewis Historical Publishing Co., 1957.

Campbell, John L. *Idaho: Six Months in the New Gold Diggings. The Emigrant's Guide Overland. Itinerary of the Routes, Features of the Country, Journal of Residence, etc., etc.* New York: By the author, 1864.

Carter, Kate B. comp. *The Development of Transportation.* [Salt Lake City]: Daughters of Utah Pioneers, 1940.

————, comp. *Our Pioneer Heritage.* Salt Lake City: Daughters of Utah Pioneers, 1958.

————, comp. *Trails and Pioneer Freighters Who Followed Them, Including Toll Gates, Bridges, and Ferries of the West.* [Salt Lake City]: Daughters of Utah Pioneers, Central Company, 1948.

Chandless, William. *A Visit to Salt Lake: Being a Journey Across the Plains.* London: Smith, Elder & Co., 1857.

Chittenden, Hiram Martin. *History of Early Steamboat Navigation on the Missouri River: Life and Adventures of Joseph LaBarge, Pioneer Navigator and Indian Trader.* New York: Francis P. Harper, 1903.

————, and A. T. Richardson, eds. *Life, Letters, and Travels of Father Pierre-Jean de Smet, S. J., 1801-1873.* 4 vols. New York: Francis P. Harper, 1905.

Clampitt, John W. *Echoes from the Rocky Mountains.* Chicago: Belford, Clarke & Co., 1889.

Clark, Barzilla Worth. *Bonneville County in the Making.* Idaho Falls: By the author, 1941.

Clark, W. A. "Centennial Address on Montana: Delivered October Eleventh, 1876." In *Contributions to the Historical Society of Montana,* vol. 2, pp. 45–60. Helena: Montana State Historical Society, 1917.

Codman, John. *The Mormon Country.* New York: United States Publishing Co., 1874.

Cowley, Mathias. *Wilford Woodruff, Fourth President of the Church of Jesus Christ of Latter-day Saints.* Salt Lake City: N.p., 1909.

Crawford, Lewis F. *Rekindling Camp Fires: Exploits of Ben Arnold (Connor).* Bismarck, N. Dak.: Capital Book Co., 1926.

Crofutt, George A. *Crofutt's Trans-Continental Tourist's Guide.* New York: American News Co., 1871.

Dale, Harrison Clifford, ed. *The Ashley-Smith Explorations and the Discovery of a Central Route to the Pacific, 1822–1829.* Cleveland: N.p., 1918.

Danielson, Marie, ed. *The Trail Blazer: History of the Development of Southeastern Idaho.* [Salt Lake City]: Daughters of Utah Pioneers, 1930.

Daughters of Utah Pioneers, Box Elder County. *History of Box Elder County.* N.p., n.d.

de Hubner, M. le Baron. *A Ramble Round the World, 1871.* 2 vols. London: Macmillan & Co., 1874.

De Voto, Bernard, ed. *The Journals of Lewis and Clark.* Boston: Houghton, Mifflin Co., 1953.

Dickson, Arthur J., ed. *Covered Wagon Days.* Cleveland: Arthur H. Clark Co., 1929.

Dimsdale, Prof. Thomas J. *The Vigilantes of Montana or Popular Justice in the Rocky Mountains.* 3d ed. Helena: State Publishing Co., 1915.

Donaldson, Thomas. *Idaho of Yesterday.* Caldwell, Idaho: Caxton Printers, 1941.

Dunraven, Earl of. *Hunting in the Yellowstone.* New York: Macmillan Co., 1925.

"Effects at Fort Benton of the Gold Excitement in Montana." Bradley Manuscript, Book 2. In *Contributions to the Historical Society of Montana,* vol. 8, pp. 126–30. Helena: Montana State Historical Society, 1917.

Eggenhofer, Nick. *Wagons, Mules, and Men: How the Frontier Moved West.* New York: Hastings House, 1961.

Federal Writers' Project of the WPA. *Idaho Lore.* Caldwell, Idaho: The Caxton Printers Ltd., 1939.

————. *Montana: A State Guide Book.* American Guide Series. New York: The Viking Press, 1939.

Ferebauer, Lulu. "The Critical Years." In *The Idaho Story,* vol. 1. N.p.: Idaho Poets and Writers' Guild, 1967.

Ferris, Warren Angus. *Life in the Rocky Mountains*. Edited by Paul C. Phillips. Denver: Fred A. Rosenstock, 1940.

Fisk Brothers. *Montana Territory: History and Business Directory, 1879*. Helena: N.p., 1879.

Fisk, Captain James L. *Idaho: Her Gold Fields, and the Routes to Them, A Hand-Book for Emigrants*. New York: John A. Gray, Printer, Stereotyper and Binder, 1863. Typescript in William Andrews Clark Memorial Library, Los Angeles, Calif.

Forsgren, Lydie Walker, comp. *History of Box Elder County*. Salt Lake City: Daughters of Utah Pioneers, 1937.

Fox, Jesse W. *General Courses and Distances from G.S.L. City to Fort Lemhi and Gold Diggings on Salmon River*. Great Salt Lake City: Deseret News Printing, 1862.

Frederick, James V. *Ben Holladay, The Stagecoach King*. Glendale, Calif.: Arthur H. Clark Co., 1940.

Fry, F. *Fry's Travelers' Guide and Descriptive Journal*. Cincinatti: Applegate & Co., 1865.

Gem State Authors' Guild. *Starlight and Syringa*. Pocatello, Idaho: Gateway Printers, Inc. 1959.

Glasscock, C. B. *War of the Copper Kings*. New York: Grosset & Dunlap, 1935.

Goodhart, George W. *The Pioneer Life of George W. Goodhart, and His Association with the Hudson's Bay and American Fur Company's Traders and Trappers; Trails of Early Idaho, As Told to Abraham C. Anderson*. Caldwell, Idaho: Caxton Printers, 1940.

Gregg, Josiah. *Commerce of the Prairies*. Edited by Max L. Moorehead. Norman, Okla.: University of Oklahoma Press, 1974.

Hakola, John. "Currency in Montana." In J. W. Smurr and K. Ross Toole, eds., *Historical Essays on Montana and the Northwest*, pp. 117-23. Helena: Western Press, 1957.

Hall, Edward H. *The Great West: Emigrants', Settlers' & Travelers' Guide and Hand-Book to the States of California and Oregon, and the Territories of Nebraska, Utah, Colorado, Idaho, Montana, Nevada and Washington*. New York: Tribune Office, 1864.

Hamilton, James M. *From Wilderness to Statehood: A History of Montana, 1805-1900*. Portland, Ore.: Binfords & Mort, 1957.

Harlow, Alvin F. *Old Waybills: The Romance of the Express Companies*. New York: Appleton-Century, 1934.

Healy, John T. *An Adventure in the Idaho Mines*. Edited by Clyde McLemore. Historical Reprints. Sources of Northwest History No. 26. Missoula: Montana State University, 1937.

Hedges, Cornelius. "Centennial Address on Lewis and Clark County: Delivered July Fourth, 1896." In *Contributions to the Historical Society of Montana*, vol. 2, pp. 107-18. Helena: Montana State Historical Society, 1937.

Herndon, Sarah Raymond. *Days on the Road: Crossing the Plains in 1865*. New York: Burr Printing House, 1902.

Historical Sketch and Essay on the Resources of Montana. Helena: Herald Book & Job Printing Office, 1868.

History of Brigham Young, 1847–1867. Berkeley: MassCal Associates, 1964.

Holmes, Oliver W., ed. *James A. Garfield's Diary of a Trip to Montana in 1872*. Sources of Northwest History No. 21. Missoula: Montana State University, [1937].

Holter, A. M. "Pioneer Lumbering in Montana." In *Contributions to the Historical Society of Montana*, vol. 8, pp. 251–82. Helena: Montana State Historical Society, 1917.

Hooker, William Francis. *The Bullwhacker: Adventure of a Frontier Freighter*. Edited by Howard R. Driggs. New York: World Book Co., 1940.

———. *The Prairie Schooner*. Chicago: Saul Bros., 1918.

Hosmer, Hezekiah L. *Montana. An Address Delivered to the Travellers' Club, New York City, January, 1866*. New York: New York Printing Co., 1866.

Howard, Helen Addison. *Northwest Trail Blazers*. Caldwell, Idaho: Caxton Printers, 1963.

Humason, W. L. *From the Atlantic Surf to the Golden Gate*. Hartford: Press of Wm. C. Hutchings, 1869.

"Instructions to Wagon Masters, and All Employees Connected for Transportation Trains." In *Rules and Regulations for the Government of Russell, Majors & Waddell's Outfit*. Nebraska City: Thorne Morton & Company, 1859.

Irving, Washington. *The Adventures of Captain Bonneville*. New York: J. B. Millar & Co., 1885.

———. *Astoria*. New York: Current Literature Publishing Co., 1912.

Jackson, William H. *Bullwhacking Across the Plains: "Told at the Explorer's Club."* New York: Albert and Charles Boni, 1931.

———. *Time Exposure: The Autobiography of William Henry Jackson*. New York: G. P. Putnam's Sons, 1940.

Johnson, Warren B. *From the Pacific to the Atlantic; Being an Account of a Journey Overland from Eureka, Humboldt Co., California to Webster, Worcester Co., Mass., with a Horse, Carriage, Cow and Dog*. Webster, Mass.: John Cort, Printer, 1887.

Kelly, William. *Across the Rocky Mountains, from New York to California: With a Visit to the Celebrated Mormon Colony, at the Great Salt Lake*. Longon, Simms and M'Intyre, 1852.

Langford, Nathaniel P. *Vigilante Days and Ways*. Introduction by Dorothy M. Johnson. Missoula: University Press, 1957.

Leeson, M. A., ed. *History of Montana*. Chicago: Warner, Beers & Co., 1885.

Lovell, Edith H. *Captain Bonneville's County*. Idaho Falls: Eastern Idaho Farmer, 1963.

Madsen, Brigham D. *The Bannock of Idaho*. Caldwell, Idaho: Caxton Printers, Ltd., 1958.

Maillet, Louis R. "Historical Sketch of Louis R. Maillet." In *Contributions to the Historical Society of Montana*, vol. 4, pp. 197–228. Helena: Montana State Historical Society, 1903.

Marcy, Randolph B. *The Prairie Traveler: A Hand-Book for Overland Expeditions.* New York: Harper Bros., 1861.

McClure, Col. A. C. "Wilbur Fisk Sanders." In *Contributions to the Historical Society of Montana*, vol. 8, p. 27. Helena: Montana State Historical Society, 1917.

McClure, A. K. *Three Thousand Miles Through the Rocky Mountains.* Philadelphia: J. B. Lippincott & Co., 1869.

McPherren, Ida. *Imprints of Pioneer Trails.* Boston: Christopher Publishing House, 1950.

Meredith, Emily R. *Bannack and Gallatin City in 1862–63: A Letter by Mrs. Emily R. Meredith.* Edited by Clyde McLemore. Historical Reprints. Sources of Northwest History No. 24. Missoula: Montana State University, 1937.

Miller, James Knox Polk. *The Road to Virginia City: The Diary of James Knox Polk Miller.* Edited by Andrew F. Rolle. Norman: University of Oklahoma Press, 1960.

Miller, Joaquin. *An Illustrated History of the State of Montana.* Chicago: Lewis Pub. Co., 1894.

Montana State Historical Society. *Contributions to the Historical Society of Montana.* 10 vols. Reprinted from the original editions. Boston: J. S. Cannor and Co., 1966.

Moody, Ralph. *Stagecoach West.* New York: Crowell, 1967.

Morton, Cyrus. *Autobiography.* Omaha: Douglas Printing Co., 1895.

Mullan, Captain John. *Miners' and Travelers' Guide to Oregon, Washington, Idaho, Montana, Wyoming and Colorado via the Missouri and Columbia Rivers.* New York: Wm. M. Franklin, 1865.

Neff, Andrew Love. *History of Utah, 1847 to 1869.* Salt Lake City: Deseret News Press, 1940.

Nevins, Allan, ed. *John Charles Frémont: Narratives of Exploration and Adventure.* New York: Longmans, Green & Co., 1956.

Noyes, Alva J. *The Story of Ajax: Life in the Bighole Basin.* Helena: State Publishing Co., 1914.

Nunis, Doyce B., Jr., ed. *The Golden Frontier: The Recollections of Herman Francis Reinhart, 1851–1869.* Austin: University of Texas Press, 1962.

Overholser, Joel F. *Centenary History of Fort Benton, Montana, 1846–1946.* N.p.: Fort Benton Centennial Association, 1946.

Ovitt, Mable. *Golden Treasure.* Dillon, Mont.: By the author, 1952.

Owen, John. *The Journals and Letters of Major John Owen, Pioneer of the Northwest, 1850–1871.* Edited by Seymour Dunbar and Paul C. Phillips. 2 vols. New York: Edward Eberstadt, 1927.

Pettite, William Stibal. *Memories of Market Lake, A History of Eastern Idaho.* N.p.: N.p., 1965.

Phillips, Paul C. ed. *Upham Letters from Upper Missouri, 1865.* Historical Reprints, Vol. 13, No. 4. Missoula: University of Montana, 1933.

Rich, E. E. *The History of the Hudson's Bay Company, 1670–1870.* 2 vols. Publications of the Hudson's Bay Record Society, no. 21. London: Hudson's Bay Record Society, 1958–59.

Richardson, Albert D. *Beyond the Mississippi.* Hartford, Conn.: American Publishing Co., 1867.

Ricks, Joel E., ed. *The History of a Valley: Cache Valley, Utah–Idaho.* Cache Valley Centennial Commission. Salt Lake City: Deseret News Publishing Co., 1956.

Riley, Harvey. *The Mule: A Treatise on the Breeding, Training, and Uses to Which He May Be Put.* Philadelphia: N.p., 1869.

Robertson, Frank C. *Fort Hall, Gateway to the Oregon Country.* New York: Hastings House, 1963.

Roe, Frances M. A. *Army Letters from an Officer's Wife, 1871–1888.* New York: D. Appleton, 1909.

Ross, Alexander. *The Fur Hunters of the Far West.* 2 vols. London: Smith, Elder & Co., 1855.

Rusling, James Fowler. *Across America: Or, the Great West and the Pacific Coast.* New York: Sheldon & Co., 1875.

Russell, Osborne. *Journal of a Trapper, Or Nine Years in the Rocky Mountains, 1834–1843.* Boise: Syms-York Co., 1921.

Sanders, Helen Fitzgerald. *A History of Montana.* 3 vols. Chicago: Lewis Publishing Co., 1913.

————, ed. *X. Beidler, Vigilante.* In collaboration with Willliam H. Bertsche, Jr. Norman: University of Oklahoma Press, 1957.

Saunders, Arthur C. *The History of Bannock County, Idaho.* Pocatello: The Tribune Company, Limited, 1915.

Sloan, Edward L., comp. *Gazeteer of Utah, and Salt Lake City Directory.* Salt Lake City: Salt Lake Herald Publishing Co., 1869, 1874.

Smith, Ralph. "Journal, 1853–1895." In *The History of a Valley: Cache Valley, Utah–Idaho.* Edited by Joel E. Ricks. Salt Lake City: Deseret News Publishing Co., 1956.

Smurr, J. W., and K. Ross Toole, eds. *Historical Essays on Montana and the Northwest.* Helena: Western Press, 1957.

Spring, Agnes Wright. *The Cheyenne and Black Hills Stage and Express Routes.* Glendale, Calif.: Arthur H. Clark Co., 1949.

Stanley, E. J. *Life of L. B. Stateler.* Nashville, Tenn.: Smith & Lamar, 1907.

Stansbury, Captain J. Howard. *An Expedition to the Valley of the Great Salt Lake: Also a Reconnaissance of a New Route through the Rocky Mountains.* Philadelphia: N.p., 1855.

————. *Exploration and Survey of the Valley of the Great Salt Lake of Utah.* Philadelphia: Lippincott, Grambo & Co., 1852.

"Steamboat Arrivals at Fort Benton, Montana, and Vicinity, 1859-1874." In *Contributions to the Historical Society of Montana,* vol. 1, pp. 317-25. Helena: Montana State Historical Society, 1876.

Stout, Tom. *Montana: Its Story and Biography.* Chicago and New York: American Historical Society, 1921.

Strahorn, Carrie A. *Fifteen Thousand Miles by Stage: A Woman's Unique experience During Thirty Years of Pathfinding and Pioneering from the Missouri to the Pacific and from Alaska to Mexico.* New York: G. P. Putnam's Sons, 1911.

Strahorn, Robert E. *The Resources of Montana Territory and Attractions of Yellowstone National Park.* Helena: N.p., 1879.

————. *To the Rockies and Beyond, or a Summer on the Union Pacific Railroad and Branches. Saunterings in the Popular Health, Pleasures, and Hunting Resorts of Nebraska, Dakota, Wyoming, Colorado, Utah, Idaho, Oregon, Washington, and Montana.* Omaha: The New West Publishing Company, 1879.

————. *The Great West: Its Attractions and Resources.* Philadelphia: Franklin Publishing Co., 1880.

Stuart, Granville. *Forty Years on the Frontier.* Edited by Paul C. Phillips. 2 vols. Cleveland: Arthur H. Clark Co., 1925.

————. "A Memoir of the Life of James Stuart." In *Contributions to the Historical Society of Montana,* vol. 1, pp. 36-79. Helena: Montana State Historical Society, 1876.

Stuart, James. "The Yellowstone Expedition of 1863 from the Journals of Captain James Stuart with Notes by Samuel Hauser and Granville Stuart." In *Contributions to the Historical Society of Montana,* vol. 1, pp. 149-233. Helena: Montana State Historical Society, 1876.

Tisdale, Henry. "Travel by Stage in the Early Days." In *Transactions of the Kansas State Historical Society, 1901-1902,* vol. 7. Topeka: W. Y. Morgan, State Printer, 1920.

Toponce, Alexander. *Reminiscences of Alexander Toponce, Pioneer, 1839-1923.* Ogden, Ut.: Mrs. Katie Toponce, Century Printing Co., 1923.

Trexler, Harrison R. *Flour and Wheat in the Montana Gold Camps, 1862-1870.* Missoula: Dustan Printing and Stationery, 1918.

Tufts, James. *A Tract Descriptive of Montana Territory with a Sketch of the Mineral and Agricultural Resources.* New York: Robert Craighead, Printer, 1865.

Tullidge, Edward W. *History of Salt Lake City.* Salt Lake City: Star Printing Company, 1886.

Tuttle, Daniel S. *Reminiscences of a Missionary Bishop.* New York: Thomas Whitaker, 1906.

Union Pacific Railroad. *The Direct Route to Colo., Ida., Utah, Mont., Nev., and Calif.* Chicago: Horan & Leonard, 1868.

Walgamott, Charles S. *Six Decades Back*. Caldwell, Idaho: Caxton Printers, 1936.

———. *Reminiscences of Early Days. A Series of Historical Sketches and Happenings in the Early Days of Snake River Valley*. Twin Falls, Idaho: N.p., 1926.

Walker, Henry Pickering. *The Wagon Masters: High Plains Freighting from the Earliest Days of the Santa Fe Trail to 1880*. Norman: University of Oklahoma Press, 1966.

Warner, Frank W. *Montana Territory: History and Business*. Helena: N.p., 1879.

The War of the Rebellion: A Compilation of the Official Records of the Union and Confederate Armies. Series I, vol. 50, pt. 1. Washington, D. C.: U. S. Government Printing Office, 1897.

Weaver, David B. "Early Days in Emigrant Gulch." In *Contributions to the Historical Society of Montana*, vol. 7, pp. 73-96. Helena: Montana State Historical Society, 1910.

Webster, N. H. "Journal of N. H. Webster." In *Contributions to the Historical Society of Montana*, vol. 3, pp. 300-30. Helena: Montana State Historical Society, 1900.

Weisel, George F., ed. *Men and Trade on the Northwest Frontier as Shown by the Fort Owen Ledger*. Missoula: Montana State University, 1955.

Wells, Fargo & Co. *California and Oregon. Express Rules, Instructions and Tariffs*. San Francisco: Excelsior Press, 1868.

——— Express. *Report of Jas. B. Hume and Jno. N. Thacker, Special Officers... Covering a Period of Fourteen Years, Giving Losses by Train Robbers, Stage Robbers and Burglaries....* San Francisco: N.p., 1885.

———, History Room. Pamphlet. San Francisco: Wells, Fargo, n.d.

White, Helen McCann, ed. *Ho! For the Gold Fields*. St. Paul: Minnesota Historical Society, 1966.

Williams, Glyndwr, ed. *Peter Skene Ogden's Snake Country Journals, 1827-28 and 1828-29*. London: The Hudson's Bay Record Society, 1971.

Woody, Frank H. "How an Early Pioneer Came to Montana and the Privations Encountered on the Journey." In *Contributions to the Historical Society of Montana*, vol. 7, pp. 140-61. Helena: Montana State Historical Society, 1910.

———. "A Sketch of the Early History of Western Montana." In *Contributions to the Historical Society of Montana*, vol. 2, pp. 93-97. Helena: Montana State Historical Society, 1917.

Word, Samuel. "Diary of Colonel Samuel Word." In *Contributions to the Historical Society of Montana*, vol. 8, pp. 37-92. Helena: Montana State Historical Society, 1917.

Periodicals

Athearn, Robert G. "Utah and Northern Railroad." *Montana Western History*, vol. 23 (Oct. 1968), pp. 2-23.

Bishop, John F. "Beginning of the Montana Sheep Industry." *The Montana Magazine of History*, vol. 1 (Apr. 1951), p. 8.

Barrows, Willard. "To Idaho and Montana: Wanderings There: Returning." *The Boston Review*, no. 26 (Mar. 1865), pp. 127-28.

Bluth, John V. "The Salmon River Mission." *Improvement Era*, vol. 3 (Sept. 1900), p. 810.

Callaway, Lew L. "John Thomas Conner: Sketch of His Life." *Montana State Historical Society Contributions*, vol. 7 (1910), pp. 222-23.

Fleming, L. A., and A. R. Standing. "The Road to Fortune: The Salt Lake Cut-off." *Utah Historical Quarterly*, vol. 33 (Mar. 1965), pp. 260-66.

Good, Nimrod. "A Close-Up of the Oxen." *Rigby [Idaho] Star* (Mar. 7, 1963).

Hailey, John. "Staging, Carrying Passengers, Express, U.S. Mail, and Fast Freight to and from Boise Basin and Boise and Salt Lake City in the Early Sixties." *Idaho State Historical Society Bulletin*, vol. 1 (Apr. 1, 1908), n.p.

Henderson, W. W. ed. "The Salmon River Mission: Extracts from Journal of L. W. Shurtliff." *Utah Historical Quarterly*, vol. 5, no. 1 (Jan. 1932), pp. 517-20.

Jackson, W. Turrentine. "A New Look at Wells Fargo, Stagecoaches and the Pony Express." *California Historical Society Quarterly*, vol. 45 (Dec. 1966), pp. 291-324.

———. "Wells Fargo Stagecoaching in Montana: Into a New Territory." *Montana: The Magazine of Western History*, vol. 29, no. 1 (Jan. 1979), pp. 40-53.

———. "Wells Fargo Stagecoaching in Montana: Trials and Triumphs." *Montana: The Magazine of Western History*, vol. 29, no. 2 (Spring 1979), pp. 38-53.

———. "Wells Fargo Stagecoaching in Montana: The Overland Mail Contract for 1868." *Montana: The Magazine of Western History*, vol. 29, no. 3 (July, 1979), pp. 56-68.

———. "Wells Fargo Stagecoaching in Montana: Final Months." *Montana: The Magazine of Western History*, vol. 29, no. 4 (Oct. 1979), pp. 52-66.

Kennedy, Michael. "'Infernal' Collector." *Montana: The Magazine of Western History*, vol. 4 (Spring 1964), pp. 17-20.

Lester, Gurdon P. "A Round Trip to the Montana Mines: The 1866 Travel Journal of Gurdon P. Lester." *Nebraska History Quarterly*, vol. 46 (Dec. 1965), pp. 293-96.

Mallory, Samuel. "Diary of Samuel Mallory. A Trip from Denver to Montana." *Montana: The Magazine of Western History*, vol. 15 (Apr. 1965), pp. 31-33.

Martinson, Lee. "The Lost Gold Poke." *The Improvement Era*, vol. 61 (Nov. 1958), p. 815.

Munson, Lyman E. "Pioneer Life on the American Frontier: Crossing the Continent from Connecticut to Montana to Establish Law and Order in the Savage Land of the Great Northwest—Experiences of a Member of Connecticut Bar on Trail of the Prairie Schooners." *Connecticut Magazine*, no. 1 (1907), p. 88.

Nealley, Edward B. "A Year in Montana." *Atlantic* (Aug. 1866), p. 236.

Oviatt, Alton B. "Pacific Coast Competition for the Gold Camp Trade of Montana." *Pacific Northwest Quarterly*, vol. 56 (Oct. 1965), pp. 169-75.

Phillips, Paul C., and Albert J. Portoll, eds. "Montana Reminiscences of Isaac I. Lewis." *Montana: The Magazine of Western History*, vol. 1 (Jan. 1951), pp. 65-66.

Richardson, A. D. "Montana and Idaho." *Beadles Monthly*, vol. 2 (Oct. 1866), n.p.

Sharp, Paul F. "Merchant Princes of the Plains." *Montana: The Magazine of Western History*, vol. 5 (Winter 1955), pp. 18-20.

Shurtleff, Lewis W. "Extracts from Journal of L. W. Shurtleff," edited by W. W. Henderson. *Utah Historical Quarterly*, vol. 5 (Jan. 1932), pp. 517-36.

Thompson, Francis M. "Reminiscences of Four Score Years." *The Massachusetts Magazine*, vol. 6 (1913), pp. 1-188.

Walker, Eugene H. "Oneida Salt." *Idaho Yesterdays*, vol. 6 (Fall 1962), p. 8.

Wells, Donald N., and Merle W. Wells. "The Oneida Toll Road Controversy, 1864-1880." *Oregon Historical Quarterly*, vol. 58 (June 1957), pp. 113-25.

Newspapers

Alta Californian, San Francisco, Calif., 1873.

Blackfoot Register, Blackfoot, Idaho, 1880-83.

Butte Miner, Butte, Mont., 1878.

Carson City Appeal, Carson City, Nev., 1873.

Corinne Daily Mail, Corinne, Ut., 1874-75.

Corinne Journal, Corinne, Ut., 1871.

Corinne Reporter, Corinne, Ut., 1871-73.

Deseret News, Salt Lake City, Ut., 1850-84.

Frontier Index, Bear River City, Wyo., 1867-68.

Helena Herald, Helena, Mont., 1866-84.

Idaho Enterprise, Malad, Idaho, 1879-80.

Idaho Statesman, Boise, Idaho, 1864-84.

Idaho World, Idaho City, Idaho, 1877-78.

Independent Record, Helena, Mont., 1878, 1964.

Jordan Times, Jordan, Mont., 1928.

Madisonian, Virginia City, Mont., 1873-74.

Montana Democrat, Virginia City, Mont., 1865-69.

Montanian, Virginia City, Mont., 1870-76.

Montana Post, Helena, Mont., 1864–69.

Montana Radiator, Helena, Mont., 1865–66.

Missoulian, Missoula, Mont., 1877.

Mountaineer, Big Sandy, Mont., 1880.

New Northwest, Deer Lodge, Mont., 1869–84.

Ogden Freeman, Ogden, Ut., 1876–81.

Ogden Junction, Ogden, Ut., 1870–79.

Omaha Herald, Omaha, Nebr., 1877.

Pocatello Tribune, Pocatello, Idaho, 1939.

Post-Register, Idaho Falls, Idaho, 1966.

Rocky Mountain Gazette, Helena, Mont., 1868–70.

Sacramento Daily Union, Sacramento, Calif., 1864–66.

Salt Lake City Independent, Salt Lake City, Ut., 1878.

Salt Lake Telegraph, Salt Lake City, Ut., 1864–70.

Salt Lake Tribune, Salt Lake City, Ut., 1870–84.

Times-News, Hailey, Idaho, 1954.

Tri-Weekly Republican, Virginia City, Mont., 1866.

Union Vedette, Salt Lake City, Ut., 1863–67.

Utah Reporter, Corinne, Ut., 1869–71.

Valley Tan, Salt Lake City, Ut., 1858–60.

Weekly Mountaineer, The Dalles, Ore., 1865–66.

World, New York City, N.Y., 1871.

Index of Subjects

Index of Names